Catskill Aqueduct Celebration Publications

A Collection of Pamphlets Published in Connection with the Celebration of the Completion of the Catskill Aqueduct, being chiefly Catalogues of Exhibitions held by Art, Scientific and Historical Museums and Institutions in New York City in cooperation with the Mayor's Catskill Aqueduct Celebration Committee in 1917.

ARRANGED BY

GEORGE FREDERICK KUNZ, Ph.D., Sc. D.,

Chairman of the Committee on

Art, Scientific and Historical Exhibitions

The Mayor's

Catskill Aqueduct Celebration Committee

New York, 1917

The Mayor of New York's Catskill Aqueduct Celebration Committee

---

Chairman

George McAneny, LL.D.

Treasurer

Isaac N. Seligman

Assistant Treasurer

Stanley G. Ranger

Secretary

Edward Hagaman Hall, L.H.D.

EXECUTIVE COMMITTEE

Chairman

Hon. Arthur Williams

William C. Breed
William Hamlin Childs
Edward Hagaman Hall, L.H.D.
George F. Kunz, Ph.D., Sc.D.
John W. Lieb
Samuel L. Martin
George McAneny, LL.D.
Hon. William McCarroll
Isaac N. Seligman
Hon. Henry S. Thompson
Charles H. Strong
Henry R. Towne

CHAIRMEN OF SUB-COMMITTEES

City Hall Exercises........William Fellows Morgan
Civic Bodies..................Robert Grier Cooke
Illuminations..................Nicholas F. Brady
Official Dinner..............Elbert H. Gary, LL.D., Sc.D.
Official Medal...............Robert W. de Forest, LL.D.
Museum Exhibits..........George F. Kunz, Ph.D., Sc.D.
Music Festivals.............Oswald G. Villard, Litt. D., LL.D.
Pageant in Central Park..William J. Lee
Public Schools ....Leo Arnstein
Religious Exercises ....Rev. Walter Laidlaw, Ph.D.

Sub-Committee on
Art, Scientific and Historical Exhibitions

Chairman
GEORGE FREDERICK KUNZ, Ph.D., Sc. D.

Universities and Colleges

Columbia University
Dr. Nicholas Murray Butler, *President*
Prof. Wm. H. Carpenter, *Librarian*
Milton J. Davies

New York University
Dr. Elmer Ellsworth Brown, *Chancellor*

Stevens Institute of Technology
Dr. Alexander C. Humphreys, *President*

College of the City of New York
Dr. Sidney E. Mezes, *President*

Learned Societies and Institutions

American Geographical Society
John Greenough, *President*

New York Historical Society
John Abeel Weeks, *President*
Robert H. Kelby, *Librarian*

New York Genealogical and Biographical Society
Capt. Richard Henry Greene, *Representative*

Long Island Historical Society
Judge Willard Bartlett, *President*

Brooklyn Institute of Arts and Sciences
Dr. A. Augustus Healy, *President*

Staten Island Association of Arts and Sciences
Hon. Howard R. Bayne, *President*

American Numismatic Society
Edward T. Newell, *President*

Cooper Union for the Advancement of Science and Art
Miss Sarah Cooper Hewitt, *Trustee*
Miss Eleanor G. Hewitt, *Trustee*

American Scenic and Historic Preservation Society
Col. Henry W. Sackett, 1*st Vice-President*

Engineering Societies

United Engineering Society
Charles F. Rand, *President*
Calvin W. Rice, *Secretary*

American Institute of Mechanical Engineers
Dr. Ira N. Hollis, *President*

American Institute of Electrical Engineers
E. W. Rice, Jr., *President*

(*Sub-committee continued on next page*)

American Institute of Mining Engineers
Philip N. Moore, *President*

American Institute of Civil Engineers
E. W. H. Pegram, *President*

Libraries

New York Public Library
Dr. Edwin H. Anderson, *Director*

New York Society Library
Frederic dePeyster Foster, *Chairman*

Museums

Metropolitan Museum of Art
Dr. Robert W. de Forest, *President*

Brooklyn Museum
William H. Fox, *Director*

American Museum of Natural History
Dr. Henry Fairfield Osborn, *President*

Museum of the American Indian
George G. Heye, *Founder*

Van Cortlandt Museum House (The Colonial Dames of the State of New York
Mrs. Hamilton R. Fairfax, *President*
Mrs. Elihu Chauncey, *Chairman*

Jumel Mansion, Washington Headquarters Association (The Daughters of the American Revolution)
Mrs. George Wilson Smith, *President*
William H. Shelton, *Curator*

Fraunces' Tavern (The Sons of the Revolution)
Henry Russell Drowne, *Secretary*

Clubs

National Arts Club
John G. Agar, *President*

City History Club of New York
Mrs. A. Barton Hepburn, *President*

Parks and Gardens

Department of Parks, Manhattan and Richmond
Hon. Cabot Ward, *Commissioner*

Department of Parks, Brooklyn
Hon. Raymond W. Ingersoll, *Commissioner*

New York Botanical Garden
Dr. Nathaniel L. Britton, *Director*

New York Zoological Garden
Madison Grant, *Vice-President*

New York Aquarium
Dr. Charles H. Townsend, *Director*

Brooklyn Botanic Garden
Dr. C. Stuart Gager, *Director*

Church

The Collegiate Church of St. Nicholas
Rev. Dr. Malcolm James MacLeod, *Pastor*

Contents

Exhibition of the City History Club of New York, 105 West 40th Street. . . . Contributed to the Catskill Aqueduct Celebration, in co-operation with the work of the Art, Scientific and Historical Exhibitions Committee .... 8 pages

The Catskill Aqueduct Exhibition in the Museum at Washington's Headquarters (Jumel Mansion) in the Charge of the Washington Headquarters Association founded by Daughters of the American Revolution. . . . October 12th to November 12th, New York, 1917........... 8 pages

Van Cortlandt House Museum. A Special Exhibition in connection with the Mayor's Catskill Aqueduct Celebration. The Colonial Dames of the State of New York. October MCMXVII..................... 16 pages

Celebration of the Completion of the Catskill Aqueduct and the Seventy-fifth Anniversary of the bringing of Croton Water into the City of New York, A. D., 1917. Exhibit of the (Collegiate) Reformed Protestant Dutch Church of the City of New York (Organized A.D. 1628) October 12th to October 20th, 1917. In the Chapel of the Collegiate Church of St. Nicholas, Fifth Avenue and Forty-eighth Street......... 12 pages

Catskill Aqueduct Celebration Number (Oct. 12-15, 1917.) Brooklyn Botanic Garden Leaflets. The Brooklyn Institute of Arts and Sciences. Series V. Brooklyn, N. Y. October 10, 1917. Nos. 12 and 13....... 8 pages

The Brooklyn Institute of Arts and Sciences, Brooklyn Museum. A Special Historical Exhibition to Celebrate the Opening of the Catskill Aqueduct. Works of American Painters, 1860-1885, in the American Gallery of the Museum. November First to November Twenty-ninth, 1917..Cover and 20 pages

Staten Island Association of Arts and Sciences. Catalog of Staten Island Exhibits. Catskill Aqueduct Celebration Exhibit prepared in co-operation with the sub-committee on Art, Scientific and Historical Exhibitions of the Mayor's Catskill Aqueduct Celebration Committee. . . . Public Museum. Staten Island, Borough of Richmond, York New City, October 11, 1917....... 4 pages

Contribution of Stevens Institute of Technology to the Catskill Aqueduct Celebration, in co-operation with the Work of the Sub-Committee on Art, Scientific and Historical Exhibitions. (Reprinted from The Stevens Indicator, October 1917)........Cover and 8 pages

The Catskill Aqueduct

and Earlier Water Supplies of the City of New York

With elementary Chapters on the Source and Uses of Water and the Building of Aqueducts, and an Outline for an Allegorical Pageant

The Mayor's
Catskill Aqueduct Celebration Committee
New York
1917

The Catskill Aqueduct

and Earlier Water Supplies of the City of New York

With elementary Chapters on the Source and Uses of Water and the Building of Aqueducts, and an Outline for an Allegorical Pageant

By Edward Hagaman Hall, L. H. D.

(Second Edition)

The Mayor's
Catskill Aqueduct Celebration Committee
New York
1917

"I will lift up mine eyes unto the hills from whence cometh my help."—*Psalms, CXXI, 1.*

Contents

ILLUSTRATIONS.

Introduction

The Catskill aqueduct, the construction of which was begun ten years ago, is now in full operation, delivering to the City of New York water brought from the Catskill mountains, one hundred and twenty miles away.

Acting upon the request of representatives of some of the leading commercial bodies of the city, the Hon. John Purroy Mitchel, Mayor, has appointed a committee of citizens to arrange a public observance of the completion of the aqueduct, and plans are being formulated for a suitable celebration beginning on October 12, 1917.

The completion of this great engineering feat is deemed worthy of commemoration for several reasons.

In the first place, when it is remembered that only three or four years ago, in a season of drouth, the city counted by days how long its reserve supply of water would last, it is a cause of inexpressible relief to the municipal authorities, and should also be to the citizens at large, that this increased supply, upon which the very life of the people depends, is now at their doors and that the necessity of "rationing" water has been averted. This is the first reason for popular congratulation; and it has been brought about so quietly that unless there is some public demonstration, few people comparatively will realize what a great blessing has come to them and the important lessons involved.

It is an occasion also for unreserved pride in American genius which has achieved a stupendous engineering triumph. Starting at an elevation of 610 feet above tide level in the Catskill mountains, and creating four large lakes on its way, the aqueduct burrows under valleys, tunnels through mountains, dives under rivers to a depth of 1,114 feet below sea-level, bores through the solid rock of Manhattan Island, and delivers pure mountain water to every borough of the city. It is 120 miles long and is capable of delivering 500,000,000 gallons of water a day. The greatest of the famous Roman aqueducts was only half as long as this one, and in technical difficulty was, in comparison, like building houses with children's "blocks." The Catskill aqueduct is three times as long as the Panama canal,* and involved problems and

* The Panama canal is 41½ miles long from shore to shore. Extension by dredging to deep water makes the nominal length of the canal about 50 miles.

difficulties unheard of in the canal's construction. Ex-Mayor McClellan, in an article published March 7, 1917, said: "The great Catskill waterway . . . is in itself certainly the greatest piece of water supply engineering, if not the greatest engineering achievement of any kind, in the world. I think that Gen. Goethals will agree with me that the Panama canal, while more spectacular in character, did not offer the engineering problems which had to be met and overcome in bringing an underground river all the way from the Catskills to . . . New York City."

Back of these physical achievements there were important moral and civic forces at work which the Mayor's Committee deems it highly profitable, from the standpoint of the public welfare, to emphasize in the celebration. The construction of the Catskill aqueduct, covering a period of ten years, affords a model of honest, clean and efficient municipal government in which every citizen should take pride. It is being finished within the original estimate of expense and is a commendable exampie of municipal economy.* It has been completed within contract time§ without a labor strike, and is a tribute alike to the Commission which directed the work, the contractors who carried it out, and the workmen who labored faithfully to build it. In its inception it was fostered by citizen bodies having the public interests at heart, and in its execution it had their invaluable support. It is a testimony of what distinterested civic spirit in co-operation with faithful public officials can accomplish. The celebration, therefore, while giving an opportunity for a merited tribute to the builders of the aqueduct, is also and chiefly an opportunity for teaching important civic lessons.

It is hoped that the celebration as a whole will cause the people of New York to realize more fully than heretofore the value of their wonderful water supply. There are other and smaller cities which have as good water, and as much in proportion to their needs, as New York; but the problem of supplying with water a city of nearly 6,000,000 inhabitants situated like New York is unique. There is nothing to be compared with it. If, by some evil magic, New Yorkers were compelled for a day to dig in the sand and wait for a few pints of water to ooze up, or to bring their water in jars from distant springs, or laboriously to pump it out of wells, they would appreciate the value of what

§ Mayor McClellan broke ground for the aqueduct on June 20, 1907.

* The aqueduct has cost to date about $140,000,000.

they have when the spell was over.* But human nature is prone to take as a matter of course blessings which come regularly and without individual effort; and it is to be feared that too few New Yorkers appreciate the great foresight and constant watchfulness exercised by the guardians of their welfare, the infinite pains and labor bestowed, the vast amount of money expended, and the wonderful scientific skill displayed, in bringing into their homes that priceless fluid upon which their very lives depend, and which they draw from a faucet by a mere turn of the hand.

If the celebration shall cause the citizens of New York to pause for a moment in their ordinary affairs, and, from the contemplation of the great work just completed, derive an adequate conception of this one of their many blessings, it will have served its not least useful purpose.

In furtherance of the various objects of the celebration, this pamphlet has been prepared. With a view to educational use, the first two chapters have been devoted to the elements of natural physics, hygiene, and sanitation, and the reasons for building aqueducts, addressed more particularly to the youthful understanding; and the seventh chapter contains an outline for an allegorical pageant appropriate to the general subject.

* On Washington's Birthday, in 1913, when President Taft broke ground in Fort Wadsworth, Staten Island, for a National Indian Monument, to be erected under the auspices of the National American Indian Memorial Association, many Indians took part in the ceremony. After the Indians had been shown the sights of the city, one of them, who came from an arid section of the West, was asked what he considered to be the most wonderful thing in New York; and he pointed to a faucet, from which water could be drawn at any time.

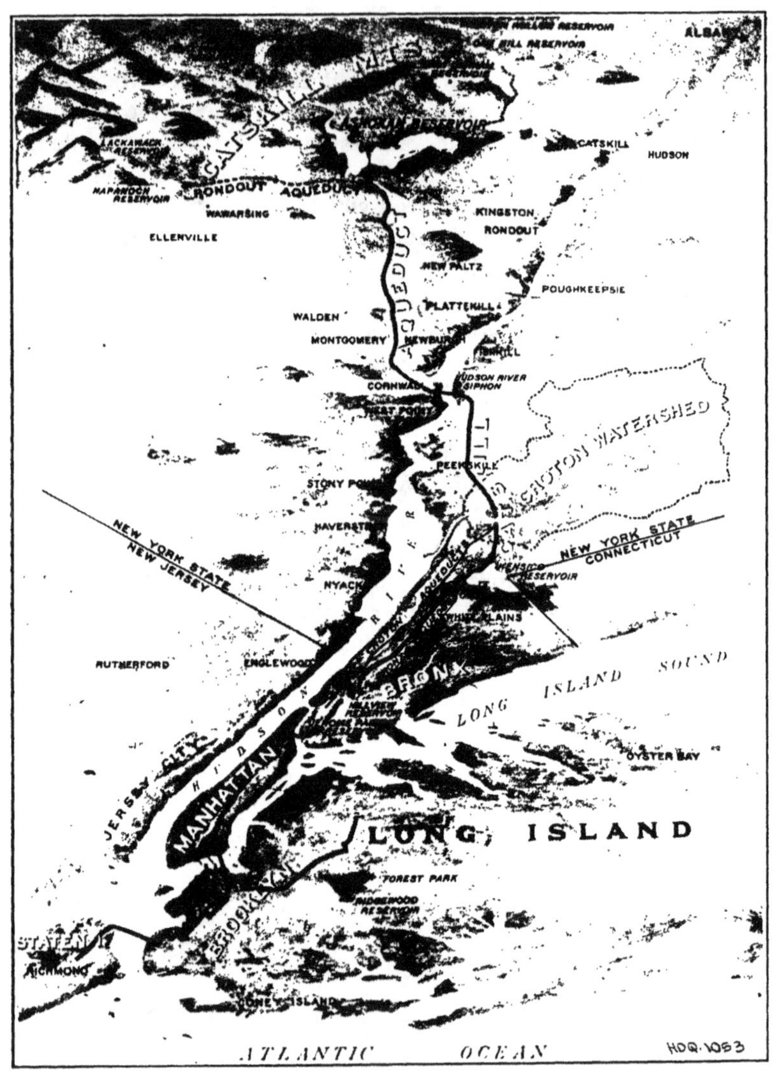

Map of Catskill Aqueduct

The Aqueduct is 120 miles long from Ashokan Reservoir to Staten Island and supplies all five Boroughs of the City of New York

Chapter I.

The Uses and Source of Water

Necessary for Life

Nothing can live without water. Where there is no water there can be no life of any kind, vegetable or animal. There is no water on the moon, therefore no living thing can exist there. If there were no water on the earth, there would be no trees, plants, or vegetables of any sort; no food to eat; nothing to drink, and therefore no human beings or lower animals. Everything would be a vast desert of rocks or sand.*

Necessary for Food and Drink

One reason why rain makes the crops grow and why we "water" plants is that they cannot take up from the earth and absorb in solid and dry form the food on which they live. The particles of earth which form their food must be dissolved in water so that the nourishing fluid can be sucked up by the little tubes in the roots and other parts of the plants.

In the same way bodies of human beings and other animals cannot live and grow on solid dry food. Food must be mixed with water so that the little particles, carried by the fluid, will pass through the organs, arteries and veins and reach every part of the body to nourish it.

Water not only serves the mechanical purpose of carrying food in plants and animals but it also helps the chemical changes in the food which make it nourishing.

About two-thirds of the weight of the human body is water. When there is not water enough in the body for its functions, one feels thirsty; and when one feels thirsty there is nothing so wholesome and satisfying to drink as water which Nature has provided for this purpose. The use of intoxicating liquor instead of water is not only bad morally, but it is bad for the health and should be avoided.

* Probably without the water of crystallization, the surface rocks would turn to dust.

Necessary for Health

As water is necessary for life, so it is necessary for health. And this is so in many ways. When a person eats and drinks, the food is digested and changed in the body; the useful part goes to nourish the body and the useless part is carried off. The useless and unhealthy particles are carried away by the aid of water just as the good particles are distributed in the body by the aid of water. Sweat, or perspiration, is one means by which the body gets rid of this unhealthy matter.* There are about 2,000,000 pores in the skin of an average person, and sweat is always coming out through them, whether it can be seen or not. Evaporation of sweat cools the body; that is one reason why fanning, or a breeze, makes one feel cool. When sweat evaporates, it leaves on the skin and in the clothing the solid particles which the body has rejected. Unless the body is washed, this accumulated matter not only makes a disagreeable odor, but it clogs the pores, interferes with their operation, and injures the health. Keeping the body clean also reduces the danger of communicating disease to, or catching disease from others.§ For similar reasons it is as necessary to wash the clothing as the body.

Necessary for Sanitation

Water is necessary for health in another way. Just as it serves to carry useless and unhealthy matter out of the body, so it serves to carry the dirt and filth out of the house and city through the sewers. There could be no sewer system without an adequate water supply. Without sewers and a water supply there could be no sinks or water-closets in our houses; the streets could not be washed; filth would accumulate; and disease and death would be the result. Great epidemics, causing the death of thousands of people, have been caused by lack of proper water supply and sewerage. For that reason the City of Mexico used to be the unhealthiest city in the civilized world. It is as necessary, therefore, to keep the rooms of houses, the door-yards and the streets clean as it is to keep the body and clothes clean.

* It is hardly necessary to mention the other natural excreta.

§ There is no disease the germs of which pass out through the pores of the skin in sweat; but for other reasons, too technical to be explained here, the danger of contagion is greatly reduced by bodily cleanliness.

Necessary for Protection from Fire

Water is Nature's great provision for extinguishing fires. Fire, when under control, is one of man's most useful friends; but when uncontrolled is one of his most destructive enemies. As civilization has progressed, the uses of fire have multiplied and consequently the dangers have increased. The Indians made fire with difficulty by rubbing two pieces of wood together; and even in the days of our own grandparents, before matches were invented, it was so difficult to make fire with flint and steel that people kept coals burning on their hearths all night so as to have fire for heat and cooking the next day; and if their coals went out, they borrowed fire from their neighbors. To-day, we have the means of making fire everywhere, and there is great danger from fire unless there is constant care to prevent it, and adequate provision for putting it out if it starts. Considering how universal the use of fire is, and how all-prevailing is the danger from it, we see how good Providence has been in providing abundant means for extinguishing it in case of necessity. Our homes and shops, churches and schools, factories and offices, and the lives of our people in them, would not be safe a day without an adequate water supply and an efficient fire department. The great damage in San Francisco in 1906 at the time of the earthquake was not due primarily to the earthquake, but to the breaking of the water pipes which prevented extinguishing the fire which started. In New York there is no danger from earthquakes, but there would be great danger from fire if it were not for the water supply and the fire department. Because of these wise provisions, New York never had a great fire like those in Chicago in 1871, in Boston in 1872 and in San Francisco in 1906.

Useful in Industry

Man increases the products of his industry and labor by employing some kind of force other than that of his own muscles. The three principal sources of power are animals, as from horses; the wind, as from windmills; and water, directly or indirectly, as described hereafter. Water is used directly for power at waterfalls, which turn wheels and run mills and factories nearby. Sometimes the water-falls run machinery which makes electricity and the electricity is sent long distances over wires to be turned into power again to run trolley cars and factories, or to make electric light or heat. Water, when heated and turned into steam, makes the steam engine go on the railroad; runs the stationary engine in the factory; produces electricity where there is no water power; and pulls the traction-plow or other machine on the farm. Water is not only used for power, but it is used in an infinite number of ways in manufacturing processes. So universal is the use of water in industry that it may be said in literal truth that not a thing is manufactured—for food, clothing, housing, transportation, or any other purpose,—of which water does not form a part or in the making of which water does not help. If we had only enough water for food and drink and none for mechanical and manufacturing purposes, nearly all forms of modern industry, and almost all the manifold activities of our lives would come to a stand-still.

Useful in Commerce

Water covers two-thirds of the surface of the earth. As man cannot walk on water, he has built boats which float on it, and thus he uses the rivers, lakes and oceans to bear the commerce of the world. New York City owes her commercial greatness largely to her situation upon a number of islands surrounded by water and upon the mainland adjacent to water; to the Erie canal* and the Hudson river, by which she is connected with the Great Lakes; and to her municipal water supply which provides not only for the life, health and safety of her great population but also for the great industries which make her the leading manufacturing city of the United States.

By reason of her water supply and her water situation, New York is enabled to employ in her manufactures more capital, to pay more wages, to use more materials, to make products of greater value, and to have a greater water-borne commerce than any other city in the Western Hemisphere—and (at the present time) probably in the world.§

* Before the Erie canal was opened in 1825, Philadelphia was a larger city than New York. It is generally conceded that the Erie canal gave New York the start which led to her commercial preëminence.

§ The following figures for the year 1914 are taken from the United States census of manufactures:

City.	*Capital*	*Salaries and wages.*	*Materials.*	*Products.*
New York City..	$1, 626, 104, 000	$510, 711, 000	$1, 229, 155, 000	$6, 292, 832, 000
Chicago...........	1, 189, 976, 000	303, 630, 000	901, 658, 000	1, 482, 814, 000
Philadelphia.......	772, 696, 000	185, 484, 000	451, 197, 000	784, 500, 000

The commerce of this port, including exports and imports, in 1916 was $3,517,987,000, which is about ten times as much as that of Boston, this city's nearest competitor.

The Source of Water

Seeing how essential water is to life and how its use contributes to our well-being in every way, it is interesting to observe the wonderful way in which Nature supplies it for the needs of man.

Water exists in three forms. As snow and ice it is a *solid;* as steam and fog, and when suspended invisibly in the air, it is a *vapor;* and as ordinary water it is a *liquid.* The same "law of gravitation" which causes a thing to fall to the ground or a ball to roll down hill causes water to seek the lowest level. Therefore all water tends to run toward the ocean.* If nature made no provision for bringing the water back again, all the water of the earth would be collected in the lowest places and the land surfaces would be dry deserts. But the Creator has provided a marvellous system by which the water keeps going back to the land as fast as it goes from the land to the ocean.§

When the sun shines on the ocean, or any other body of water, some of the water is turned into vapor. This vapor, which is generally invisible at first, rises into the air and is carried by the winds to different parts of the earth. If the vapor meets cooler currents of air, or if in rising the air expands so that the invisible water becomes heavier than the air, the vapor condenses and becomes visible as clouds. Clouds are water floating in the air. A rainbow also consists of drops of water which refract the sunlight in beautiful colors. When the clouds become dense enough, the water which forms them falls either as snow or rain. The rain and melted snow make our fresh water.

When the rain falls on the hills and fields, the roofs and streets, it immediately begins to soak through the ground or run down hill, always trying to reach a lower level. Falling and running water, or water in the form of glaciers, has enormous power to wear away the surface of the earth. It is Nature's great sculptor, which† has carved the hills and valleys and the rocks into all the beautiful shapes which we see in the landscape.

* This statement is sufficiently exact as a generalization. If all waters do not reach a common level it is because of some physical obstruction or evaporation. The surface of the Dead Sea is 1,292 feet below sea-level, while that of Great Salt Lake in Utah is 4,200 feet above sea-level; but physical barriers prevent their waters and those of the ocean coming to a common level. The only escape of the waters of the Dead Sea and Great Salt Lake is by evaporation.

§ Solomon said: "All the rivers run into the sea, yet the sea is not full; into the place from whence the rivers come thither they return again."—*Ecclesiastes, i, 7.*

† Aided by aerial erosion.

One of the most wonderful examples of the power of water to carve the earth is the Grand Canyon of the Colorado river in Arizona, which is over a mile deep and measures from ten to fifteen miles from rim to rim. As the water runs over the surface or soaks through the ground it gradually collects in streams and lakes which in turn empty eventually into the ocean, and thus the water gets back to the starting point. And so it keeps up its eternal round.

When, in soaking through the ground and flowing over the surface, the water dissolves and wears away the rocks and soil, it deposits the heavier particles in lower places, but retains some minerals in solution. Upon the proportion of these minerals depends the purity of the water. When the minerals are abundant in water it is called mineral water. Water with much lime or iron in it is called "hard" water. The water from the Catskill mountains is very free from minerals and therefore is a "soft" water, very good for drinking, cooking and washing. The most common mineral which water collects in its journey to the ocean is salt. When the water evaporates from the ocean, or from a lake which has no outlet, like the Great Salt Lake, the salt is left behind, so that sea water is salty and cannot be drunk; and it is the rain which supplies fresh water for all the beneficial uses of man.

Religious Observances

Water is such a great blessing to mankind and so indispensable to his life and happiness, that all peoples of all ages, from the aborigines to the present time, have, in the forms of their various religions, prayed to God for it and thanked Him for it. The Indians of Arizona perform very beautiful "flute ceremonies" around their water pools and the Hopi Indians have a most remarkable ceremony for rain in the form of a Snake Dance, in which their priests dance around holding big snakes in their mouths. The New York Indians used to have a Rain Dance and a Corn Planting Dance; and when they passed Niagara Falls and other waterfalls they would empty a wooden plateful of tobacco into the waterfall as an offering to the Great Spirit. It was also a very ancient practice in the Old World, to throw offerings into springs, rivers and lakes that were sacred. Extraordinary proof of the antiquity of this custom was discovered in 1852 when the Jesuit fathers, who owned the cele-

Ruins of Ancient Aqueduct on the Campagna at Rome

brated sulphur springs called "Sorgenti di Vicarello" (by the ancients called the Waters of Apollo), on the western border of the Lake of Bracciano in Italy, sent from Rome a gang of masons to clear the mouth of the central spring and put the whole in order. In draining a well only a few feet below the ordinary level of the waters they came across a layer of brass and silver coins of the fourth century after Christ. As they continued to dig, they found offerings of earlier periods, gold and silver coins, silver cups, etc. The farther down they went the cruder the offerings were. Under the earliest known Roman coins were found shapeless pieces of copper, an early kind of currency, and lowest of all they found a stratum of stone arrowheads, polished stone knives, etc., of the stone age long before Rome was founded.*

Another curious illustration of more modern date, showing veneration for water, is cited by Clemens Herschel in his work on Frontinus' "Two Books on the Water Supply of the City of Rome." He mentions that in the seventeenth century, it was one of the "rules of the bath" at Baden, near Vienna, to salute the water on entering and leaving it. A guest was fined if he omitted this ceremony or spoke of the bath as mere water.

The Babylonians in their religion associated Wisdom with Water and symbolized this belief in the form of a fish-god. Whatever may be thought of the Babylonian religion, it is safe to say that they were pretty near the truth in recognizing some relation between Water and Wisdom. Great and beneficent Wisdom has given water to man for his use and those people are wise who use it freely and properly.

* Lanciani's "Ancient Rome," p. 46.

Chapter II.

Aqueducts and Why They Are Built

Definition of the Word Aqueduct

The word "aqueduct" comes from two Latin words, "aqua" which means "water," and "ducere" which means "to lead." An aqueduct, therefore, is a thing built to lead water.

Reasons for Building Aqueducts

When a place is first settled, as will be seen in a subsequent chapter on New York's early water supply, the people depend upon local springs, streams and wells for their water supply. As the town grows, and the number of people increases, the supply from those primitive sources is not sufficient and it is necessary to get water from some other place. At the same time, with the growth of the settlement, the local sources of water become defiled and cannot be used. Therefore it is necessary to seek pure water elsewhere and to conduct it to the town through a channel so protected that it cannot be spoiled on the way.

There is another very important reason for building an aqueduct. Rain does not fall equally in all parts of the world; the same amount does not fall in all years; and the rain at a given place does not fall evenly at all times of the year. For instance, in some parts of southwestern Arizona the average annual rainfall or "precipitation"* in some years is only an immeasurable trace, and in others only an inch. In a considerable section of the area comprising southern Nevada, southeastern California, western Arizona and southwestern Utah, the average annual rainfall is only 2 inches or less. On the other hand, in the Mount Olympus region in northwestern Washington there is an average annual rainfall of 120 inches. The average for the whole United States is variously estimated at from 29 to 31.46 inches. The average for New York City is 44.63 inches a year.

Now a total annual precipitation of 44.63 inches over the

* "Precipitation" is measured by catching the rain and snow in a vessel with vertical sides and open at the top, and measuring the depth of the water and melted snow in inches. The sum of all the measurements during a year is the total precipitation.

area of 315.9 square miles of New York City would amount to 204,125,707,138 gallons, or an average of about 559,000,000 gallons a day; and even if it could be collected and used it would not be sufficient, for the average daily consumption of the city is nearly 600,000,000 gallons. But it could *not* all be collected; and if it *could*, it would not be fit to use. Furthermore, it does not fall in regular daily quantities of just 559,000,000 gallons. On October 8-9, 1903, about one-fifth of the total precipitation of the year occurred in 24 hours. So that if the city depended on the rainfall within its own area, it would have more water than it needed some days and none at all on other days. Again, in 1916, the total annual precipitation in New York City was only 33.17 inches, or only three-fourths that of the average year, and it would have been insufficient even if it could have been collected and used. It becomes necessary, therefore, to build an aqueduct leading water from an adequate and never-failing source; or to build in connection with the aqueduct dams which will hold back the water in reservoirs when there is too much and let it out for use when otherwise there would not be enough. In the accounts of the Croton and Catskill aqueducts given hereafter it will be seen how great artificial lakes have been made for this purpose of equalizing the supply.

An aqueduct has so many advantages over a local and natural water supply that they cannot all be described in these pages; but two or three may briefly be mentioned. One is, that by taking the water from high sources, it rises to a certain height in our buildings by its own pressure; which saves the expense and trouble of pumping. Water supplied by an aqueduct can also be handled, controlled and distributed more efficiently than water derived from innumerable local sources; and it can be kept purer, by preventive measures and by chemical treatment, than a local supply.

Early Aqueducts

People began at a very early period to realize, in a dim way, some of these truths and to take artificial measures for securing water. Sometimes, like the American Indians and other primitive peoples, they built reservoirs and ditches for irrigation.* As civilization advanced and cities began to grow up, channels were

* An interesting example is the so-called Mummy Lake, recently discovered in the Mesa Verde National Park, Colorado, which was never a lake, but a reservoir for prehistoric irrigation.

built to supply water for domestic use. In fact, the degree of intelligence with which any people, ancient or modern, has used water may almost be taken as a measure of its civilization. Both Mexicans and Peruvians had attained a stage of culture which led them to build aqueducts before the advent of Europeans in the New World. The best known Mexican aqueduct was that which led water from Chapultepec to Mexico City. It was about a league long. But the Peruvians, whose culture excelled that of the Aztecs, built aqueducts of great length. Prescott says, "One that traversed the district of Condesuyu measured between four and five hundred miles." It is not known when these early Americans began to build aqueducts.

The earliest aqueduct of which the present writer has found a precise record was built about 700 years before Christ by Hezekiah (King of Judah, 720-689 B. C.) to supply Jerusalem with water. There was formerly a surface conduit which conducted the water of the river Gihon to the city, but in anticipation of an attack from the Assyrians, Hezekiah built an underground tunnel about 1,700 feet long to carry the water of that stream to a reservoir or pool called Siloam. The Pool of Siloam was in the highway of the fullers' field on the west side of the city. It was hewn out of solid rock and measured 71 feet north and south and 75 feet east and west. Stone steps led down into it. This was called the upper pool. Lower down the valley Hezekiah built another pool to receive the overflow of Siloam. The aqueduct was discovered by Dr. Schick in 1886. About 25 feet from the Pool of Siloam an old Hebrew inscription tells realistically of the meeting of the two parties working toward each other in constructing the tunnel. Interesting references to this primitive aqueduct are to be found in II Kings xviii, 17, and xx, 20; II Chronicles, xxxii, 30; and Isaiah, vii. 3.

It is not intended to give here a history of aqueducts, but to cite a few instances in order that the reader may realize, by comparison, the magnitude of the Catskill aqueduct. With the general statement that the building of aqueducts had been practiced in Greece and the older civilizations of Asia for centuries before the first Roman aqueduct was built, we may glance at those justly famous works which in ancient days supplied the Eternal City with water.

The greatest public works of ancient Rome, to which the

city and empire owed much of their greatness and power, were roads, aqueducts and drains. As for the aqueducts, we are indebted to a great Water Commissioner of the first century for a description of them. In the year 97, Emperor Nerva appointed as Superintendent of Water Works Sextus Julius Frontinus, a remarkable administrator. In order that he might intelligently perform his duties, Frontinus made a study of the Roman aqueducts and wrote a description of them in two books entitled "De Aquiis Urbis Romæ" ("Concerning the Waters of the City of Rome.")* Near the beginning of his work he names the nine aqueducts then existing. He says:

"From the foundation of the city for 441 years†† the Romans were content with the use of the waters which they drew either from the Tiber, or from wells, or from springs. Springs have held, down to the present day† the name of holy things, and are objects of veneration, having the repute of healing the sick; as, for example, the Springs of the Camenae (Prophetic Nymphs), of Apollo, and of Juturna. But there now run into the city: the Appian aqueduct, Anio Vetus, Marcia, Tepula, Julia, Virgo, Alsietina which is also called Augusta, Claudia and Anio Novus."

The lengths of these aqueducts are not accurately known. The inscriptions on them indicate certain distances; Frontinus gives others; and measurements based on existing remains indicate others. The differences may be due to subsequent changes of locations, or to different bases of calculation. The following are their dates of construction and approximate lengths:§

Name	*Built*	*Miles Long*
Aqua Appia	312 B.C.	10
Aqua Anio Vetus	272-269 B.C.	43
Aqua Marcia	144-140 B.C.	58
Aqua Tepula	125 B.C.	17
Aqua Julia	33 B.C.	17
Aqua Virgo	19 B.C.	12
Aqua Alsietina	10 A.D.	20
Aqua Claudia	38- 52 A.D.	43
Aqua Anio Novus	38- 52 A.D.	62 (?)

* A facsimile of the original, a translation and an interesting commentary thereon are to be found in "The Two Books on the Water Supply of the City of Rome of Sextus Julius Frontinus, Water Commissioner of the City of Rome A. D. 97," by Clemens Herschel, hydraulic engineer, published in 1899 by Dana Estes & Co., of Boston.

† About the year 98 A. D.

§ Other aqueducts were built after Frontinus' time. Of the four aqueducts which now supply Rome—Vergine, Paola, Marciapia, and Felice—three of them are duplicates or reconstructions of Virgo, Alsietina, and Marcia.

†† Until the year 313 B. C.

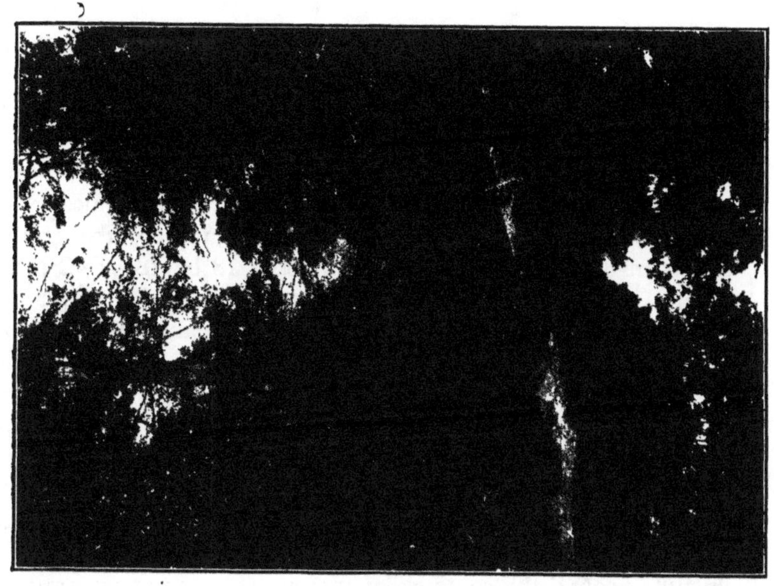

Ancient Water-courses of Manhattan Island Still Flowing in Central Park

It will be seen that the longest of these was only about half the length of the Catskill aqueduct. Other details also show that even the best of them was not comparable with the Catskill aqueduct as an engineering achievement.

The oldest of them, called Appia, took its water from a spring, and was a low-level aqueduct. All of its ten miles except about 300 feet was built just below the surface of the ground. It was made of rough-hewn stones about 18 by 18 by 42 inches in size, enclosing a passageway about 2½ feet wide and 5 feet high; and was not much more than a walled and covered sewer except that it carried clean water.

Anio Vetus took its water from the river Anio. It was about 90 feet higher than Appia but was still a low-level work. Of its 43 miles, a portion of about 1,100 feet was on an artificial structure above ground. It was built of massive masonry, laid in cement and plastered on the inside. Its channel was about 3.7 feet wide by 8 feet high. It was a true aqueduct, being carried skilfully around the contours of mountains so as to maintain the elevation necessary to carry the water to the city.

Marcia was the first true high-level aqueduct. It carried spring water to the city a distance of nearly 58 miles. It had an elevation of 195 feet above sea-level. It was built of rough-hewn stone, but Mr. Clemens Herschel characterizes it from the remains he has examined, as showing "the commonplace work of the rustic ditch-builder." Its interior was 5.7 feet wide and 8.3 high at one place, and varied to 3 feet by 5.7.

Tepula, about 17 miles long, was built of homogeneous concrete, and marks the beginning of the use of that material in which the Romans were very skilful. It was 2.7 by 3.3 feet in cross section. It conducted warm water from volcanic springs.

Julia was about the same length as Tepula, and followed the same course, being built directly on top of the earlier aqueduct and of the same material. Its source was some cold springs a little beyond the warm springs of Tepula.

Virgo was a low-level aqueduct, its springs being only about 80 feet above sea level. It was only about 1.6 feet wide by 6.6 feet high, built of concrete and brick.

Alsietina brought water from a lake of that name about 20 miles from Rome and about 680 feet above the sea level. Concrete and brick were its principal materials.

Claudia took its waters from three springs not far from the source of Marcia, but was only about 43 miles long. A short distance from its intake its cross section was about 3.3 feet by 6.6 feet high. This aqueduct is particularly interesting, because it marks the highest development of the skill of the Romans in hydraulic engineering. It was constructed mainly of stone cut to regular dimensions. Built at the same time with Anio Vetus, the two cost 55.5 sestertii or nearly $3,000,000, or about $6 a running foot, with slave labor. It had a tunnel about 3 feet wide by 7 feet high and three miles long through Mount Affliano. The tunnelling through the rock was by the primitive means of chiselling, and by heating the rocks and chilling them with water, causing them to crack. Claudia crossed the Campagna on stately stone arches the ruins of which are standing today and look like the High Bridge of the Croton aqueduct across the Harlem River, except that the arches of Claudia have only 18 or 20 feet span and the piers are only about 8 feet thick in elevation, while the High Bridge arches have spans of 50 and 80 feet according to location and the piers are proportionately thick.

Anio Novus was built of brick lined with concrete and was about 62 miles long. Some authorities say only 52. Its cross section was 3.3 feet wide by 9 feet high. It took its waters from a series of reservoirs constructed by damming rivers very much after the fashion of modern storage reservoirs, only on a smaller scale. Part of the way it was built on the structure of Claudia. In fact, some of the old Roman ruins show portions of four or five different aqueducts built on top of each other.

The Roman aqueduct represented the open cut, cut-and-cover, tunnel and overhead forms of construction and employed as materials rough stones rudely mortised together (Anio Vetus), stones cut to regular dimensions, bricks and concrete. Sometimes the exterior was ornamental with a kind of masonry called "opus reticulatum," consisting of stones about six inches square, inlaid in concrete with their lines diagonal, producing a tile-like effect. The roofs of the conduits were sometimes flat, sometimes arched, and sometimes shaped like an inverted V, the latter being made of slabs of stone inclined against each other. These different forms of roof were used promiscuously in the same works and do not appear to have any chronological value. The interior of the aqueducts was lined with concrete to make them water-tight. At intervals there were chambers called "piscinæ," evidently used for collecting sediment; and shafts for ventilation, inspection and cleaning. The speed of the current of water was checked in some of the aqueducts by contracting the size of channel, or by abrupt turns in the course of the aqueduct. Inscribed stones were set up at various places, giving distances from the city, dates of construction and repair, and names of rulers.

The Romans knew the principle of the inverted siphon and used it on a small scale in their distribution system, but rarely resorted to it in their main conduits. The Catskill aqueduct employs this principle to such an elaborate extent in passing under deep valleys and rivers that none of it is above ground. The great inverted siphon of the Catskill aqueduct which passes under the Hudson river at Storm King 1,114 feet below sea-level is infinitely beyond any accomplishment of the Romans.

The cross-sections of the Roman aqueducts indicate their smallness compared with the Catskill aqueduct which has diameters as great as 17½ feet. The cross-section area of the Catskill aqueduct is six or seven times the size of the largest Roman aqueduct. As to capacity, Mr. Clemens Herschel, in his work before mentioned, estimates that when all nine Roman aqueducts were in operation—which was not always the case, as two or three might be out of commission at the same time—they had an aggregate capacity of about 84,000,000 gallons a day; but as much water was lost or stolen on the way, or purposely diverted outside the city, only about 39,000,000 gallons a day on the average was delivered inside the walls of the city in the time Frontinus. The single Catskill aqueduct has a capacity of 500,000,000 gallons a day.

When the Roman aqueducts crossed the low Campagna on masonry arches they have left impressive monuments. The Catskill aqueduct has avoided such exposed structures for purposes of safety, and instead of building arcades to pass over valleys and rivers, has inverted siphons to pass under them. The aqueduct ruins on the Campagna (see page 15), like the Roman aqueduct at Segovia, Spain, and the Pont du Gard near Nismes, France,* and others which might be mentioned, give an impres-

* The aqueduct at Segovia, built A. D. 109, is 8 feet wide and 2,700 feet long and at places consists of a double tier of stone arches 95 feet high. It is still in use. The Pont du Gard is part of a Roman aqueduct built in the year 19 B. C. It crosses the Gard river on a three-storied arcade 180 feet high and 873 feet long. It is estimated that the ruins of over 200 aqueducts built by the Romans in their extensive provinces still exist.

sion of massiveness and durability, and, above all, of the force of intellect that was behind them and extended the Roman Empire to such vast dimensions.

Frontinus, in his "De Aquiis Urbis Romae" sarcastically compares the "idle pyramids and the other useless but much renowned works of the Greeks" with the great utilitarian and indispensable structures of these aqueducts, when he says: "Tot aquarum tam multis necessariis molibus pyramidas videlicet otiosas conpares aut cetera inertia sed fama celebrata opera Graecorum."

But wonderful as the Roman aqueducts were, they were not the equals, in size or the difficulty of the engineering difficulties overcome, of the Catskill aqueduct, which is the greatest engineering feat of its kind in the world.

Chapter III.

Manhattan's Primitive Water Supply

The Era of Pumps and Wells

The natural water supply of New Amsterdam and of New York City in its early years was derived from the ponds, brooks and springs which abounded on the island of Manhattan before they were obliterated by the construction of streets and buildings. Some of the ponds afforded good fishing, and there are people living today who remember the existence of Sunfish pond at Madison avenue and 32d street, Stuyvesant's pond and Cedar ponds, which as late as 1860 were favorite resorts for skating.*

Most of these ponds, springs and streams which once sparkled in the landscape have been obliterated by modern improvements, but a few of them may still be observed in Central Park, and on the unbuilt portions of the upper end of the island. (See page 21.)

The earliest artificial supply was derived from wells. The geological formation of the lower end of Manhattan island was not favorable for obtaining good water, however. The rock bottom of the island is covered with alluvial deposits which appear to have been permeated easily with water from the salt rivers; while at the same time the absence of a sewer system in the early history of the town permitted much unwholesome matter to find its way into the ground. When we read that "tubbs of odour and nastiness" were emptied in the street§ it is not surprising that the wells were not only generally unpleasant to the taste, but, as we shall see, were also undoubtedly at times highly unsanitary.

The wells were of the kind in the use of old country at that period, surmounted by a long pole which was balanced at one end with a counterpoise and had at the other end a chain rope to which the bucket was attached.

As may well be imagined, the abundance of water from both the wells and the natural springs was subject to fluctuations on account of the weather. As a single instance, we may cite the

* Haswell's Reminiscences, p. 541.

§ Common Council minutes, 1700.

Holland's View of Broad Street looking northward toward Federal Hall in 1797, showing Street Pumps

experience of the British troops on the upper end of the island in the year 1782. In September of that year, there was a great drouth which generally inconvenienced and alarmed the troops. Lieut. Von Krafft of Von Donop's Hessian regiment, who kept a diary, records under date of September 3, of that year:

"This afternoon our foragers and sharpshooters returned. They had measured at the camp but could find no water on account of the great heat of this year which had dried up everything."

The next day men were sent out to dig wells, but they could not find anything but the faintest and poorest springs, even at a depth of 30 or 40 feet. "All the wells and ditches round about were dried up." On September 27 "There was a general complaint that all the men would die soon for want of water."

The earliest wells were private enterprises, dug within the owners' enclosures, although it was the custom for several neighbors to join in meeting the expense of a well which they used in common. The establishment of a public well was first proposed in 1658 during the incumbency of Peter Stuyvesant as Director General. At the meeting of the Burgomasters held on July 11, 1658, the "Burgomasters resolved to communicate with the General relative to having a public well made in the Heere straat."* The Heere straat was Broadway. It does not appear whether this proposed well was constructed. It is a remarkable fact that at the time of the surrender of Fort Amsterdam to the English in 1664, there was no well or cistern in the fort, although just before the appearance of the English, "it was hastily provided with 20 or 24 water barrels or pitched casks removed from the ships and filled with water."§ In 1667, Gov. Nicolls repaired this defect by digging a well in the fort which supplied excellent water, much to the surprise of the old inhabitants, whose previous neglect in this respect may have been due to their belief that potable water could not be found there. Later a well was dug outside the sally-port of the fort at the foot of Bowling Green and it became a great resort for the inhabitants who were not otherwise supplied. The pump installed in this well is the first recorded in the city's history.

In 1677, under the English, the Common Council began the systematic construction of wells in the public streets. On Febr-

* Records of New Amsterdam, vii, 190.

§ Stuyvesant's answer. Doc. Rel. Col. Hist. N. Y., ii, 441.

uary 28, 1676-77 they ordered that "Severall Weells bee made in the places hereafter menconed (for the publique good of the Cytie) by the inhabitants of Each Street where the said wells shall bee made, Viztt:"—one in the street opposite the butcher Roeoliff Johnson's house; one in Broadway opposite Hendrick Van Dyke's; one in Smith street opposite John Cavileer's; one in the Water Side opposite Cornelis Van Borsum's; and one in the back yard of the City Hall at 73 Pearl street. The latter was the first stone well.

On September 10, 1686, the Common Council ordered nine more wells to be built. These were built of stone, "one halfe of the Charge of them to be borne by the inhabitants of every Streete proportionately and the other halfe by the Citty." One or two citizens were appointed to have charge of each well. The practice of dividing the expense between the beneficiaries and the city was continued as long as the public well system existed.

Some of the wells at the end of the 17th century became well known by name and their locations have been pretty well identified. Among them were the following:

Name.	*Location.*
De Riemer's Well	Whitehall street, near Bridge.
William Cox's Well	Near Stadt Huys, at head of Coenties Slip.
Ten Eyck and Vincent's Well	Broad street between Stone and South William streets.
Tunis de Kay's Well	Broad street, north of Beaver
Frederick Wessel's Well	Wall street, west of William street.
Rombout's Well	Broadway, near Exchange Place street.
Suert Olpherts' Well	Near last mentioned.

Many other wells were dug in later years and may be identified by reference to the Common Council minutes and maps.

Pumps came into fashion in the first half of the 18th century and rapidly displaced the old well-sweeps. After the city had bought its first fire-engines mentioned hereafter, it became particularly necessary to maintain the water supply and in November, 1741, the Assembly enacted a law (chapter 719) entitled "An act for mending and keeping in repair the publick wells and pumps in the City of New York." This law provided for the appointment of Overseers of Wells and Pumps, the levying of taxes for their maintenance, etc. Disorderly persons frequently cut the ropes of the wells, broke the pump-handles and did other mischief of a similar nature, and the same law provided penalties for such offences.

Sometimes a public spirit citizen would give a well and pump to the city if the corporation would agree to keep it in repair. Henry Rutgers made such an offer to give a well and pump in the Out ward in December, 1785. But generally the expense of the well and pump was jointly borne by the City and the neighborhood.

To give an idea of how these matters were managed at the beginning of the American period after the evacuation of New York by the British we may cite a few transactions of the Common Council.

On August 26, 1784, for instance, the inhabitants of Frankfort street petitioned for a well and pump and it was granted. The city's share of the first cost of this well and pump was £39:16:15. The cost of digging a well varied according to circumstances. In October, 1784, Silvanus Seely was paid £4:11:3 for digging a well in the South ward, but Phil Arcularius was paid £40:19:6 for digging one in Frankfort street in 1785. On November 11, 1784, the Common Council authorized a well in Catharine street and voted to contribute £7 toward it, later adding £8 more. In July, 1785, the inhabitants of Greenwich street were given permission to sink two wells at their own expense, the corporation furnishing the pumps. In a similar way in August, 1785, the inhabitants of Chambers street were permitted to make a well and stone it at their expense, the pump being at the expense of the corporation.

These street pumps were landmarks, very much like street monuments to-day, and formed convenient points of reference. For instance, when the Common Council decided in May, 1785, to grade Broadway southward from Exchange place, it voted that there should be a "gentle descent from the upper pump to the Bowling Green." The "upper pump" was at Broadway and Exchange place. (See picture of pumps in Broad Street on page 27.)

On April 5, 1785 William Smith contracted to keep the wells and pumps in repair at the rate of £140 per annum; but Smith's job was not a profitable one; the number of pumps and wells was rapidly increasing and the cost of repair mounting with equal pace. The Common Council, therefore, devised the system of electing two Overseers of pumps and wells for each ward; but evidently these new functionaries occasionally neglected their duties, for on September 16, 1789, the Common Council "Ordered that whenever the Overseers of the Public Wells and Pumps neglect or refuse to do their duty that the Aldn & Assist of the Ward direct the necessary Repairs; lest by the want of water from the public wells and pumps the City may be endangered in case of Fire."

During the year 1789 the Common Council approved for payment bills for repairs to wells and pumps amounting to £408:15:5½.

The Tea Water Pump

The water from the wells in the lower part of the city served well enough for ordinary domestic uses, except drinking, but, as we said before, was brackish and disagreeable to the taste. Some time during the first half of the 18th century, however, a spring of fresh water on the north side of the present Park row, between Baxter and Mulberry streets, began to attract popular attention. This spring was probably supplied by the same underground sources that supplied the neighboring Fresh Water or Collect pond. The water was so desirable for making tea that it became famous in history as the Tea Water Pump. Indeed, it became a regular landmark and has left its impress on the real estate records of that neighborhood. The property described in deeds as the "Tea Water Pump" was a parcel 75 feet by 120 feet on the north side of Chatham street (Park row) beginning 28 feet east of Baxter street. A deed containing a reference to it as the "Tea Water Pump," is dated June 1, 1795,* and there is another of the same description in liber 169, page 334. The description there is: "Which said three lots, pieces or parcels of ground are known by the name or description of the 'Tea Water Pump' or the Estate of Gerardus Hardenbrook, Sr., deceased." The same description or a similar one is found in later deeds, among which are those to be found in liber 55, page 395; liber 65, page 102; liber 66, page 454, and liber 68, page 225. The property was afterwards sold in parts. Gerardus Hardenbrook left a will dated 1755 and recorded in liber 33 of wills, page 533. About 1796 William C. Thompson, a grandson, acquired the majority interest and is undoubtedly the Mr. Thompson referred to hereafter and in Valentine's Manual for 1856, page 438. Abraham Shoemaker referred to hereafter and

* Liber 170 of deeds, p. 7.

on the same page in Valentine's Manual afterwards acquired at least the central part of the 75 foot tract from Thompson and others. Valentine's authority for designating the property as No. 126 Chatham street (the old name for Park row), does not appear. No. 126 Chatham street as shown in deeds of the middle of the nineteenth century would be east of Mulberry street. If there was a numbering of the street that would bring No. 126 near Baxter street, it has not been found. The site of the pump, however, is well established by the deeds referred to.

The first mention of the Tea Water spring is in the diary of Professor Kalm, a learned and observant man who visited the City in 1748. He says:

"There is no good water to be met with in the town itself; but at a little distance there is a large spring of good water, which the inhabitants take for their tea and for the uses of the kitchen. Those, however, who are less delicate on this point make use of the water from the wells in town, though it be very bad. The want of good water lies heavy upon the horses of the strangers that come to this place for they do not like to drink the water from the wells of the town."

Shortly before the Revolution the Tea Water spring and its vicinity were made into a fashionable resort at which beverages adulterated with pure water could be obtained. A high pump with a prodigiously long handle was erected over the spring, and the grounds around it were laid out in ornamental fashion and called the Tea Water Pump Garden.

The tea water from this source was so popular that not only did people come to the pump for it, but it was delivered around town in carts which looked something like modern sprinkling-wagons without the sprinkler. The distributors of this water were called "tea-water men," and became so numerous and active that on June 16, 1757, the Common Council had to pass "A Law for the Regulating of Teawater men in the City of New York."

At length, the big pump projecting over the street and the crowd of water-wagons gathered there became so great an obstruction to the street that in 1797 a petition for an abatement of the nuisance was presented to the Common Council. The committee to whom the subject was referred reported as follows:

"The committee on the subject of the petition complaining of the obstruction in Chatham street caused by the Tea Water Pump delivering its water in the street and by the water carts

This is a fair copie of ye Ingen arrived
from London and now in ye City Hall
7 feete wide on ye baard and 9 feete
worke poole 73 feete long in ye whole-
manned by 12 tugmen eleven buckett
men and 1 pipe man

Stoutenburgh's Sketch of the First Fire "Ingen," 1732.

(See page 38.)

drawn up across the street when about to receive water, report that they have viewed the premises and find the matters and things set forth in the petitions to be true. That the committee have maturely considered the premises and are of opinion that the said obstruction may be removed at no great expense to Mr. Thompson, the present occupant and part proprietor of the premises, by causing the spout of the said pump to be raised about two feet and by lengthening it so as to deliver the water at the outer part of the paved walk, which would permit passengers to pass under without inconvenience; and if the water carts were ordered to draw up abreast of the spout near the gutter and receive the water in rotation it would remove the obstruction in the street." The committee recommended also that the sidewalks in that vicinity be paved.

The recommendations of the committee, except that relating to paving, were adopted, the paving being postponed for the time being.

In 1805 Abram Shoemaker petitioned to the Common Council for leave to erect works so as to conduct the water of the late Tea Water Pump into carts in Orange street (now Baxter street) as they formerly took the water from Chatham street, by which inconvenience would be avoided, and the petition was allowed during the pleasure of the Common Council.

It is amusing, in these modern days when the city authorities are concerning themselves with a great aqueduct system capable of delivering 500,000,000 gallons of water a day to the city, to read of the Common Council passing solemn resolutions about the length of the Tea Water Pump spout.

The Primitive Fire Department

While the primitive conditions of the water supply just described existed, there was an equally primitive system of fire extinguishing. When one recalls the inflammable character of the earliest buildings in New Amsterdam and the inadequate means for fire protection, it is a wonder that the infant city was not destroyed several times.

During the Dutch regime there were a few stone storehouses and several brick houses belonging to the more wealthy residents; but most of the buildings were of wood. To add to their inflammability, the roofs of a majority of the early houses were thatched with straw or reeds, and their chimneys were made of wood or of interwoven twigs plastered with clay.

No machine for projecting water upon a fire existed in New Amsterdam. If a fire broke out, a bucket brigade was formed. Men stood in single or double file between the fire and the nearest source of water, and passed buckets filled with water to the scene of the conflagration, sending the empty buckets back by the second line of men if there was a second line.

Twenty-two years after New Amsterdam was settled, the occurrence of fires in two houses, owing to carelessness in the care of fire-places and chimneys, aroused the authorities to the necessity of organizing means of protection. They therefore ordered on January 23, 1648, that from that time forward no more wooden or platted chimneys should be erected between the "fort and the fresh water,"—that is to say, between the sites of the present United States custom house and the Tombs prison, —and four fire wardens were appointed to see that the ordinance was enforced. The fines for violating this ordinance were to be devoted to the purchase of fire ladders, hooks and buckets, to be procured in Holland at the first opportunity. In 1657, the following notice was given:

"Notice is hereby given, that for the purpose of preventing calamities by fire, they long since condemned all flag roofs, wooden or platted chimneys within this City, and to that end they appointed Fire Wardens and Inspectors of Buildings, which ordinance has been and is at present neglected by the inhabitants and in consequence thereof several fires have occurred and more are to be apprehended—yes, indeed, to the entire destruction of the City,—so that it is necessary to make provision in the case. To which end, the Director General and Councillors do ordain that all flag roofs, wooden chimneys, hay barracks and hay stacks shall be taken down and removed within four months after the publication of these presents, under the penalty of twentyfive guilders for every month's delay; and this penalty shall be claimed for every house, great or small, with reed roof, hay barrack or hay stack, or wooden chimney within the walls of the City. Hen-houses and hog-pens shall be included."

But the safety of the city was not to be secured by ordinance alone. Fire extinguishing apparatus was necessary. Therefore, in December, 1657, the Burgomasters and Schepens adopted the following order, reflecting the custom of the old country in that matter:

"Whereas, in all well-regulated cities it is customary that fire-buckets, ladders and hooks are in readiness at the corners of the streets and in public houses for time of need, which is the more necessary in this City on account of the small number of stone houses and many that are built of wood, therefore it shall be required immediately that for every house small or large shall be paid one beaver or eight guilders in seawant,* out of which funds shall be procured from fatherland 250 leather fire-buckets; and we shall also have made some fire-ladders and fire-hooks. In order to maintain the same in good order, there shall afterwards be a yearly demand of one guilder for every chimney in a house."

It was proposed that instead of sending to Holland for the buckets they be made in the City and on August 1, 1658, four shoe-makers of the town,—an important as well as necessary craft at that time—were requested to meet the authorities and consider the matter. The contract was tendered to Coenraet Ten Eyck, but he declined it. Pieter Van Haalen declared that he had not the materials with which to make the buckets. Reinout Reinoutsen, however, undertook to make 100 buckets and Arian Van Laar 50 buckets between that date and All Saints day (November 1). The buckets were all to be made of tanned leather in the most complete manner, and for each they were to be paid six guilders and ten stuyvers, half in beaver-skins and half in wampum. By January 20, 1659, 125 of the 150 buckets were finished, taken to the City Haall or Stadt Huys at No. 73 Pearl street and numbered.

It was ordered that the 150 be distributed as follows, the assignments really totalling 152.

From 1 to 50.	In the City Hall	50
From 50 to 62.	Daniel Litscho	12
From 63 to 74.	Abraham Planck's house in Smith's Valley	12
From 75 to 86.	Joannes Pietersen Verbruggen	12
From 87 to 98.	Paulus Leenderzen Vander Grift	12
From 99 to 110.	Nicasius de Sille in the sheep's pasture	12
From 111 to 122.	Pieter Wolferzen van Couwenhoven	12
From 1 to 12.	Jan Janzen the younger	10
From 13 to 24.	Hendrick Hendrickzen Kip, the elder	10
From 25 to 36.	Jacobus Backer	10

David T. Valentine, in his Manual for 1856 at pages 253-254, locates the above places with reference to modern streets as follows: Litscho's tavern in Pearl street near Wall; Planck's (or Verplanck's) house in Pearl street near Fulton; Verbruggen's in Hanover square; Van der Grift's in Broadway nearly

* Wampum.

opposite Exchange place; DeSille's on the southeast corner of Broad street and Exchange place; Van Couwenhoven's on the northeast corner of Whitehall and Pearl streets; Kip's on the north side of Bridge street between Whitehall and Broad; and Backer's on the east side of Broad between Stone and South William.

Under the English regime the pump, well and bucket system was somewhat elaborated in detail, but remained the same in principle for many years. In 1687 every inhabitant who had a house with two chimneys was required to provide one fire-bucket for his house, and if he had more than two hearths he was required to keep two buckets. Bakers were obliged to have three buckets and brewers six. At an alarm of fire, everybody who had buckets ran to the scene, and it was inevitable that their buckets should get mixed up. It was therefore customary after a fire for the Town Crier to give notice of a general exchange of buckets which had gotten into the wrong hands.

As the eighteenth century advanced, the inadequacy of the "bucket brigade" began to impress itself on the citizens as the news of Newsham's pumping engines in England became better known, and on October 17, 1730, the sentiment in favor of the introduction of fire-engines into this country took shape in an act passed by the Assembly (chapter 550) which contained the following declaration among others:

"The Repairing of the said City Hall,* Repairing and Enlarging the Goals and Prisons, Erecting of Watch-Houses and defraying other Necessary and Contingent Charges for the keeping of the Peace and Preserving good Rule and Government within the said City, and the purchasing of two fire Engines which are greatly wanted for the better Securing the said City from the Danger & Accidents of fire, will amount to a Larger sum of money than the Yearly Revenue of the said Corporation can Supply."

Therefore it was enacted that the city be authorized to raise money for those purposes by taxation. This legislation was promptly followed up by an ordinance of the Common Council, adopted May 6, 1731, levying the necessary tax. On the same day, the Common Council adopted the following:

RESOLVED that this Corporation do with all Convenient Speed Procure two Complete fire Engines with Suction and Materialls there unto belonging, for the Publick Service. That the Sizes

* The second City Hall, in Wall street at the head of Broad street.

thereof be, of the fourth and sixth sizes of Mr. Newshams fire Engines, and that Mr. Mayor, Alderman Cruger, Alderman Rutgers and Alderman Roosevelt or any three of them be a Committee to Agree with some proper Merchant or Merchants to send to London for the same by the first Conveniency and Report upon what Terms the said Fire Engines &c.: will be delivered to this Corporation.

On June 12, 1731, the committee reported that Stephen De Lancey and John Moore were willing to send to London by the ship Beaver for two engines of Mr. Newsham's "New Invention of the fourth and sixth sizes, with suctions, Leather Pipes and Caps and Other Materialls thereunto belonging," charging the city 120 per cent advance on the invoice price; and the committee was authorized to order the engines accordingly. The commission was promptly executed and in a few months the novel machines were in the city. On November 18, 1731, the Common Council ordered that provisions be made for keeping hooks, ladders, buckets and the fire-engines in convenient places, and on December 1 workmen were employed to fit up a convenint room in the City Hall for the engines. A couple of weeks later Alderman Johannes Hardenbroeck and Assistant-Alderman Gerard Beekman were appointed a committee "to have the Fire Engines Cleaned and the Leathers Oyled and put into Boxes that the same may be fitt for Immediate use."

The engines thus procured consisted each of a wooden box tank on wheels, upon which was mounted a suction pump. One engine was operated with a long handle-bar or brake by men standing on a platform on top of the tank. See Engineer Stoutenburgh's sketch of the first "Ingen" on page 33. The other was operated with a long crank handle protruding from the side of the machine by men standing on the ground. Sometimes the water was conveyed to the engine by the bucket brigade and forced through a short leather hose and nozzle or "goose-neck" upon the fire; sometimes the engine was placed close to a pump so that the water could be pumped into the tank; and sometimes a suction hose was used to draw water from a well.

The next important step in the evolution of the fire protection system was the establishment of a regular Fire Department. This was done pursuant to a law (chapter 670) enacted December 16, 1737. This law provided that the Common Council could

Hand-Pump Fire-Engine, Period of 1732

"Double-Decker" Fire-Engine, Period of 1840

elect a sufficient number of "Strong able Discreet honest and sober men" not exceeding 42 in number, who should be ready at a call by either night or day to use the fire-engines and other tools and instruments for extinguishing fires. It was provided that these persons "shall be called the firemen of the City of New York." These were in addition to the engine-men who were regularly employed. The firemen were exempt from jury and militia duty and from serving as Constables and Surveyors of Highways. The same law provided that when a fire broke out, the Sheriff, Constables and Marshals should "immediately repair to the place where the said fire shall happen with their Rods, Staves and other Badges of their authority," to aid the firemen and to cause other people to do the same, in extinguishing the fire and protecting goods from theft.

In such humble ways the great Fire Department of the City of New York, now the finest in the world, began. It would require a volume in itself to follow the growth of the department through the stage of hand-pumping engines to steam, chemical and automobile engines and the high pressure water systems which represent its highest development to-day. (See illustration on pages 39 and 45.) But enough has been said with respect to water supply for domestic use and fire extinguishing purposes to indicate how poorly equipped the early city was for the prevention of disease and fire by water.

Great Fires and Epidemics

The movement for a municipal water supply received powerful stimulus, from time to time, from great fires and epidemics. It will conduce to a better understanding of the events recorded in succeeding chapters to mention some of these unfortunate occurrences.

On September 21, 1776, six days after the British captured the city, a fire broke out at the foot of Whitehall street and spread to Broadway, burning up on the east side as far as Mr. Harrison's brick house and on the west side to St. Paul's chapel. Trinity church and 493 houses were destroyed.

On August 7, 1778, a fire originating on Cruger's wharf (in the block now bounded by Water and Front streets, Old slip and Coenties slip) consumed about 50 houses in that vicinity. This was during the British occupation and the military took exclusive control of the situation.

On December 18, 1804, a fire broke out on Front street south of Wall street and burned the whole block in Water street from Coffee House slip at the foot of Wall street to the next door to Gouverneur's lane, including all the buildings in Front street to the water; and also some buildings on the northeast side of Coffee House slip. The famous old Merchants Coffee House, built in 1737, on the southeast corner of Wall and Water streets, was burned.

On May 19, 1811, a fire began near the northwest corner of Duane and Chatham street (now Park row), and spread rapidly with a wind from the northeast. Between 80 and 100 buildings were burned. The steeple of the old Brick church, in the block bounded by Beekman street, Park row, Printing House square and Nassau street, and cupola of the old jail in City Hall park, caught fire, but were not seriously damaged.

The "Great Fire" broke out on the night of December 16, 1835, in the premises of Comstock & Andrews, at No. 25 Merchant (now Beaver) street and burned over the area bounded approximately by the south side of Wall street from William street to the East river, by William and South William street to Coenties lane; by Coenties lane and slip to the river; and by the river from Coenties slip in Wall street. In this area, 674 stores and other buildings were destroyed, causing a loss stated at $17,000,000. The Merchants Exchange (site of the National City bank) and the old Dutch church in Garden street (now Exchange place) were among the structures destroyed.

A notable fire in the early years of the Croton system occurred on July 19, 1845, when 345 buildings were destroyed and about $5,000,000 loss was caused in lower Broadway, Whitehall street, and in Exchange place and other cross streets to the southward.

There were epidemics of yellow fever in 1795, 1798, 1805, 1819 and 1822, and of cholera in 1832, 1834, 1849, and 1855. The epidemic of 1805 was particularly severe. John Lambert's diary says that in that year 26,000 persons moved from the interior of the City to escape the plague. Those who could not go far went to Greenwich village on the west side of the island "about two or three miles from town" where merchants and bankers had other offices for the transaction of business.

Chapter IV.

Early Pipe-Line Projects

Christopher Colles' Water-Works

The earliest proposal to supply the city with water conducted underground through pipes was made by Christopher Colles just before War of the Revolution.

Colles was born in Dublin, Ireland, May 9, 1739, and came to America in 1771.‡ He was certainly a man of genius and foresight as his water-works project sufficiently attests. He was an expert in mathematics, gunnery, and drawing, upon which subjects the Common Council allowed him to lecture in the Exchange,§ and he was a chemist, as indicated by the reference hereafter to his manufacture of "fig blue." He was also a pioneer in canal development, and as early as 1784 petitioned the Legislature to connect the waters of Lake Ontario with the Hudson by a canal through the Mohawk Valley.* He was an American patriot, suffering many privations during the American Revolution, and his memory is deserving of high respect.†

On April 22, 1774, Colles proposed to erect a reservoir near the Collect or Fresh Water pond where he had reason to believe that he could get an adequate supply of fresh water, and to distribute it through the streets by means of pipes made by boring a hole longitudinally through the trunks of small trees. The water was to be pumped into his reservoir from a well by a steam engine, and to flow by gravity through the pipes.

When the proposition first came to the Common Council it was so novel that there was uncertainty as to its practicability and advisability. The Council therefore put the subject off and deliberated on it for three months. When it came up for action on July 21, opinion was still divided; but the majority were in

‡ Transcript from family Bible received from Dr. Christopher J. Colles of New York.

§ Common Council Minutes of August 22, 1787.

* Sketch of Colles by John W. Francis in "The Knickerbocker Gallery," 1855.

† Francis errs in dates. Those above are correct. Colles died October 4, 1816, in the New York Institution in Chambers street, New York, which at that time included the Academy of Arts, the Historical Society, the City Library and the American Museum. Francis says he was buried in the Hudson street (St. John's) cemetery, and others say in St. Paul's churchyard, but the Rector of Trinity Parish says the parish has no record of burial in either. Colles was a man ahead of his time. He conceived many ideas for which others received credit. His culture is reflected in living descendants who are prominently connected with the social, intellectual, art and civic life of the city. The New York Historical Society has a fine portrait of him by John W. Jarvis.

favor of the experiment and voted 8 to 2 to undertake it. At the same time, they voted to issue notes to the amount of £2,600 for the undertaking. Subsequent issues brought the amount up up to £9,100.

These notes were about the size of the "shin-plasters" of the Civil War period, being about 2 1/3 by 4 inches in size. A specimen of which we have a copy before us bore on its face the following inscription.

NEW YORK WATER WORKS
(No. 1911.)
This Note shall entitle the Bearer to the sum of
Four Shillings
current money of the Colony of New York, payable on Demand, by the Mayor, Aldermen and Commonalty of the City of New York, at the office of Chamberlain of the said City, pursuant to a Vote of the said Mayor, Aldermen and Commonalty, of this Date. Dated the Sixth Day of January, in the Year of our Lord One Thousand Seven Hundred and Seventy Six.
By order of the Corporation.
N. Bayard.
J. H. Cruger.

On the back of the note was the picture of a pumping engine and two fountains.

It cannot be said that the Common Council proceeded with rash haste in this enterprise, for when Augustus and Frederick Van Cortlandt offered to sell to the city a site for the reservoir on the east side of Great George street, now Broadway, at what is now White street, at the rate of £600 an acre, they personally went to the new well sunk on the property and tasted the water. One can almost imagine these dignified gentlemen going to that then remote spot on the west side of the Fresh Water pond, adjacent to the marshy Lispenard meadows abounding in bullfrogs and game birds in season, sipping the water from the new well like connoisseurs of some rare vintage, smacking their lips, looking at each other wisely, and finally pronouncing a favorable verdict. Concluding "the same to be of very good quality," they accepted the Van Cortlandts' offer and told Mr. Colles to go ahead with his work.

On August 29, 1774, the Common Council appointed a committee of eight members to superintend the construction of the works, and in November they contracted with Isaac Mann and Isaac Mann, Jr., of Stillwater, now in Saratoga county, to furnish 60,000 linear feet of pitch or yellow pine timber for the making of the pipes. The original contract, which is on file in the document room of the City Clerk in the Municipal building, provided that the logs should be from 14 to 20 feet long and that one-fourth of them should be 12 inches in diameter at the small end of the log "exclusive of the sap thereof" and three-fourths 9 inches in diameter at the small end, and all should be "streight and free from shakes and large knots." The contractors were to deliver one-third of the timber on July 1, 1775, one-third on August 1, and one-third on October 1, and were to receive therefor £1,250.

While waiting for the timber for the pipes, Mr. Colles went ahead diligently with the construction of his well, reservoir and pumphouse on a slight eminence on the east side of Broadway between Pearl and White streets. The reservoir had a capacity of 20,000 hogsheads. The well was 30 feet in diameter. And the engine pumped 200 gallons of water 52 feet high per minute. After the war, Josiah Hornblower was paid £12 for "attending and making report of the fire-engine for the water works about to be erected in 1775." The pump-house was a substantial structure, roofed with pantiles (curved tiles, laid alternately with the convex and concave sides upward) and the bills for iron-work, braziers work, rope, etc., which the city had to pay after the war, indicate that all the works were built in a durable manner.

But while the water-works were being built, the city was thrown into a turmoil of excitement by the news from Lexington and Bunker Hill. The work of construction, however, continued into 1776, but with the critical events of that year, the project was completely interrupted, never to be renewed. Mr. Colles with his family fled from the City and endured great privations, rather than submit to the British rule; and during the period of the war his water-works became totally ruined.

After the war, he returned to New York and soon after the Common Council assembled he presented a petition for the payment of moneys due him. His original memorial, dated October 27, 1784, is in the records room of the City Clerk in the Municipal building. It is a document of peculiar historical interest:

Horse-Drawn Steam Fire-Engine, Period of 1865

Self-Propelled Steam Fire-Engine, Period of 1917

To the Honorable the Mayor, Aldermen and Common Council of the City of New York.

The Humble Memorial of Christopher Colles of said City Engineer Sheweth.

That your Memoralist in the year 1774 presented a proposal to this honorable corporation for erecting works for supplying this city with water for the sum of eighteen thousand pounds.

That this honorable board after sufficient enquiry concerning the practicability of the design Resolved to agree with the said proposal and directed your memorialist to proceed in the execution of the work.

That your memorialist did accordingly proceed in the execution of the work and erected a reservoir capable of containing twenty thousand hogsheads of water; dug, walled, covered and completely finished a well of thirty feet diameter at the inside, from which he pumped by means of a steam engine which he also erected, two hundred gallons of water, fifty-two feet high perpendicular per minute, into the said reservoir.

That previous to the said resolve of the corporation your memorialist furnished them with an estimate of the expense of the different parts of the work, agreeable to which the part executed amounted to the sum of three thousand six hundred pounds.

That the several sums advanced for the prosecution of the work amounted to three thousand pounds, consequently, that there remains a balance of six hundred pounds, one hundred and fifty pounds of which is due to different artificers for work and the remaining four hundred and fifty pounds is due to said Colles.

That your Memorialist in common with other citizens, friends of society and the interest of mankind, suffered the most poignant afflictions during the late war, and with the utmost difficulty procured the common necessaries for his family; and being now returned to the city, where he hopes to devote the remainder of his days in promoting the welfare of the city and country, he prays the corporation to use their endeavors to pay him the balance above referred to, by which he may be enabled to support his numerous family in credit, and in some degree of comfort.

May it therefore please your honors, to take the premises into consideration, and grant him that justice and assistance, which to your judgment shall seem meet.

CHRISTOPHER COLLES.

The Common Council did not at first act on this petition and on July 20, 1785, Mr. Colles begged the Board again to give him relief declaring that "his distresses are of such a poignant nature as to compel him to request some (though small) yet present assistance."* In August, 1785, the Council granted him £100 on account.

On November 23, 1785, he appealed to the Council for £50 more on account. This petition gives an interesting indication of Mr. Colles' abilities. He said that he was desirous of applying part of the money "so as to enable him to support his family with credit," and to that end "he has erected a horse-mill and other works for the purpose of carrying on in this City the Manufacture of Fig Blue, which manufacture he proposes to have carried on by his eldest son in case he shall be engaged in the prosecution of the navigation of the Mohawk River." He said that he had already made and sold to grocers and others this product "which upon trial is proved to be fully equal in quality to any imported, although he can afford to sell it at less price."

The foregoing petition was granted and he was given the £50 asked for. Finally, on January 16, 1788, he consented to accept £50 in settlement of all demands. Meantime, the corporation had allowed him to use the room at the Exchange to give lectures on gunnery, drawing, mathematics, etc., which indicate that the delay and apparent penuriousness in paying him were not due to any underestimate of his character and abilities.

Projects of Ogden, Livingston, Rumsey and Others

While the Common Council was still paying bills for the dead enterprise of Mr. Colles, it received successive propositions of a similar nature from other sources.

The first, dated March 24, 1785, came from Samuel Ogden. The original document, which is in the document room of the City Clerk in the Municipal building, reads as follows:

"To the Mayor, Aldermen and Commonalty of the City and County of New York in Common Council.

The Memorial of Samuel Ogden of said City
Sheweth:

That as the late war hath totally ruined the fire engine and water works which were erected for the purpose of supplying this city with water, your Memorialist begs leave to propose to the consideration of the corporation the following proposals. That he will at the expense of himself and associates erect and establish at or near the place where the former one was built† which

* Original in records office of city clerk, Municipal building.

† The word "works" evidently omitted.

shall supply the reservoir with 144,000 gallons of water per day, and that he will in pipes lead and conduct the same water through the streets of this city, in such manner as shall be hereafter explained provided such compensation and reward be secured to your Memorialist and his associates as shall hereafter be agreed upon. On the subject of which your Memorialist begs a conference at such time and place as you may think proper to appoint.

SAML. OGDEN.

New York, March 24, 1785.

This petition came before the Common Council April 5, and Aldermen John Broome and William Neilson and Assistant Alderman Daniel Phoenix were appointed a committee to confer with him.

Before any conclusion was reached on this proposition, and on January 30, 1786, Chancellor Robert R. Livingston, who later encouraged Robert Fulton in his steamboat invention and who had a considerable interest in mechanical engineering himself, made a proposition to the Board to contract to convey fresh water to the city. Aldermen John Broome and Jeremiah Wool and Assistant Aldermen William Malcom, George Janeway and Abraham Van Gelder were appointed a committee to confer with him.

On February 6, 1786, both committees made reports, but consideration was postponed, and on February 15, Chancellor Livingston and John Lawrence, who was associated with him in his proposal, appeared before the Board in support of their proposals. On the latter date, the Board decided to return the proposals previously received and to advertise for new ones, to be received prior to January 1, 1787. The latter date was subsequently changed to April 20, 1786.

On April 19, 1786, the day before the date set for opening proposals for the water-works, a strong sentiment was shown at the Common Council meeting against letting out the water-supply to private enterprise. The Clerk reported that he had received three sealed packets containing proposals to erect the water-works; but the Board ordered that they remain unopened until further orders. Meanwhile, the aldermen and assistants were requested, "to set on foot in their respective wards representations to this Board in writing and subscribed by the citizens in order more fully to ascertain their sense whether the corporation ought to grant to individuals the privilege of supplying the city with water or whether the same ought to be undertaken by the corporation and that the moneys necessary for the purpose should be raised by a tax on the citizens."

Nothing, however, came of these projects and the matter dragged along almost two years without any further progress or further movement on the part of the citizens. On February 27, 1788, a large number of inhabitants represented to the Common Council "the inconveniencies which arise from the present mode of supplying the city with water" and prayed the Board "to adopt such measures for supplying it with water by means of pipes agreeable to a plan or proposal set on foot by Christopher Colles or such other plan as to the Board shall appear most expedient." But this petition was as ineffectual as its predecessors. The fact was, that the city was passing through a period of reconstruction after the war. The minds of the members of the Common Council and the financial resources of the corporation were engaged to the limit with other municipal improvements—the laying out of streets, the laying of pavements, the building of sewers, the remission or settlement of rents, and the straightening out of the numerous affairs tangled by the interruption caused by the war. It is not surprising therefore that the water-works improvement was held in abeyance.

On January 30, 1789, the Common Council received a letter from Benjamin Wynkoop, Levi Hollingsworth and G. Turner, the Corresponding Committee of the Rumsian society of Philadelphia, stating that Mr. Rumsey had invented an engine superior to any other for supplying towns with water; that he had applied to the Legislature for a patent; and when it was granted, the society would come forward with proposals for supplying New York with water by contract. The Board received the suggestion with every encouragement, but declared that it had no moneys which it could use for the purpose at that time.

During the next nine years, the subject was taken up fitfully by the city government and by individuals, with no better results. In February, 1792, Zebrina Curtis and others made proposals which were referred to the Street committee and were heard of no more. In March, 1795, Amos Porter made a like proposal. This year, Samuel Crane submitted a specific plan to lead water from the Tea Water Pump through Roosevelt street; and Benjamin Taylor advanced still a different project. In February, 1796, the Common Council directed a committee to advertise for proposals; and in December, Dr. Joseph Brown and associates offered to supply the city with water through pipes. Again in 1797, sealed proposals were advertised for, and seven or eight applications were received. One of them was from Christopher Colles. They were referred to a committee and lost sight of. In 1798, R. J. Roosevelt and Judge Cooper of Otsego made new applications; and so did Dr. Joseph Brown.

The originality of Dr. Brown's project in 1798 lay in the fact that he proposed to go to the Bronx river for the water, and this was apparently the first suggestion of going off the Island of Manhattan for this purpose. On December 17, 1798, the committee of the Common Council, which was appointed to investigate this suggestion reported in its favor, and made three specific recommendations.

First, that William Weston, who had been the engineer for the canal companies in this state and was a man of known abilities, be requested to examine the river, the grounds for the aqueduct, etc., and report his opinion;

Second, that in view of the importance of the matter to the comfort and health of the inhabitants, and the fact that private parties would not undertake the enterprise except with the prospect of gain at the expense of the citizens, the water-works should be under the control of the corporation as the immediate representative of the citizens in general; and

Third, that the Legislature be requested to pass a law giving the city power to undertake the work and to raise the necessary funds by taxation.

Mr. Weston was consulted, as above suggested, and on March 14, 1799, he made a report which is of great civic and historical interest, recommending the Bronx river as a source. His report also gives an indication of the state of hydraulic science nearly a century and a quarter ago. Its full text is to be found in Valentine's Corporation Manual for 1860, at pages 580-588.

The Manhattan Company's Water-Works

The first successful pipe-line system of water-works was that of the Manhattan company, which was incorporated in 1799. Upon the assembling of the Legislature that year, Aaron Burr and several other men applied for a charter for the purpose of "supplying the City of New York with pure and wholesome

Reservoir of the Manhattan Company in Chambers Street, 1825

water," and on April 2, 1799, the bill was passed, incorporating the Manhattan company. The capital of the corporation was $2,000,000—a great sum for those days—and as the cost of the proposed water system could not accurately be foreseen, there was a clause in the charter permitting the company to employ its surplus capital in financial transactions not inconsistent with the constitutions and laws of the state of New York and the United States.

It has been a common tradition that the banking privilege contained in this charter, apparently as a subordinate feature, was really the main object of the projectors, and was thus introduced covertly to avoid the opposition which Burr was certain to encounter from Alexander Hamilton and the Federal party. Hamilton had organized the first banking organization in New York when in 1784 he formed the Bank of New York which was chartered in 1792. For fifteen years, Hamilton's bank and the Branch bank of the United States were the only banks doing business in the City of New York. This monopoly was of value to the political party which was then in control and with which Hamilton was allied, and consequently Burr's effort to obtain a charter, which was quickly perceived to contain a clause which permitted banking, was earnestly opposed. The opposition was unsuccessful, however, and the Manhattan company secured its charter.

Whether the tradition before mentioned as to the leading motives of Burr and associates was well founded or not, the fact remains that the company did go ahead with the water-works undertaking, built reservoirs, and laid an extensive system of distributing pipes in the then small city. These pipes were hollow logs, many of which have been dug up in recent years in the streets south of Chambers street. The first meeting of the directors was held at the house of Edward Barden, inn-keeper,* on April 11, 1799, when there were present Aaron Burr, John Broome who was long an Alderman, John B. Church who fought a duel with Burr on September 2, 1799, John B. Coles, Richard Harrison who was Recorder of the city, William Laight, Brockholst Livingston, Daniel Ludlow, Samuel Osgood, Pascal N. Smith, John Stevens and John Watts. The only absentee was William Edgar. Mr. Ludlow was elected President.

* The Merchants Coffee House.

At the meeting of April 11, 1799, a resolution was adopted declaring that the principal object of the corporation was to obtain a supply of pure and wholesome water for the city and a committee was appointed to report means for obtaining such a supply. So rapidly did the plans mature that on May 6 following the water committee was empowered "to contract for as many pine logs as they may think necessary for pipes and also for boring the same."

Meanwhile, if the water supply was the chief object of the company, the banking privilege was not neglected, and on April 17, 1799, a committee was appointed "to consider the most proper means of employing the capital of the company." On June 3 the committee reported in favor of opening an office of discount and deposit and a house was bought on the site of the present No. 40 Wall street (then having a different number) in which, on September 1, 1799, the bank of the company began business. This venerable corporation is still doing business at No. 40 Wall street under the style of the Bank of the Manhattan company.

In prosecuting the water-works business, the company sank a number of wells, built tanks and reservoirs, and extended its distributing system generally throughtout the city below Chambers street. In 1836 the system was extended northward along Broadway as far as Bleecker street, when the company had about 25 miles of mains and supplied about 2,000 houses. The maximum amount of water supplied by this company was about 700,000 gallons a day. The company continued to operate its system until about the time the Croton system came into use in 1842.

One conspicuous landmark of the old water-works was the Chambers street reservoir. It had sloping walls, similar in style to the Croton reservoir which later stood on the site of the present public library on the west side of Fifth avenue between 40th and 42d streets. It stood on the north side of Chambers street between Broadway and Center street. Its facade was unrelieved except by an entablature which was supported by four Doric columns and upon which was a figure of "Oceanus, one of the sea-gods, sitting in a reclining posture on a rising ground pouring water from an urn which forms a river and terminates in a lake." This was the physical embodiment of the device of the corporation seal of the company adopted May 8, 1799.

Another landmark of the company was the tank which stood on the northwest corner of Reade and Center streets until July, 1914, when it was demolished. This tank, which was erected over one of the earliest wells of the company, was circular in form and measured 41 feet in diameter. It had a massive stone foundation rising 23 feet above the original ground level, which was surmounted by a circular tank, 41 feet in diameter and 15 feet high, the sides and bottom of which were composed of iron plates bolted together. Later the reservoir was enclosed in a three story building. Water was originally pumped into the tank by a steam engine. When the tank was taken down in July 1914, the black sediment on the bottom of the reservoir—the accumulation of dust which had slowly settled in the tank notwithstanding it was surrounded and covered by the building,—was about one foot thick. Among the traditions which grew up around the old reservoir was one to the effect that the Manhattan company was obliged to pump water into the tank every day in order to keep alive its charter. As the reservoir is now gone and the company continues to do business, the tradition appears to be effectually set at rest. When the building and tank were torn down in 1914 to make room for a modern building and the old reservoir was exposed to view, all sorts of strange tales were circulated about it. One story alleged that it had been a fort in the war of the Revolution and another that it had been an ancient prison, neither of which legends was true.

The wooden pipes of the old Manhattan company are frequently met with in excavating for modern water-mains, gas-mains, sewers, electric conduits and subways; and sections of them are preserved at the New York Historical society building and elsewhere as great curiosities. One of the latest sections to be exhumed to the knowledge of the present writer was located at Pearl street and Coenties slip and was removed by the contractors in June, 1917.

The Municipal Water Supply of 1829.

During the first quarter of the nineteenth century, while the Manhattan company was supplying the city, there was repeated agitation of the subject of a larger water-supply, some people proposing private projects and some advocating a municipal water system. In 1804, under the mayoralty of De Witt Clinton, a committee was appointed to report upon the practicability of supplying the city with pure and wholesome water, and especially to confer with the Manhattan company as to the terms upon which it would cede to the corporation its works and privileges of supplying water; but nothing seems to have come of it, and things ran along until March, 1816, when it was voted to ask the Legislature to give the city power to establish a municipal water-supply. Still, nothing was accomplished. In 1819 Robert Macomb memorialized the Common Council, proposing to bring water from Rye pond to a reservoir at Harlem river, and distribute it to the city. A favorable report was made on this suggestion in 1820, but it was not carried out. In 1821 and 1822, when Stephen Allen was Mayor, the subject was renewed and in the latter year Canvas White was employed to survey the whole line from the city to the main source of the Bronx river. While he was at work, in 1823, a project for bringing water from the Housatonic river to New York by canal was advanced. In 1824, Canvas White reported in favor of bringing water from the Bronx river, taking it at the Westchester cotton factory pond, but this plan was abandoned. In 1825 the New York Water-Works company was incorporated by the Legislature, but its charter proved unworkable and it was surrendered in 1827. In the latter year the New York Well company was incorporated and tried to get water from artesian wells, but the plan proved to be impracticable.

At length, in 1829, the city adopted the recommendation of Alderman Samuel Stevens to establish a reservoir in the small block between Broadway, Fourth avenue, 13th and 14th streets, for the distribution of water for fire extinguishing purposes. The reservoir was an elevated tank, with a capacity of 233,000 gallons, its surface being 104 feet above sea-level. Its water came from a well at Jefferson Market, at the intersection of Sixth and Greenwich avenues, which was supplied by conduit galleries converging from different directions at the well. In 1832, a 12-horse-power steam engine was installed at the well to force water through a main pipe to the reservoir.* The water was not good enough for domestic use; but the committee urged the laying of iron pipes, instead of the old-fashioned wooden pipes, arguing that when the long desired object of supplying the city with water for domestic purposes should be carried into effect, these same

Haswell's Reminiscences, pp. 264, 285.

pipes would serve. A reluctant assent to these recommendations was wrung from the Common Council, and a committee was empowered to provide the necessary site for a reservoir, and to contract for iron pipes. This was the feeble and economical beginning of the city-owned water supply.

The provision of 1829 was confessedly inadequate, and during the next seven years events rapidly moved toward the Croton system. In 1830, projects for bringing water from the Croton river, Rye pond, and from the Passaic river, N. J., were advanced, with the strongest drift toward the Croton.

In December, 1832, De Witt Clinton arrived at the conclusion that an adequate supply could only be obtained from the Croton. He advocated an open aqueduct or canal for that purpose.

A curious proposition was made in 1834 by Bradford Seymour of Utica who proposed to dam the Hudson river opposite Amos street and generate 30,000 horse-power of which 3,000 horse-power was to be used for pumping water to a reservoir on Manhattan island, and 27,000 horse-power for industrial purposes.

Surveys having shown a closed masonry aqueduct from the Croton river to be practicable, the people decided in 1835 by a popular vote of 17,330 to 5,963 to issue $2,500,000 of "water stock" and go ahead with the work.

In July, 1836, the Common Council ordered pipe to be laid preparatory to the introduction of the water, and in October John B. Jervis was appointed Chief Engineer. The work of construction began early in 1837.

Laying 90-inch Pipe of Croton Aqueduct on High Bridge in 1861

High Bridge in 1917

Chapter V

The Croton Aqueduct

The Old Croton Dam

The work on the old Croton aqueduct which was commenced in 1837 began at a point on the Croton river about six miles from its mouth with the construction of a dam. This dam was designed to raise the water 40 feet above the level of the head of the aqueduct and 166 feet above mean tide.

The rock formation at the site is Fordham gneiss, and the rock bottom of the river was so deep as to give the engineers trouble at the very start. Even after shifting their plans, it was necessary to make an artificial foundation for part of the dam where they could not build it on the living rock. The southern abutment was of natural rock, and the aqueduct being on the southern side of the river, the water was conducted to its head by a tunnel out 180 feet through the rock. The gateway was also located in the solid rock, unexposed to the floods of the river. A waste culvert was built in the north abutment, with suitable gates for drawing down the reservoir for repairs and to discharge the river at ordinary times during the course of construction. From this abutment the old channel of the river was filled by an embankment, with a heavy protection wall on the lower side which was raised fifteen feet above the waste weir of the dam and designed to be thirty feet wide on top. While this was in course of construction in January, 1841, the water rose until, when near the surface, it began to pass between the frozen and unfrozen earth about 20 inches from the top. Then, after the breach was made, heavy masses of ice came down from the reservoir and broke down the unfinished protection wall, with the result that the whole embankment was carried away. The masonry of the dam and abutment, however, suffered little damage. It was then decided to fill the breach thus made, about 200 feet long, by a structure of hydraulic stone masonry, adapting 180 feet of it for a waste weir. This was effected with great difficulty in those days, it being necessary to lay an artificial foundation. The greatest height of the dam was 40 feet above low water level and

55 feet above the bed of the river. The masonry at low water line of the river was 61 feet long.

Three hundred feet below the main dam a second dam, 9 feet high, was built for the purpose of setting the water back over the apron of the main dam to form a pool of water which should receive the impact of the water passing over the main dam.

The old Croton dam impounded the water of the river in a reservoir five miles long and covering about 400 acres.

High Bridge Over Harlem River

From the Croton dam a masonry aqueduct was built through the country and the villages of Sing Sing, Tarrytown, Dobbs Ferry, Hastings and Yonkers to the Harlem river opposite 174th street, Manhattan, a distance 32.88 miles. At this point, the next monumental structure of the aqueduct, namely High bridge, was erected. The valley of the Harlem river here, at the aqueduct level, is 1450 feet wide, and it required a structure of that length to conduct the water across the river to the Island of Manhattan. The width of the river at ordinary high water mark was then 620 feet, but at low ebb tides was reduced to about 300 feet. It has since been narrowed by filling out the shores. The southeastern shore is bold and rocky, rising from the water's edge at an angle of about 30° to a height of 220 feet. On the northwestern shore, a strip of table land extends back from the water about 400 feet to the foot of a rocky hill which rises at an angle of about 20° to a considerable height above the level of the aqueduct.

Across this interval was constructed a picturesque masonry bridge, supported, in the Roman style, by piers connected by half round arches. There are fifteen of these arches. Eight of them, over the river proper, have a span of 80 feet each. The others are of 50 feet span. Across the structure, above the arches and below the roadbed, were originally laid two 36-inch cast iron pipes. A third pipe 90-inches in diameter was added in 1860-61. The Chief Engineer, John B. Jervis, explained that "the object of using pipes in this case is more effectually to secure the conduit from leakage that might eventually injure the masonry of the bridge, and it incidentally allows the bridge to be constructed of less height."

The whole length of High bridge is 1450 feet; the height of the river piers above high water is 60 feet to the spring of the arches and the height from high water mark to the under side of the arches at their crown 100 feet. The height to the top of the cornice was originally 114 feet above high water and 149 feet above the lowest foundation of the piers, but it was raised about six feet in 1860-63. The width across the top is 21 feet.

High bridge was not completed until about six years after the other parts of the aqueduct had been finished, and water did not pass over it until May, 1848. Meanwhile, the water had been carried through an inverted siphon under the Harlem river so that it was introduced into the City in 1842 as stated hereafter. The cost of High bridge was stated in 1849 to have been $963,427.80. The following inscription is on the southern face of one of the eastern piers of the bridge:

Aqueduct Bridge

Begun 1839 Finished 1848

Stephen Allen
Saul Alley
C. Dusenberry
W. W. Fox
T. T. Woodruff } Water Commissioners

John B. Jervis, Chief
H. Allen, Princ. Assist.
P. Hastie, Resident
E. H. Tracy, Assistant } Engineers

George Law
Samuel Roberts
Arnold Mason } Contractors

On the south face of the westernmost pier is the following inscription:

Aqueduct Bridge

Finished December 31, 1848.

Philip Hone
Nathaniel Weed
M. O. Roberts
J. H. Hobart Haws
A. C. Kingsland } Water Commissioners

John B. Jervis, Chief
P. Hastie, Resident
E. H. Tracy, Assistant } Engineers

I. Vervalen, Inspector of Masonry

George Law
Samuel Roberts
Arnold Mason } Contractors

Within 20 years the capacity of High Bridge had to be increased by adding to the original two cast-iron conduits a wrought-iron pipe 90 inches in diameter. In order to cover this additional pipe, the sides of the bridge were raised about six feet and the structure was covered with a flat brick arch which serves as the pavement of the promenade. The latter, although wide enough for vehicles, is restricted to the use of pedestrians. A wrought iron fence 41½ inches high surmounts the cornice on either side of the promenade. The improvement is recorded in an inscription on the gate-house at the Manhattan end as follows:

The improvement of this bridge by adding the large
pipe raising the side walls and covering the whole
work with an arch was commenced Oct. 1860.
The new pipe was put in operation Dec. 1861.
The masonry completed 1863.

CROTON AQUEDUCT BOARD

Thos. Stephens
President Commissioner.

Thos. B. Tappen
Assistant Commiss'r to Dec. 4, 1862

Rob't L. Darragh
Assistant Commiss'r from Dec. 4, 1862

Alfred W. Craven
Commissioner and Engineer in Chief

Engineers

Geo. S. Greene
Engineer in Charge to Jan. 31, 1862

Wm. L. Dearborn
Engineer in Charge from Feb. 1, 1862

Contractors

Thos. F. Rowland for the pipe

J. P. Cumming for the masonry

High Bridge was the sole means of conveying Croton water from the mainland to Manhattan Island up to July 15, 1890, when water was first supplied through the new siphon under the Harlem river near Washington bridge.

The Yorkville Reservoir in Central Park

From the Manhattan end of High bridge, the masonry aqueduct continues two miles along the line of Tenth avenue to the high ground on the north side of Manhattan valley at Manhattan street. This valley is 0.792 of a mile wide at the aqueduct level below which it descends 102 feet. The names of the landmarks in Chief Engineer Jervis' description of seventy years ago sound archaic to-day. He says that at Manhattan valley "the conduit of masonry here gives place to iron pipes which descend into the bottom of the valley and rise again to the proper level on the opposite side; from which point the masonry conduit is again resumed, and crossing the Asylum ridge and Clendenning valley is continued 2.173 miles to the receiving reservoir at York hill."

Asylum ridge was the name for Morningside heights where Columbia University now stands and where the Bloomingdale asylum formerly stood. Clendenning valley was a depression between 101st and 99th streets, named after John Clendenning, whose house was at the present 104th street and Columbus avenue. And York hill, named after the neighboring Yorkville, is now included in Central Park (which did not then exist) between the lines of 79th and 86th streets.

The old Yorkville reservoir, as it was called, is rectangular in shape, 1,826 feet long and 836 feet wide. Its area at the water line is 31 acres, including embankments 35.05 acres, and with accessories 37.05 acres. It has a storage capacity of 150,000,000 imperial gallons according to Mr. Jervis' figures, but more recently stated at 180,000,000. Of the 37 acres occupied by the reservoir, 27½ acres were common lands of the city, and 9½ acres were acquired in two blocks of 4¾ acres each from Hickson W. Field and William Matthews. The City paid $11,000 for each of these blocks or $22,000 for 9½ acres. The water was admitted into the Yorkville reservoir with due ceremony on June 27, 1842, in the presence of the Mayor, the Common Council, the Governor, the members of the Court for the Correction of Errors (then the highest court of appeals in the state), and a great gathering of people. A feature of the celebration was the arrival of the boat Croton Maid. This boat, large enough to hold four persons, had been launched at the Croton reservoir thirty-eight miles distant and sent through the aqueduct to High bridge, where it arrived June 23. On the 27th it was carried across the Harlem and put into the aqueduct again and arrived at Central Park soon after the artillery salute of thirty-eight guns had announced the arrival of the water. The boat was presented to the fire department with an appropriate speech by the President of the Board of Water Commissioners.

On December 17, 1860, the Croton Aqueduct Board assented to the removal of the wall at the southwest corner of the reservoir, where the Belvidere was subsequently erected, on condition

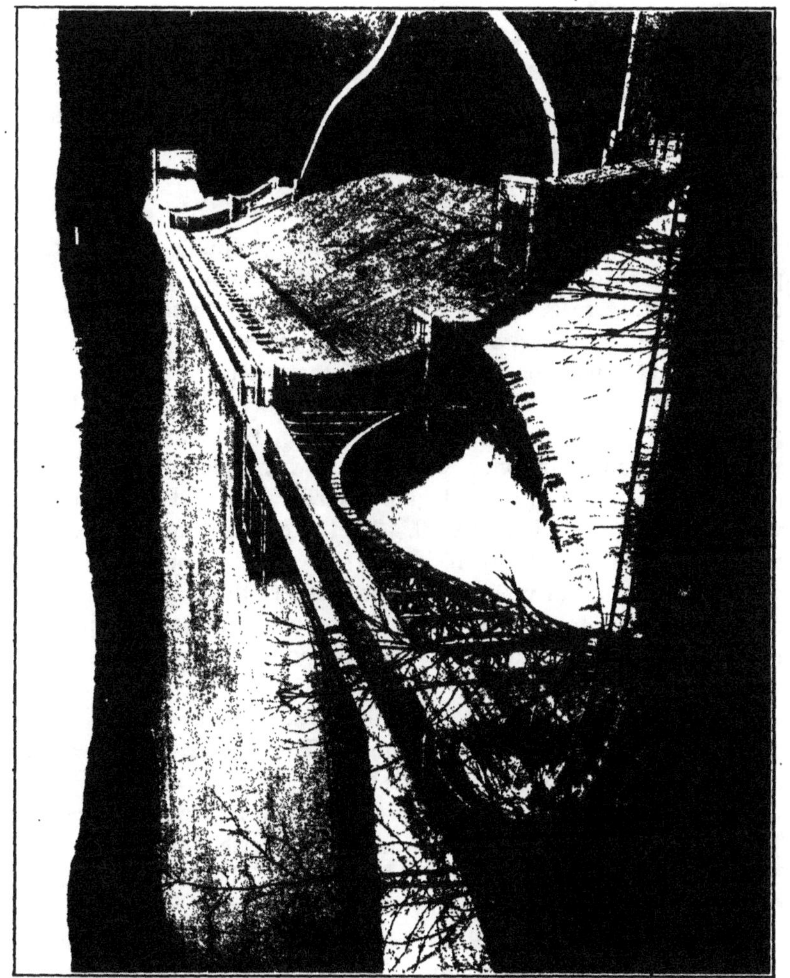

New Croton Dam in Westchester County

that the Park Commissioners should place some suitable monument to mark the line of the aqueduct property; that no public walk be made on the property; and that no objection would be made at any time to the reoccupation of the corner by the aqueduct commissioners. This reservoir is soon to be abandoned for aqueduct purposes and the Mayor's Catskill Aqueduct Celebration Committee is developing plans for adding it to Central Park as a permanent memorial of the aqueduct.

The Murray Hill Reservoir

From the upper reservoir at Yorkville, a double line of iron pipes 3 feet in diameter was laid to Fifth avenue and thence to the distributing reservoir which formerly stood on the west side of Fifth avenue between 40th and 42nd streets. This reservoir was 420 feet square on the cornice of the exterior wall and contained 4.05 acres. It had an average elevation of 44.5 feet above the street level, the greatest height being 49 feet. The walls were of hydraulic masonry, constructed with openings to reduce the quantity of masonry and give a larger base. The reservoir was composed of a double wall. The outer wall had a bevel of one to six and was uniformly four feet thick. The inner wall, which had a vertical inner face, was six feet thick at the bottom and four at the top. There were cross walls and arches in the interspace. On the outside walls an Egyptian cornice was laid, which was in keeping with the sloping architecture. The reservoir was designed to hold a depth of 36 feet of water, or a capacity of 20,000,000 imperial gallons. The surface of the water, when the reservoir was full, was 115 feet above mean tide. The water was admitted to this reservoir with formal ceremonies on July 4, 1842. The reservoir was then described as being "at Murray hill, a short drive from the city." The total length of the aqueduct from Croton dam to this point is 45.562 miles.

In the spring of 1899, a contract was let for the removal of the reservoir to make room for the New York Public Library which now occupies its site, but the process of removal was slow, and portions of the massive walls remained standing long after the library building had been begun. The cornerstone of the library was laid on November 10, 1902, and the completed building was dedicated on May 2, 1911. By the thoughtfulness of Mr. Thomas Hastings, architect, the memorial inscription from the old reservoir is preserved in the Public Library.

Extension to City Hall Park

On October 14, 1842, the water was admitted to the fountain in City Hall Park with still further ceremonies, including a procession seven miles long. The fountain was situated in the triangular area now occupied by the post-office. At that time, there was an unobstructed view from the junction of Broadway and Chatham street (Park row) in front of St. Paul's chapel to the City Hall. The larger park was embowered with trees, in the midst of which the Croton fountain was for many years a graceful ornament.

In a statement of the real estate belonging to the City of New York published in the Corporation Manual for 1852, the value of the Croton water-works at that time was stated as follows:

Croton aqueduct	$14,200,000
Yorkville reservoir	134,000
Murray Hill reservoir	152,000
	$14,486,000

Since that time the Croton water-supply and the water-works system have been enormously increased, and it is impossible here to follow out its details. One or two further features, however, may be mentioned.

Lake Manahatta in Central Park

One enlargment of interest was the building of the new reservoir or Lake Manahatta in Central Park. In less than a decade after the introduction of the Croton water supply, the city realized that it did not have storage capacity enough in its reservoirs to protect it against a serious drouth, and on February 5, 1851, the Common Council directed the Croton Aqueduct Board "to purchase without unnecessary delay enough suitable ground for a new reservoir of sufficient capacity with those already built to contain a supply for at least sixty days' consumption." The Board thereupon carefully examined the island and on February 9, 1852, voted to appropriate for that purpose the rectangular area comprised between Fifth and Seventh avenues and Eighty-sixth and Ninety-sixth streets, as those streets were laid out on the city plan by the Commissioners of 1807. On May 21, 1852, the Board recommended to the court the following named gentlemen as Commissioners of Estimate of the value of the ground to be taken: Daniel Dodge, Samuel B. Ruggles, Ezra P. Davis, Jacob S. Baker, Jedediah Miller and Anthony J. Bleecker.

Before work was begun on the reservoir, Central Park was created, including the reservoir area, and the Park Commissioners proposed an exchange of territory by which the new reservoir, instead of being rectangular, would follow natural contours and by avoiding some rock excavation, would save from $200,000 to $250,000 in the cost of construction. The Croton Aqueduct Board, therefore, on June 6, 1857, consented to the change and the reservoir was built as it now exists. The land for this reservoir, purchased under an act of the Legislature of June 30, 1853, comprises 106.726 acres, and the reservoir, which covers ninety-six acres, has a capacity of 1,030,000,000 gallons. On April 14, 1858, the sum of $729,964.50 was awarded for the site.

This new reservoir, called on a map of 1859, Manahatta Lake,* in the records of the Aqueduct Board the Grand Reservoir, and popularly the New Reservoir, was completed in 1862 and the water was admitted on August 19th with due ceremony. The minutes of the Croton Aqueduct Board of that date read as follows:

"The water was let into the new Grand Reservoir on this day at 3 P. M. The signal was given by Chief Engineer Alfred W. Craven, Esq., when the ten influent gates were raised simultaneously, and the Croton flowed through to the delight of the thousands that were present to witness the great event. His Honor the Mayor then introduced Myndert Van Shaick, who delivered an address, after which Mr. McChesney recited an ode prepared for the occasion, and with an address by Mr. Marsh and music by Mr. H. Dodworth's band the ceremonies ended and the assembled multitude dispersed to pay their respects to the contractors, Messrs. Fairchild, Walker & Company, at their office."

New Croton Aqueduct

On account of the phenomenal growth of the city, it became necessary not only to build additional reservoirs from time to time, but also to build another aqueduct from the Croton valley to conduct the increased supply of water to Manhattan island. Such a new conduit was built in 1885-1893. It is almost entirely

* Mayor Tiemann so named it at the ceremonies attending the induction of the water, saying: "Our new lake of the Manahatta will far surpass the dimensions of the old kolch" (or fresh-water pond).

a tunnel from Croton lake to the terminal gate-house at 135th street and Convent avenue, a distance of 31 miles. At this gate-house the old aqueduct is connected with the new. The old Croton aqueduct, with a capacity of 90,000,000 gallons a day and the new Croton aqueduct with a capacity of 300,000,000 gallons a day, were supplemented in 1880 and 1885 by an additional supply of 22,000,000 gallons a day by a conduit bringing water from the Bronx and Byram rivers.

The Cornell or New Croton Dam

When the plans were made in 1882-1885 for an enlarged water-supply, they included the project for a high masonry dam across the Croton river about two miles from its mouth, at the side of the old Quaker bridge. Owing to local opposition to this site, another location was selected about 1¼ miles farther up-stream on the land of A. B. Cornell and others. The dam here constructed was at first called the Cornell dam, but later was designated as the New Croton dam, to distinguish it from the old Croton dam 3½ miles farther up-stream.

The rock at the dam site is gneiss on the north side of the valley and limestone in the center and on the south side.

The contract for building the dam was awarded August 26, 1892; work was begun in the fall of 1892; the first stone in the foundation was laid May 26, 1896; the dam was nearly finished and the gates were closed January 28, 1905, beginning the storage of water, the work was completed January 1, 1906; and by November 5, 1907, the reservoir was full to high water mark.

The total length of the masonry and earth dams across the channel is 1600 feet; the total height from bottom of foundation about 240 feet; and the maximum thickness of masonry at the bottom 206 feet. The thickness of masonry decreased toward the top until it is only about 15 feet thick under the roadway. The roadway has a width of 19½ feet by being carried out on corbels. The reservoir thus formed is about 19 miles long and stores about 33,815,000,000 gallons.

The plans for the new Croton dam were prepared under the direction of the late Alphonse Fteley, Chief Engineer of the Aqueduct Commissioners. They were modified as the work progressed. The construction was carried on under his supervision until January 1, 1900; then under Mr. William R. Hill until

October 14, 1903; Mr. J. Waldo Smith until August 1, 1905; and Mr. Walter H. Sears until completion.

The cost of the dam, not including engineering, land and legal expenses, was $6,886,872.

Even this provision was not adequate to the growing needs of the City, and two more sources were added in 1908 and 1911, making the total storage capacity of the Croton system as follows:

Reservoir	Service Begun	Gallons of Storage Capacity
Old Croton Lake	1842	
Boyd's Corners	1873	2,727,000,000
Middle Branch	1878	4,155,000,000
East Branch (Sodom)	1891	5,243,000,000
Bog Brook	1891	4,400,000,000
Titicus	1893	7,617,000,000
West Branch (Carmel)	1895	10,668,000,000
Amawalk	1897	7,086,000,000
New Croton	1905	33,815,000,000
Cross River	1908	10,923,000,000
Croton Falls	1911	15,753,000,000
		102,387,000,000

Ashokan Reservoir, Looking Westward Across Reservoir

Chapter VI

Other Borough Water-Supplies

Borough of Brooklyn

The town of Brooklyn was settled in 1636, ten years after the first permanent settlement of New Amsterdam, and the early histories of the water-supplies of the two communities were very much alike, both depending on natural springs, streams, ponds and wells. But on account of the differences in geographical and geological situation, the two developed very differently after the beginning of the nineteenth century. Old New York City, lying on a rocky island only 13 miles long and from 1 to 2¼ miles wide, had small natural resources for water and was early driven to seek an artificial supply. Brooklyn, situated on an island which is 115 miles long and from 12 to 24 miles wide, and which is composed largely of sand and gravel, was able longer to use natural sources, and, as a matter of fact, she relied exclusively upon springs, streams, ponds and wells up to the year 1859 and largely so up to the present time.*

The first suggestion of a general water-supply was made in 1832, two years before the village of Brooklyn was incorporated as a city; and after Brooklyn became a city, the subject was discussed over and over again without substantial results for twenty years. Numerous committees were appointed and made reports. Some recommended co-operation with New York in using Croton water; others advocated using the streams of Long Island; and still others the construction of wells in or near the city. In 1851, a supply from the Bronx river was added to the sources proposed.

In these discussions, the underground water condition of Long Island was the subject of earnest and at times contentious discussion. There were those who thought that the water existed in veins; others who thought there were subterranean rivers; and others who held that the whole island was saturated with water. When William J. McAlpine in 1852 recommended artesian wells, Prof. William W. Mather's report on the geology of New York

* I. M. de Varona, in his "History and Description of the Water Supply of Brooklyn," 1896, says that prior to the introduction of Croton water in New York City, Brooklyn wells were largely drawn upon for New York's water supply.

was quoted to refute it. There were those who believed that a well fifty feet deep would draw salt waters. At one time an opei canal was advocated. The best plan that the municipal authorities could evolve after nearly 20 years of discussion was submitted to the people in 1853 and voted down.

While these futile efforts were being made by the public authorities, an enterprising private water corporation was formed, somewhat parelleling New York's early experience with the Manhattan Company. In 1852, the Williamsburgh Water Works company was incorporated, with a view to taking water from a well within the city limits and from springs on the north side of Long Island, and made a formal offer to supply the City of Brooklyn. This raised the question whether the city should depend upon a private company for its water or should possess its own supply. In the exigencies of the situation, the Common Council held secret sessions and public interest was greatly stirred. In one of these secret sessions, a plan recommended by Mr. McAlpine was approved. The plan provided for collecting at Baisley's pond the water of certain streams emptying into Jamaica and Hempstead Bays; conducting it in a conduit 9 miles long to a pump-well where it was to be pumped into a reservoir on Mount Prospect, near Prospect Park. In 1853, a modified plan was submitted to the people's vote and rejected. In 1854, the annexation of the City of Williamsburgh and town of Bushwick to Brooklyn gave renewed impetus to the subject.

Meanwhile, the Williamsburgh Water-Works company had undergone changes, its name being changed first to the Long Island Water-Works company, and then (in 1855) to the Brooklyn Water company. In the latter year, the Nassau Water company was incorporated, with power to absorb the Brooklyn Water company. All this time, the company had been gradually acquiring water rights, until it became necessary for the city either to buy it out or use its water, although the city too had been buying land and water rights here and there for its own use.

In 1856 the Common Council subscribed $1,300,000 to the stock of the Nassau Water company upon condition that it should construct works capable of supplying 20,000,000 gallons a day; that it should purchase the lands bought by the city which were necessary for the purpose; and that the city should have the privilege of buying out the whole plant at cost. This was the beginning of the Ridgewood system; and the inaugural celebration was held on the site of the Ridgewood reservoir July 31, 1856. In the following year the city availed itself of its privilege and bought out the Nassau Water company and finished the work itself. On November 18, 1858, water was first pumped into the Ridgewood reservoir; water was admitted to the distributing mains on December 4, and on December 16 it was used for the first time in the city to extinguish fires. On April 27 and 28, 1859, the successful completion of the main features of the plan was marked by a public celebration. Prior to this event, Brooklyn water had come exclusively from wells and cisterns.

In 1872 the construction of the Hempstead reservoir was begun and the water-supply was further augmented from time to time by pumping stations at various ponds. In 1889, the construction of a new reservoir at Millburn, a 48-inch pipe line connecting it with the engine house at Ridgewood, and various supply ponds and intermediate conduits were contracted for.

The Ridgewood system was expanded at successive periods until 1898 it embraced practically all the water-shed of Queens county, bounded in the north by the ridge forming the backbone of Long Island, on the east approximately by Suffolk county, on the south by the salt meadows bordering Hempstead and Jamaica bays, and on the west by Kings county.

While the events above narrated were occurring, private water-works were organized in New Lots, Flatbush, New Utrecht and Gravesend.

The plant at New Lots, belonging to the Long Island Water-Supply Co., was located on New Lots avenue at the head of Fresh creek and was built in 1881.

The New Utrecht Water Co., had its plant at the corner of East 14th street and Avenue E. It was acquired by the City of Brooklyn in 1895.

The Gravesend Water-Works, built by the town of Gravesend about 1892, was located on 17th street between Avenues R and S. It became the property of Brooklyn in 1895.

The works of the Flatbush Water company were built in 1882 at the head of Paerdegat creek, near the intersection of New York avenue and Avenue E.

The Flatbush Water-Works is still a private company serving the 29th ward.

Another private concern, the Blythebourne Water company, serves a portion of the 30th ward.

Up to the year 1896, just before her consolidation with Greater New York, Brooklyn had bought 2,706 acres of land at a cost of $1,261,271, and spent $22,102,700 for the construction or purchase of water-works. She then had an average water-supply of about 75,735,000 gallons a day from the Ridgewood system, which the subsequent completion of the Millburn works increased to about 99,000,000 gallons a day. She owned fifteen supply ponds with an area of 215 acres and storage capacity of 264,489,000 gallons, as follows: Baisley's, Springfield, Simonson's, Clear stream, Watt's, Valley stream, Pine's, Hempstead, Smith's, Millburn, East Meadow, Newbridge, Wantagh, Seaman's, and Massapequa pond.

In 1916, Brooklyn had an average water-supply of 73,000,000 a day from drawn wells of a depth of from 30 to several hundred feet; 34,000,000 gallons a day from infiltration galleries laid for nearly six miles about ten to fifteen feet below the water-table; and 20,000,000 gallons a day from surface supplies.

Borough of Queens

For the Borough of Queens no municipal water-works of magnitude have been constructed. Prior to 1913 the First ward was served by three local municipal pumping stations and by private water companies. Between 1913 and 1917 it was served largely from the Brooklyn watershed. The Third ward, prior to 1917, was served by two municipal pumping stations, while the Second, Fourth and Fifth wards were and still are supplied by private water companies, their sources of supply being entirely ground water collected by means of driven wells. The Citizens' Water Supply company of Newtown and the Urban Water company furnish water for the Second ward, the Jamaica Water Supply company and the Woodhaven Water Supply company for the Fourth ward and the Queens County Water company for the Fifth ward. About 400,000 citizens of Brooklyn and Queens Boroughs, consuming nearly 40,000,000 gallons a day, are still dependent on private water companies.

Borough of the Bronx

The region now comprised within the Borough of the Bronx

was favorably situated with respect to its natural water resources. Traversed by more than a score of rivers and creeks of considerable size, among which may be mentioned Bronx river, Tippett's brook, Cromwell's creek, Westchester creek and Eastchester or Hutchinson's river, and with a soil well adapted for springs and wells, the early settlers did not lack good water for domestic use or sufficient volume to turn the wheels of several considerable mills. Among the best known of the latter were the Van Cortlandt grist mill in what is now Van Cortlandt Park and the Lorillard Tobacco mill in Bronx Park.

On January 1, 1874, that portion of Westchester county west of the Bronx and south of the Yonkers line was annexed to the City of New York; on July 1, 1895, the 24th ward was somewhat enlarged on the east of the Bronx; and on January 1, 1898, the remainder of the present borough was added to the ctiy.

With these successive additions of territory, the responsibility of the city with respect to its water supply increased, and in October, 1880, it began to develop the Bronx and Byram watersheds for the supply of the higher levels of the Annexed District. The plan comprised a dam at the outlet of Little Rye pond converting the two Rye ponds into a reservoir holding 1,050,000,000 gallons; a dam across the Bronx river near Kensico station on the Harlem railroad, making a reservoir holding 1,620,000,000 gallons; a dam across Byram river a fifth of a mile north of the state line, making a reservoir of 180,000,000 gallons, and a 48-inch conduit fifteen miles long from Kensico reservoir to a reservoir on Gun hill near Williamsbridge, which latter had a capacity of 120,000,000 gallons. In addition to the above, Byram pond held 550,000,000 gallons. The connection between Kensico and Williamsbridge reservoirs was made September 4, 1884, and the other developments gradually followed. In 1902 connection was made with the old Croton aqueduct by means of a 48-inch pipe for supplying lower levels in the Bronx; and there were some connections from Manhattan under the Harlem river for supplying some of the nearer areas of the mainland borough.

There was one private water-supply company in the Bronx borough area, the Westchester Water Company, which supplied Westchester Village and vicinity. Between 1900 and 1902 the city bought out the interests of this company within the city line, but it still serves water to communities just outside the city.

Ashokan Reservoir, Looking Westward from Middle Dike

There are still many private wells in use in this borough.

Jerome Park reservoir, an adjunct of the Croton system was begun in 1895 and its western basin was finished in 1905. It holds 773,000,000 gallons. Its eastern basin was never completed, and in 1911 the Legislature authorized the use of part of the ground for an armory.

In recent years, nearly three-fourths of the Bronx borough supply came from the Croton and the remainder from the Bronx and Byram watersheds. As stated hereafter, the old Kensico reservoir has been merged in the new Kensico reservoir of the Catskill system, and at that point, the supplies from the Bronx and Byram watersheds become merged in the Catskill supply.

Borough of Richmond

Prior to 1917 the Borough of Richmond was dependent for its supply on ground water drawn from wells. Until 1909, except at Tottenville, it was served by private water companies, the principal of which were in that year acquired by the city.

Chapter VII.

The Catskill Aqueduct

The Evolution of the Project

The history of the evolution of the Catskill aqueduct project is full of intense interest and civic significance, and to write it fully would require a volume by itself. For the purposes of this pamphlet, only a few leading events must suffice.

All history is an endless chain of cause and effect, and the question of the water-supply of any growing community is never-ending. Nevertheless, one is able to point out quite definitely the origin of the Catskill aqueduct idea.

With a population which was approaching 3,500,000 souls in the area of Greater New York at the time of municipal consolidation in 1898 and which was increasing at the rate of a million a decade; with the Croton water supply developed to its fullest extent and confessedly running behind the needs of Manhattan and the Bronx; with Brooklyn, Queens and Richmond boroughs relying on local supplies largely derived from wells and in many cases purveyed by private companies; and with alarming deficiencies in rainfall in 1895 and 1896, it was plainly manifest that something must be done and done quickly to avert a calamitous shortage of water in the near future.

This realization came with especial force to certain individuals and civic organizations. On November 2, 1896, the Manufacturers Association of Brooklyn, under the leadership of Mr. Charles N. Chadwick, took the active initiative by appointing a committee, of which Mr. Chadwick was Chairman, to investigate the problem of Brooklyn's water-supply. The reports of this committee are very suggestive of the civic foresight and the thoroughness of research which Andrew H. Green, "The Father of Greater New York," manifested in his writings in advocacy of municipal consolidation. Lacking,—as the committee's report of March 15, 1897, stated,—the power to bring rain from the clouds by incantations like the Indian Rainmaker, or to bring water from the rocks by smiting them with a rod like Moses, or to discover subterranean streams by means of the forked witch-hazel stick, Mr. Chadwick investigated the subject with all the practical thoroughness that human limitations would permit. He made a particular study of the water-supplies of 200 cities in this country and Europe, including that of the Metropolitan district which was soon to become Greater New York. He found that the sister cities and smaller communities in this area never had a settled plan for developing water-supply and had lived only in a hand-to-mouth way with inadequate appropriations for any large provision for the future. He believed the question should be handled in a broader way than ever before, and out of his studies he developed four fundamental ideas: First, that the new water-supply should be comprehensive enough to include the whole of the future Greater City; second, that it should be financed by separating the water debt from the constitutional debt limit of the city; third, that in planning and providing this larger water-supply, there should be continuity of administration outside of the field of political influence; and fourth, that provision should be made looking to the needs of the Metropolis for at least half a century to come. The influence of these ideas may be traced through all the formative events which followed the report of the Manufacturers Association.

It is also a significant fact, which deserves to be dwelt on at greater length than the limits of these pages will permit, that while the project of the Catskill aqueduct encountered great apathy and even opposition in many quarters, it received the helpful and indispensable co-operation of other civic bodies, notably the Chamber of Commerce of the State of New York, the Merchants Association of New York, the City Club, the New York Board of Trade and Transportation, the Brooklyn League, the Flatbush Taxpayers Association, the Citizens Union, the New York Board of Fire Underwriters, the People's Institute, the East Side Civic Club, the West End Association, etc. It was a citizens' movement throughout, animated by the highest and most disinterested motives.

In 1897, the possible new sources of water under consideration were the Ten Mile river and Housatonic river as a continuation of the Croton watershed; the Delaware river at Port Jervis, N. Y.; the Ramapo watershed; and the Catskill Mountains, with the Adirondacks ultimately in view. As a last resort, more particularly for Brooklyn, the Long Island watershed was not forgotten.

A serious obstacle to a free survey of all possible sources, however, was presented by the existence of the Ramapo Water Company. This company, which had been incorporated by certificate in 1887, had in 1895 secured the passage of a law entitled "An act to limit and define the powers of the Ramapo Water Company." Instead of "limiting" its powers, the act enlarged them so that it was authorized to acquire lands in the Ramapo watershed by condemnation in the same manner as a railroad company; and to construct reservoirs and water-works and to supply water for municipal, domestic, manufacturing and agricultural purposes. It was also authorized to lay pipes under the navigable streams of the state. These broad powers aroused intense public criticism and an effort was immediately begun for their repeal. In this campaign, which proved successful, the Merchants' Association, under the leadership of the late William F. King, performed public service of inestimable value, working through a large Citizens' Committee, one of the members of which was Mr. Henry R. Towne*, who served on the engineering sub-committee. As a result of these efforts the Legislature, in 1901, repealed the Ramapo Act of 1895.

Meanwhile, on March 23, 1900, Mr. John R. Freeman, civil engineer, reported to the Comptroller that the Croton, Bronx and Byram watersheds would supply Manhattan and Bronx Boroughs for only five years. This was fresh evidence of the need for expedition; and in the Legislature of 1901 the Manufacturers Association secured the introduction of a bill, drafted by Mr. Chadwick, providing for the appointment of a Board of Water Commissioners with mandatory powers to go ahead and provide an enlarged water-supply. The bill failed to pass and was reintroduced in 1902, slightly amended, and providing, among other things, for the appointment of the members of the board by the Mayor. Again the bill failed to pass, but efforts were not relaxed.

On November 30, 1903, Prof. William H. Burr, Mr. Rudolph Hering and Mr. John R. Freeman, constituting a Commission on Additional Water Supply, made a notable report which not only added impetus to the movement but was also immensely helpful in later selecting the Catskill watersheds.

In 1904, two important strides were made toward the attainment of the goal. The first was the getting together of the civic organizations in concerted work. The second was the enlistment of Mayor McClellan's interest.

* Mr. Towne's services were not confined to this one phase of the subject. As Chairman of the Committee on Water Supply of the Merchants' Association, its President for nearly six years, and one of its Directors during the whole period, he has been one of the ablest and most untiring advocates of the Aqueduct, and his aid in shaping public sentiment and in securing proper legislation entitle him to special credit as one of the "fathers" of this great public work.

The first of these was achieved at a joint conference held at the City Club on June 9, 1904. All of the civic organizations mentioned on page 78 preceding were represented. Prof. Burr and Mr. Hering explained to the conference the situation which confronted the City; and Mr. Chadwick emphasized the necessity of getting down to practical work and formulating a plan. He also urged the necessity of separating the water-debt from the debt limit, so that the project could be amply financed; and of creating a commission with large powers, like the Rapid Transit Commission, to carry on the work. The meeting resulted in the appointment of a representative committee of these civic bodies, and from that time forward there was splendid "team work" between them. The meetings of the representatives of the civic bodies at the City Club continued for a period of six months or more.

In July, 1904, the gravity of the situation was brought to the attention of Mayor McClellan by a sub-committee of the conference, consisting of Mr. Horace E. Deming of the City Club, Mr. Charles N. Chadwick of the Manufacturers Association, Mr. Robert Van Iderstine of the Citizens Union, Mr. Abner S. Haight of the Brooklyn League, Mr. George W. Brush of the Flatbush Taxpayers Association, Mr. Henry Evans of the New York Board of Fire Underwriters, Mr. A. B. Hepburn of the Chamber of Commerce, Mr. Oscar S. Straus of the Board of Trade and Transportation, and Mr. Lawrence Veiller of the City Club, in behalf of their own and the associated organizations. Mayor McClellan's interest was instantly enlisted and proved a powerful factor of the success which soon followed.

On January 3, 1905, with the backing of Mayor McClellan, a new bill for the creation of a Board of Water Supply was introduced in the Legislature. Gov. Higgins did not at first regard the measure favorably, as he was an advocate of the development of all the water resources of the State under State auspices. On February 16, 1905, Mr. Chadwick went to Albany and saw the Governor by appointment, explained the situation, removed the Governor's objections and secured his endorsement of the general provisions of the bill; and from that time forward, Gov. Higgins was a firm advocate of the measure.

The situation in the Legislature, however, was not altogether promising, and a special effort was made to carry conviction at a

Ashokan Reservoir, showing Ashokan Bridge, Dividing Weir, and Gate Chambers

legislative hearing held February 20, 1905. Mayor McClellan, ex-Mayor Low, Corporation Counsel Delaney, and a committee of representatives of the joint conference of civic bodies of which Mr. Horace E. Deming was Chairman, went to Albany on this occasion. In addition to the influence of this notable delegation, Governor Higgins, on that very day, threw into the scales the weight of a special message to the Legislature urging the passage of the bill.

One of the strongest supporters of the Mayor's bill at this critical time was the Chamber of Commerce. An able report made to that organization on February 28, 1905, by Mr. A. B. Hepburn, Chairman of the Committee on Internal Trade and Improvements, said, among other things:

"The Mayor's bill . . . contains within itself everything necessary to secure with the utmost possible speed the additional water-supply so much needed, to put the control of the undertaking from start to finish in the hands of a small efficient, non-political business body, responsible directly to the city, and at the same time establishes rules of justice and fair dealing readily enforceable in the courts.

"The securing of an adequate additional water supply for the city will cost probably $100,000,000 and the undertaking demands a consistent and continuous business policy that will last through several city administrations. This means, on the one hand, that the city should control the spending of so vast an amount of the money of the citizens, and, on the other, that the control of so stupendous a business enterprise should be removed absolutely from the exigencies of political parties or political partisanship."

In the mutations through which the bill passed while in the committee stage in the Legislature, the loss of one feature caused much concern. One of the primary objects which had been kept in mind by the projectors of the movement from its very inception in 1897 had been to keep on a high civic plane and outside of partisan politics the administration of the commission which was to build the aqueduct; and it was conceived that if an impartial selection of commissioners could be assured, it would tend to remove much of the opposition to the bill. A provision had therefore been inserted in the Mayor's bill requiring the appointment of the three members of the proposed Board of Water Supply from lists supplied by the Chamber of Commerce, the Board of Fire Underwriters and the Manufacturers' Association. This had been stricken out, however, as unconstitutional, but the deletion was compensated for by a timely and important public declaration by Mayor McClellan. At a dinner given to him at the Hamilton Club in Brooklyn on April 6, 1905, he said:

"I promise with all sincerity that is in me that if the bill is amended giving to the Mayor absolute and unqualified power of appointment I shall immediately on the enactment of the bill call upon the Chamber of Commerce of New York, the Board of Fire Underwriters and the Manufacturers' Association for a list of three names each, and from those names I shall appoint Commissioners, one from each list; and should any vacancies occur later during my administration, I shall fill those vacancies in the same manner as I shall appoint the original Commission. I want to make a precedent so strong and establish a tradition so binding that none of my successors can in any circumstances violate this tradition or precedent."*

This declaration had the desired effect. The bill passed the Assembly April 11 and in the last days of the session it passed the Senate. It became a law (chapter 724 of the laws of 1905) by the Governor's signature on June 3, 1905.

The last obstacle in the stony path of the movement was removed when, on November 7, 1905, by popular vote, the constitution was amended by inserting in section 10 of article VIII a provision excepting from the constitutional debt limit of municipalities "debts incurred by the City of New York after the 1st day of January, 1904, . . for the supply of water." This amendment went into effect January 1, 1906, but was retroactive to January 1, 1904.

Chapter 724 of the laws of 1905 provided that the Mayor should appoint three Commissioners to be called the Board of Water Supply. An unusual feature of the law, designed to secure continuity of administration, is that it prescribes no limit to the term of office of the Commissioners, who are not to be removed except for incompetency or misconduct. The Board chooses its own President, and any two of them constitute a quorum for the transaction of business. This Board was given power to appoint its own engineers, surveyors, and other employees; and was charged with its duty of ascertaining the most available sources of an additional water supply for the city of New York, its recommendations being sub-

* Mayor Gaynor did not follow this precedent.

ject to modification by the Board of Estimate and Apportionment. Upon the approval of its plans and after certain formalities concerning the filing of maps, etc., the Corporation Counsel was authorized to institute condemnation proceedings for the acquisition of the lands needed and the Board of Water Supply was authorized to build the aqueduct. By the terms of the act, the City of Kingston and any municipality in Westchester county may use water from the Catskill aqueduct, at the same rate of consumption per capita as New York city, upon payment to the city of New York at the same rate charged to New York city consumers.

On June 5, 1905, Mayor McClellan called Mr. Chadwick to his office and appointed him a Commissioner as from the Manufacturers' Association. Not then having the nominations of the Chamber of Commerce and Board of Fire Underwriters, the Mayor deferred appointments of the other two until June 9, on which date Mr. Chadwick was formally commissioned, with Mr. J. Edward Simmons of the Chamber of Commerce and Mr. Charles A. Shaw of the Board of Fire Underwriters.

The full list of the Commissioners who for twelve years have had this great responsibility of evolving a definite and comprehensive plan of water-supply and of carrying out that plan, is as follows, the Presidents of the Board being indicated by asterisks.

Name	*Appointed*	*Resigned*
*J. Edward Simmons	June 9, 1905	Jan. 28, 1908
Charles N. Chadwick	June 9, 1905	Incumbent
Charles A. Shaw	June 9, 1905	Jan. 12, 1911
*John A. Bensel	Jan. 30, 1908	Dec. 31, 1910
John F. Galvin	Jan. 23, 1911	Incumbent
*Charles Strauss	Feb. 7, 1911	Incumbent

The Board spent two months in considering the plan and details of organization. Before the engineers could be appointed it was necessary to secure their exemption from civil service rules by the state and municipal Civil Service Commissions.

On July 7, 1905, Mr. John R. Freeman was appointed Consulting Engineer.

Mr. J. Waldo Smith was made Chief Engineer and assumed his duties August 1, 1905. The selection of Mr. Smith for this responsible position was extremely fortunate for the success of the undertaking. He had begun his engineering career twenty-seven years before, at the age of 17, as Chief Engineer of his home town of Lincoln, Mass.; and after having directed works of increasing importance in that and other states, had been Chief Engineer of the Aqueduct Commissioners of New York from 1903 to 1905, and had charge of the completion of the new Croton dam—the largest masonry dam in the world. He was therefore thoroughly familiar with the water problem of New York City. In his work on the Catskill aqueduct, he surrounded himself with very able men as executives and consultants, and directed the work with such skill as an engineer that every problem—and many were entirely new—was solved as it was encountered. In addition to his professional ability, he displayed remarkable tact. All of his associates became very fond of him personally, and their esprit de corps and loyalty contributed greatly to the success of this crowning work of his genius.

Mr. Charles R. Harrison was appointed Deputy Chief Engineer and was later succeeded in turn by Mr. Merritt H. Smith and Mr. Alfred D. Flinn. On August 8, 1905, Prof. William H. Burr and Mr. Frederic P. Stearns were appointed Consulting Engineers, and some years later Messrs. Thaddeus Merriman, George G. Honness, Ralph N. Wheeler, Frank E. Winsor, Robert Ridgway, Carleton E. Davis and Walter E. Spear were appointed Department Engineers.

The organization at the present time is as follows:

Commissioners

Charles Strauss, President

Charles N Chadwick	John F. Galvin

Administration and Claims Bureaus

George Featherstone, Secretary	William S. Haupt, Chief Clerk
Ralph T. Stanton, Asst. Secretary	Walter LeC. Boyer, Chief of Bureau of Claims.
Henry C. Buncke, Auditor	

Engineering Bureau.

J. Waldo Smith, Chief Engineer

Alfred D. Flinn, Deputy Chief Engr.	Thaddeus Merriman, Department Engr.
John R. Freeman, Consulting Engr.	George G. Honness, Department Engr.
William H. Burr, Consulting Engr.	Ralph N. Wheeler, Department Engr.
Frederic P. Stearns, Consulting Engr.	Walter E. Spear, Department Engr.

Prof. William O. Crosby, formerly of the Massachusetts Institute of Technology, Prof. Charles P. Berkey, Ph. D., of Columbia University, and Prof. James F. Kemp, Sc. D., LL. D., of Columbia University, were the experts on geological questions.

The Catskill Mountains

And now, to quote "The Pilgrim's Progress," "they came to the Delectable Mountains." With the aid of previous studies, it did not take the Board long to determine the general question of the source from which the water was to be obtained, and exactly four months after its appointment, the Board recommended to the Board of Estimate and Apportionment a plan for taking water from the watersheds in the Catskill mountains and foot-hills tributary to the Catskill, Schoharie, Esopus and Rondout creeks. The Rondout watershed, embracing an area of 131 square miles, begins about seventy-five miles in an air line from New York City Hall. The Esopus watershed, containing about 255 square miles, lies next to the northward; the Schoharie, 315 square miles, next; and the Catskill, 163 square miles, farthest north, its northernmost boundary being about 130 miles from City Hall.

The Catskill mountains in which these watersheds lie are an excellent illustration of the mechanical agency of water referred to in the opening chapter. In the Middle and Upper Devonic periods of Palaeozoic time, perhaps 43,000,000 years ago,* when all the interior of New York state and much of the continent was submerged under the sea, the sandstones and shales of the Catskills were formed by particles and fragments of ancient rock washed from adjacent heights and deposited on the shore and bottom of the Devonian sea. In the lapse of these millions of years, there has been a gradual elevation of the land surface,—probably several alternate elevations and depressions, which, as their net result, lifted the ancient seashore and sea-bottom in a great plateau several thousand feet above sea-level. As it emerged, the rains, aided somewhat by the winds, and later the glaciers, began to wear it down and carved it ultimately into the shapes which we now call mountains. The highest of these, Hunter mountain, is 4025 feet high, although it was once much higher, and we can recognize on these high mountain-tops the sands of the ancient sea-shore.

Preliminary Explorations

Having selected the general source of the water supply, it

* Geologists do not reckon geological time by years, but by periods, characterized by certain forms of rocks and evidences of life. The above rough estimate of the age of the Catskills is based on Lord Kelvin's estimate of 100,000,000 years of elapsed time since the Archaean, and Dana's ratios of the different periods.

Ashokan Reservoir: Dividing Weir Bridge

was necessary to determine the route of the aqueduct, the location of the reservoirs, and the general character of the works to be constructed. The work was divided into five departments, namely, the Departments of Reservoirs, North Aqueduct (from Ashokan to Peekskill), South Aqueduct (from Peekskill to New York City), City Tunnel, and Headquarters, in charge of department engineers. The Chief Engineer over the whole work was Mr. J. Waldo Smith.

The survey covered about 3000 miles before the line of 92 miles between the Ashokan reservoir and the city line was determined. Additional surveys and explorations were necessary to locate the 28 miles of tunnel in the bed rock in the city itself. It was decided at the outset not to build the aqueduct anywhere on structures above ground. There were to be no picturesque arcades of masonry like the Roman aqueducts or the Harlem river High bridge. Bridges were to be only for highway purposes. The aqueduct itself was to be underground, for safety. Rivers and valleys, therefore, had to be crossed by inverted siphons passing under them, and as the pressure of water at low depths is enormous, these siphons and certain other parts of the aqueduct had to be built in solid rock; and to determine the subterranean rock conditions, hundreds of borings were made with a diamond drill The diamond drill used was a hollow cylindrical steep pipe, 1¾ inches in diameter, in the end of which were set seven black diamonds. Each diamond was valued at about $100, making the diamonds alone worth $700 in each drill. In the operation, a pipe somewhat larger than the drill was first driven down through the top soil to the rock. The drill was then let down in the pipe, lengths being added to the drill as required, until the end with the diamonds rested on the rock. The drill was then revolved by machinery, cutting down through the rock somewhat as an apple-corer cuts through an apple, leaving a core of rock inside the drill. Occasionally the drills were pulled up and the rock cores removed, labeled and carefully saved for study. The cores came out in fragments varying in length from a few inches to ten feet, and their aggregate length exceeded 25 miles. They constitute a distinct contribution to geological science generally. Every phase of the work was done under the supervision of three experts in geology, namely, Prof. William O. Crosby, formerly of the Massachusetts Institute of Technology,

Prof. Charles P. Berkey, Ph.D., of Columbia University, and Prof. James F. Kemp, Sc.D., LL. D., of Columbia University. The information furnished by the studies and reports of these experts concerning the rock-cores enabled the engineers to know where to locate the rock tunnels in rock strong enough to resist the bursting pressure of the water, how deep to sink their shafts, etc.

The Ashokan Reservoir

Although the experimental shaft at the Storm King end of the siphon under the Hudson river was begun February 23, 1907, the work of construction dates officially from June 20, 1907, on which day Mayor George B. McClellan turned the first sod, with appropriate ceremonies, near Indian creek and Garrison road in Phillipstown, about midway between Cold Spring and Garrison.

The work of construction proceeded simultaneously on several different parts of the aqueduct; and for convenience of description, we will follow the geographical rather than the chronological order, beginning at the Catskills and proceeding southward.

Of the four Catskill watersheds which we have mentioned, it was decided to develop first the Esopus watershed, capable of supplying 250,000,000 gallons of water a day, but to build the aqueduct with a capacity of 500,000,000 gallons a day, and to develop the other watersheds as needed. The Esopus development has been completed and the work on the Schoharie watershed, which is expected to supply the second 250,000,000 gallons a day, is now in progress.

In looking around for a suitable place for the storage reservoir of the Esopus watershed, a site was found about eleven miles west-northwest of the City of Kingston in a portion of the Esopus valley which in pre-glacial times was probably a lake. In the glacial period, the lower side of this lake was ground down by the ice-sheet and the lake was emptied into Esopus creek. By throwing a dam across the Esopus creek at Olive Bridge the engineers found they could re-create this ancient lake for New York City's water-supply. This site, embracing about 15,000 acres, was therefore selected,—10,000 acres being for the water area and 5000 acres for the marginal reservation. Within this area were nine villages with private houses, boarding houses, stores, churches, school houses, and all the activities of country life. The villages were West Hurley, Ashton, Glenford, Brown Station, Olive Bridge, Brodhead, Shokan, West Shokan and Boiceville. The oldest of these village names, Shokan, is an abbreviation of the Indian place-name Ashokan,* which latter is very appropriately preserved in the name of the reservoir built on this site. There were also 32 cemeteries, containing over 2800 graves, some dating back over 200 years. It was necessary to acquire all this land, remove the villages and cemeteries, relocate 11 miles of the Ulster & Delaware railroad track, discontinue 64 miles of old highways, build 40 miles of new highways and construct 10 highway bridges, to make way for the reservoir. Some of the property involved was purchased by agreement; but the prices asked in most cases were so exorbitant that most of the area was secured by condemnation proceedings. One man, who formerly owned a boarding-house which was condemned, complained bitterly after he had spent the money received for his house and had neither house nor money left. Being asked if he had not been compensated for it, he replied in the affirmative, but said he had lost his business and he wished the City of New York had never come. Most of the former inhabitants went to Kingston and the others scattered to the four winds.

The problem of the cemeteries was a serious one because of the sentiment attaching to them. The owners of the cemetery lots were paid for their land and fences, and were given a suitable allowance for the expense of removing the bodies and for new headstones; and were given two years in which to vacate. An evidence of the transitoriness of human life or the indifference of the living generation to the memory of their ancestors is afforded by the fact that the relatives of many of those buried in the cemeteries had either died, could not be found, or took no pains to transfer the bodies in the cemeteries, and after the two-year notice had expired the bodies which remained were removed by contract and reverently reinterred in other cemeteries.

The ground having been cleared, the engineers built across the Esopus creek a dam which created a reservoir 12 miles long from east to west and from 1 to 3 miles wide, covering about 10,000 acres with water which at its deepest place near the dam is 190 feet deep but which on the average is 50 feet deep. It has

* In the Marbletown records of 1677 this name is spelled Shokaken. In "Aboriginal Place Names of New York," published by the New York State Museum, it is stated that the name may be derived from "chogan," meaning "black-bird," or, preferably, from "sokan," meaning "to cross the creek."

a shore line of 40 miles and a storage capacity of 132,000,000,000 gallons, or enough water to cover Manhattan Island 30 feet deep. This dam, built of cyclopean masonry—that is, great boulders laid in a solid bed of concrete—is 240 feet high, 190 feet thick at the base, and 1,000 feet long. With wings on each side, each consisting of a core wall covered by an embankment, the total length of the dam is nearly 1 mile from hill to hill. In addition to this dam, a dike about 5 miles long is built along the south line of the reservoir.

The dike has a concrete core going down to rock, and is banked with earth which was wet and rolled as every six inches of height was added, making a solid mass through which water cannot pass. This dike is so compact that a cubic foot of it weighs 150 pounds, only 20 pounds less than a cubic foot of granite. There are several other dikes at low depressions around the reservoir on the east end, while on the north and west are the Catskill peaks, so that there is now another large lake where its pre-glacial predecessor once lay.

At the extreme east end of the reservoir, there is a concrete spillway over which the excess water escapes and flows down through a valley to the Esopus creek.

The reservoir is divided by an embankment called the dividing weir into two parts, called the East basin and the West basin, from either of which the water can be allowed to flow through the gate-house into the aqueduct. Crossing the reservoir on the dividing weir is the Ashokan bridge, built of reinforced concrete. The bridge is 1,120 feet long, and has 15 arches of 67½ foot span.

Another notable bridge is at Travers Hollow. It is a three-hinged arch bridge of 200-foot span.

In planning this reservoir, very careful attention was given to the subject of the purity and taste of the water. When a reservoir of potable water is built on ground covered with vegetable mould, it is usually considered desirable to remove the top soil to prevent the harmless but disagreeable tastes and odors which minute vegetable organisms give to the water at certain seasons. Such an operation at Ashokan reservoir would have cost five and a quarter million dollars. But as the bottom of the reservoir was principally rock and peat, the engineers decided that they could attain the same result at less expense by building an aeration plant. This consists of a small reservoir, 500 feet long and 250 feet wide, on the bottom of which are laid water pipes four or five feet apart. At intervals of five or six feet in each pipe are nozzles, through which the water, under pressure, rises into the air in jets from 40 to 60 feet high and falls back into the reservoir as spray. The mixture of air with the water in this process causes oxidation of the vegetable organisms and removes the tastes and odors. This water garden forms an attractive feature of the landcape treatment of the reservoir site. Set among thousands of evergreen and deciduous trees and surrounded and crossed by forty miles of wonderful highways and bridges, Ashokan reservoir presents a scene of landscape beauty which is pronounced by those familiar with European scenery to rival the lakes of Switzerland.

Humanitarian Work

As the work on the various parts of the aqueduct progressed, men were employed in increasing numbers until as many as 17,243 were at work at one time on the entire line. Comparing the Catskill aqueduct with the Roman aqueducts again, it is interesting to contrast the treatment of these workmen with those of the Romans. The Roman workmen were slaves. The Catskill aqueduct workmen were freemen in the fullest sense of the word. Although a large proportion of them were Italians, the padrone system was completely eliminated and the men and their families were so well cared for that there was not a single labor strike during the whole ten years during which the aqueduct was being built. The Board of Water Supply inserted in all contracts provisions requiring stringent sanitary precautions for the health of employes, local communities in the neighborhood of the aqueduct and people using water from the drainage areas upon which the work was being conducted. Ample supplies of wholesome water and good food, comfortable housing and careful sanitary conditions for the employes, were also insisted upon, and employes violating the sanitary regulations were discharged. At places where particularly large numbers of workmen were concentrated, still further care was taken for the welfare of the workmen.

As an illustration may be cited the camp at Ashokan reservoir. Here 3,000 men lived with their families near the work in a camp built by the contractors under the supervision of the

Bonticou Grade Tunnel, 17 feet high, 13 feet four inches wide, typical of other grade tunnel work

Board of Water Supply. The maximum population here was 4,500. The camp was laid out with streets, and the negroes, Italians and other white employes were separated into different quarters. Good dwellings, generally of wood, one-story high, with screens on all doors and windows, were built and there was a special sewage disposal plant. Electric lights, telephones, a savings bank, a general store, a bakery, a hospital, police and fire protection, a post office, a kindergarten and school for children, churches, and a Young Men's Christian Association also provided for the material and moral welfare of the workmen and their families. There were smaller camps at other places, notably at Valhalla, near Kensico reservoir, but the same humanitarian spirit pervaded all.

One interesting branch of the work in these camps was the camp-schools for grown men and kindergartens for children, which were in addition to the regular public schools for children, and which were supported by private philanthropy. Commissioner Charles N. Chadwick started this movement by an address at Lake Mohonk on August 26, 1908, after which Mr. Albert Smiley took up a collection. This was supplemented by contributions by the Commissioners of the Board of Water Supply, the engineers, Mayor McClellan, and others. Valuable co-operation was given by the Italian Government, the Society for Italian Immigrants, the American Civic League, and similar organizations. Miss Anne Morgan was one of several prominent women who supported the movement. Other women who lent practical aid, as supervisors or teachers, were Dr. Jane E. Robbins, Miss Sarah W. Moore, Miss Anne Young, Miss Kennedy and Mrs. A. E. Talbot. Besides the classes of instruction these schools provided medical attendance, gymnasium classes, moving pictures, dances, foreign and American newspapers, libraries, story-telling for children, old-fashioned games (but not cards), etc., for the welfare and happiness of the camp communities, all free of charge.

The result of all these wise provisions for adults and children was reflected in both the health and general morale of employes and their families. The death rate among them, exclusive of accidents, was only 3.5 per thousand.

The reason for the camp schools for men was that under the restrictions of the 8-hour law, to secure as nearly as possible

100 per cent. of efficiency, it was necessary to take into consideration not only physical conditions but also some field of mental activity and employment that would reasonably occupy the laborer when he was not at work. This suggested what are called camp schools for grown men. As there was no provision under the act for the support and maintenance of such schools, it became necessary to raise the money from outside sources. The workmen in these schools were taught to read and write the English language, and incidentally were given some knowledge of the laws and institutions of the country. This work of pointing out to the men of foreign extraction the advantages of becoming good and law-abiding citizens was aimed at the root of the immigration problem. It was also believed that if the men's time were properly employed during their recreation hours they would pay closer attention to their work during their eight hours of labor. Through the medium of a common language, a prolific source of misunderstanding between employer and employees was done away with. All these things contributed to the completion of the work without a strike. The situation in connection with the administration, engineering, construction and other problems may be summarized in the one statement that the human side of the workmen was considered.

The Five Types of Aqueduct Construction

The aqueduct which conveys the water from the Ashokan reservoir to the City of New York is of five different types of construction, namely, cut-and-cover, grade tunnel, pressure tunnel, steel pipe siphon and flexible-jointed pipe siphon—the latter being used only at one place, namely, across the Narrows of New York harbor.

The term "cut-and-cover" is used to describe that type of aqueduct which is built by cutting a trench in the surface of the ground, laying the conduit in the trench, and covering it with earth. In section it is horse-shoe shaped with a slightly curved bottom called the "invert" and a high arched top. The interior diameter is 17 feet 6 inches wide and 17 feet high. The conduit is made of concrete, varying in thickness from one foot at the top and bottom to five feet at the bottom of the arch. This is the least difficult and least expensive type, and has been used wherever the elevation and nature of the land permitted, where the grades are comparatively moderate, and therefore where the bursting pressure of the water is not great. The gradient of the cut-and-cover tunnel is about one foot to the mile. An aggregate of fifty-five miles of the aqueduct is of this type. Most of the old aqueducts which supplied the City of Rome were built by the cut-and-cover method, although the Roman conduits were made generally of stone or brick, lined with concrete.

Grade tunnels were driven through hills and mountains where it would have been impracticable or uneconomical to circumvent them by the cut-and-cover method. They followed the general grade of the aqueduct, but had a gradient of about two feet to the mile. They are also horse-shoe shaped, and the same height as the cut-and-cover type, namely, 17 feet, but are narrower, being only 13 feet 4 inches wide. In explanation of the smaller diameter of the grade tunnel, and the still smaller diameter of the pressure tunnel mentioned hereafter, it may be explained for the benefit of those not familiar with hydraulics, that by increasing the "head" or the rate of descent, the same amount of water can pass through a conduit of smaller size in the same time that it would take to pass through the larger. By a comparison of cost between "head" and excavation, it was found to be cheaper at certain places to increase the gradient and to decrease the calibre of the tunnel than to continue the lesser gradient and larger diameter. The grade tunnels are built of concrete, which solidly fills all the space between the inner surface of the conduit and the rock through which the tunnels are blasted. There are 24 of these grade tunnels, aggregating 14 miles in length. (See illustration.)

Pressure tunnels were built where it was necessary to pass under broad valleys and deep rivers, and in the City of New York, and where suitable rock could be found through which to build them. It may be stated in passing that all rock is not suitable rock for an aqueduct tunnel for it is impracticable to construct through disintegrated and badly fissured rock a tunnel which has to stand great bursting pressure due to the depth of the tunnel below the initial level of the water. The pressure tunnels are circular in form, built of concrete and are generally 14½ feet in diameter in those portions north of New York City. The city tunnel begins with a diameter of 15 feet which is gradually reduced as it goes southward to 11 feet. There are seven pressure tunnels aggregating 17 miles in length north of the city, and the city tunnel is 18 miles long, being the longest tunnel in the world for carrying water under pressure or for any other purpose. The normal gradient of the pressure tunnels is about 3 feet to the mile. (See illustration.)

Wonderful skill was shown by the aqueduct builders in constructing the grade and pressure tunnels. The marvelous precision of the engineers in the single matter of surveying may be illustrated by a comparison with the old Romans. When the Aqua Claudia was being built in the first century, the Romans decided to drive a tunnel three miles long through Mount Affliano. Their chief engineer set the line for the tunnel and put two parties of men at work, one at each end, to tunnel toward each other, in the expectation of meeting in the middle of the mountain. While they were thus at work, the chief engineer was captured by bandits and held a prisoner for a long time. When he was released and went to see how the tunnel was progressing, he found that the two working parties had passed each other and did not know it. He said that if he had not discovered their error in time they would have had two tunnels instead of one. In contrast with this experience may be mentioned two typical examples of Catskill aqueduct engineering. In crossing the Hudson river at Storm King, two parties of workmen on opposite sides of the river, over three-fifths of a mile apart, bored vertically down to a depth of 1,114 feet below sea-level, then started toward each other, and met under midstream with the variation of not more than half an inch. In building the Bonticou grade tunnel through the mountain between the Rondout and Walkill creeks on the west side of the Hudson, two parties started from opposite directions and met under Bonticou mountain with equal precision, each having worked a distance of about 3,500 feet, or a total distance of over a mile and a quarter. Such feats, repeated many times, were not so difficult as overcoming the many new and unforeseen problems presented by unexpected geological conditions, illustrations of which will be mentioned hereafter.

The fourth principal type of construction is the steel-pipe siphon. This form of construction is used to pass under valleys where the rock is not sound and where for other reasons presure tunnels would be impracticable. Each siphon consists of three cylindrical steel pipes from 9 feet to 11 feet in diameter made of plates varying from 7/16 to ¾ of an inch thick riveted together. They are lined with two inches of cement mortar and are enveloped with concrete. Only one of the three pipes of each siphon has been laid thus far, the others not being needed at present. There are 14 steel-pipe siphons, aggregating 6 miles in length. They are not true siphons but are so-called because of their resemblance in shape to an inverted siphon. The Romans knew the principle of the inverted siphon, but, not having cast iron and steel, were unable to employ it on their main aqueducts. The best they could do was to use small lead pipes as inverted siphons in their distribution system.

The fifth type of Catskill aqueduct construction is the flexible pipe-line across the Narrows of New York harbor, an ingenious invention which will be more fully described hereafter. It is nearly two miles long.

About 8 miles of by-pass and miscellaneous construction brings the total length of the aqueduct at present up to about 120 miles. About 18 miles more of tunnel will be built north of Ashokan reservoir under the Shandaken mountains to bring the Schoharie water into the Ashokan reservoir.

From Ashokan Reservoir to Hudson River

When the Ashokan reservoir is full, the surface of the water is 590 feet above tide level. Through the gate chamber at the dividing weir of the reservoir the water is let down to the aqueduct proper which begins at the level of 492 feet. The first mile of aqueduct constituting the "headworks," is mostly of the cut-and-cover form of construction. The general direction of this and succeeding portions, until otherwise stated, is southeastward.

For about two-fifths of a mile from the headworks, the aqueduct drops down about 120 feet in order to pass under Esopus creek by means of an inverted siphon, coming up again to about the same level of 492 feet on the other side of the creek. Three-fifths of a mile of cut-and-cover brings it to Tongore creek, under which it passes by an inverted syphon about 80 feet deep. It then runs 4½ miles, by cut-and-cover, through the Esopus valley to Peak Mountain, a formation of Hamilton shale, through which it passes by means of grade tunnel about five-eighths of a mile long. A mile and a half more of cut-and-cover brings it to the great Rondout siphon.

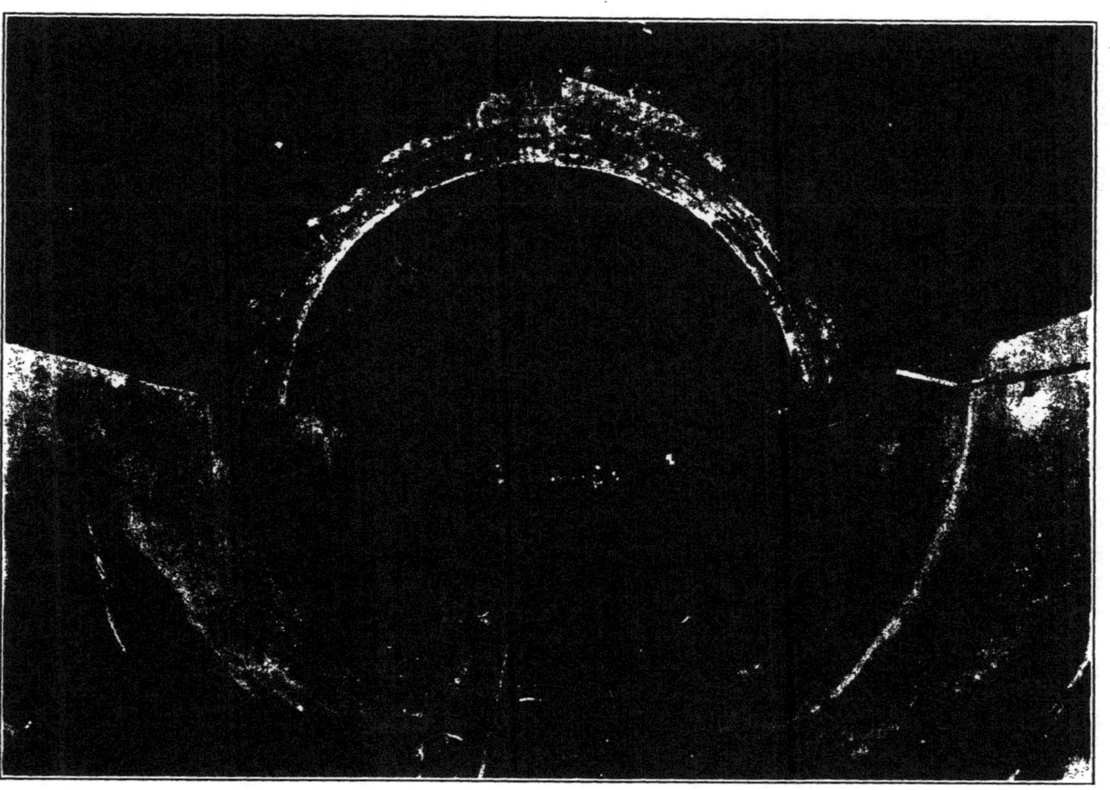

Rondout Pressure Tunnel, 14½ feet in diameter, typical of other pressure tunnel work

The Rondout siphon is not a steel pipe siphon but a pressure tunnel, 14½ feet in diameter. It is 4½ miles long between the down-take and up-take shafts, and descends from an elevation of 478 feet to a point 249 feet below sea-level—a drop of 727 feet—in order to pass under the Rondout creek and valley. Between the down-take and up-take shafts, six construction shafts were sunk in order that construction parties might tunnel in both directions and thus expedite the work. At shaft 4 a peculiar condition was met. Here the workmen encountered fissures through which 2,000 gallons of water a minute leaked into the tunnel and greatly inconvenienced the work. The trouble was aggravated by a sulphuric condition which gave a bad taste to the water and so permeated the air that it irritated the eyes and lungs. The problem was ingeniously solved by boring around the crevices and filling them with concrete. The excavation of this tunnel also revealed violent folding of the rock strata. The intake shaft passes down through Hamilton shale to Marcellus shale, then the tunnel passes horizontally through Marcellus shale. Binnewater sandstone, High Falls shale, Shawangunk grit, Hudson river shale, Shawangunk grit again, and again through Hudson river shale. The Shawangunk grit was particularly unfavorable for tunnel construction, and necessitated going down to greater depth in order to avoid it as far as possible. Twelve different kinds of rock were found. Some was limestone and in many cases the drills penetrated limestone caves of unknown depth and were lost. Rock weakness was developed in one locality in the Rondout tunnel, and it was counteracted by reinforcing the lining for a short distance with an interlining made up of steel channel rings, welded together and lined with concrete.

The uptake of the Rondout siphon comes up through Hudson shale to an elevation of about 463 feet, and then passes through Bontecou mountain, of the same formation, in a grade tunnel about 1¼ miles long. A stretch of about 3¾ miles of cut-and-cover work brings the aqueduct to the Walkill siphon.

The Wallkill siphon carries the aqueduct under the Wallkill creek and valley by means of a pressure tunnel, 14½ feet in diameter and 4½ miles long. In this performance it drops 577 feet to a depth of 90 feet below sea-level, and comes up again to about 440 feet above tide water.

Cut-and-cover work for a distance of fifteen miles almost

due southward brings it to a point between Washington Square and Little Britain in the town of New Windsor, where it passes under a stream with a siphon about 3/5 of a mile long; and then continues for 1½ miles with cut-and-cover to the Moodna pressure tunnel. The level here, at a distance of 40 miles from Ashokan, is 418 feet.

At the edge of the Moodna valley a vertical down-take shaft 586 feet deep and an additional drop of about 50 feet in grade takes the aqueduct down to a depth of 218 feet below sea-level. In the five miles distance under the valley and creek and under Storm King Mountain, it drops ten feet more and arrives at the Hudson river at a depth of 228 feet below sea-level.

The Hudson River Crossing

The crossing of the Hudson river was a brilliant achievement, to appreciate which one must understand something of the geological conditions encountered.

The geological history of the Hudson valley through the Highlands is different from that of its other sections. The Highlands are primitive rocks which were among the first to be lifted up out of the primeval flood at the beginning of geological time. They are part of the "Appalachian protaxis," so-called, a great mountain ridge extending from Georgia on the southwest to Canada on the northeast which, with the Adirondack mountains of New York and the Laurentian mountains of Canada, were elevated above the sea when almost all the rest of the continent was yet submerged. They are more than sixty millions of years older than the Catskills.* In the alternate rise and fall of the land through long periods of time, deep valleys were cut across this protaxis, one of them being the pass through which the Hudson river now flows. After this pass was worn through the rocks, the land became depressed until the bottom of the rock gorge, which was once approximately at tide level, reached a point eight or nine hundred feet below the level of the sea, and became largely filled up with sand, gravel and boulders brought down by water and glaciers. Such is the condition between Storm King mountain on the west side of the Hudson and Breakneck mountain on the east side where the engineers decided to bring the aqueduct across. But it had to be built in solid rock, and nobody

* See note on page 86 preceding.

at that time knew exactly how deep the rock gorge was at this point. (See illustration.)

To solve this riddle, a series of explorations and borings was made. Scows were placed in the river between the two shores and test pipes sunk through the water and the drift which formed the river bottom. At a distance of about 800 feet from each shore, rock was found at a depth of about 600 feet, but beyond these points toward the middle of the river, no rock was found. From the scow in the middle of the river, a boring 750 feet deep met with no better success, nothing but boulders, gravel and sand being encountered. It then became necessary to attack the problem from a new point of view. Shafts were sunk to a depth of 300 feet on each shore near the river, a working chamber was hollowed out at the bottom of each, and from each a diamond drill was started to work toward the middle of the river at a downward angle of about 45° with the horizon. These two borings, one 2,000 feet long and the other 1,831 feet long, met in solid rock 1,500 feet below the surface of the river. As the boring from the scow in midstream had found no rock at a depth of 750 feet, and as the diagonal borings had shown it to exist at a depth of 1,500, it was thus ascertained that the bottom of the gorge was somewhere between those depths; but it was necessary to know more than this in order to ensure building the tunnel far enough below the bottom of the gorge to enable it safely to resist the great bursting pressure of the water in the aqueduct at that depth. Therefore, another pair of diagonal borings at a lesser angle was made and met in rock 950 feet below the surface of the river. The engineers therefore knew that they had a zone of rock at least 550 feet thick through which to bore their tunnel, and they decided to locate it 1,114 feet deep.

As an illustration of the cleverness of the engineers in making these diagonal borings, we may mention the device which they employed to ascertain the position of their drills. The drills showed a curious tendency to turn upward instead of following a straight line at the initial angle, and it is evident that unless the engineers knew the amount of departure or corrected the deflection they could not know the vertical depth of their drills. They therefore inserted in the drill a small bottle partly filled with hydrofluoric acid, which etches glass. When this was let down in the boring and allowed to remain long enough to etch the bottle, the angle between the horizontal etched line and the axis of the bottle enabled the engineers to calculate the true position of the drill and make corrections accordingly.

Still another question had to be answered before it was safe to begin the tunnel across the river. From the data furnished by the borings and from deductions therefrom, Professor Crosby concluded that the profile of the cross-section of the rock gorge was U-shaped on the east side and V-shaped on the west side, with concave scarfs facing the southward, and it was necessary to ascertain if such scarfs existed, lest the tunnel should emerge from the rock into a concavity filled with glacial drift. Horizontal borings were therefore made from the shafts, with reassuring results. The selected route was considered safe and the contracts for construction were let.

As previously stated, the Moodna pressure tunnel reached the Hudson under Storm King mountain at a depth of 228 feet below sea-level. To construct the pressure tunnel under the Hudson, it was necessary to send an access shaft down from the surface of the ground to the pressure tunnel, and to carry the latter down 886 feet farther to a point 1,114 feet below sea-level before the actual crossing could be begun. The first access shaft was found to be too near the side of the mountain to enable it to resist the bursting pressure of the water which was to run in it, and a second shaft was sunk farther back from the river.

This siphon under the Hudson river is of the pressure tunnel type, cylindrical in section, 14½ feet in diameter, and built of concrete fitting compactly against the inside of a tunnel excavated through solid granite rock. The aqueduct comes up on the east side of the river to a height of 395 feet above sea-level, making the total depth of the up-take over 1,500 feet. The access shaft on the west side has been sealed with concrete, but the up-take shaft on the east side is to serve as the drainage and access shaft for the whole Moodna-Hudson-Breakneck pressure tunnel, and is closed with a removable steel cap, weighing 50 tons, bolted down with 34 bolts 50 feet long and 2½ inches in diameter, to resist the terrific pressure of the water.

The middle of the Hudson river siphon is 45 miles from Ashokan reservoir.

From Hudson River to Kensico Reservoir

From the up-take at Breakneck mountain, the aqueduct

starts off again in a southeasterly direction, with a tunnel of 1/5 of a mile through the mountain, half a mile of cut-and-cover, a mile tunnel through Bull hill (granitic gneiss) and ¾ of a mile of steel-pipe siphon under Foundry brook.

It then turns in a more southerly direction and for about 4 miles is cut-and-cover, with one short tunnel and one short siphon.

About a mile and a half east of Garrison and a short distance south of Philipse brook, a grade tunnel nearly 2⅛ miles long carries it through granitic gneiss.

Continuing in a generally south-southeasterly direction, in the next 3½ miles it has first a stretch of cut-and-cover, then passes under Sprout brook by siphon, through Cat hill by tunnel, along the surface by cut-and-cover to Peekskill creek, and then under Peekskill creek by steel pipe siphon. In passing under the creek, a distance of 6,620 feet, the aqueduct drops from a level of about 380 feet to about 50 feet above sea-level, rising again to 370 feet on the south side of the valley. At present only one of the three pipes of this siphon has been laid. It is 9 feet 2 inches in diameter and is sufficient for the present supply of 250,000,000 gallons a day. When the Schoharie supplement of 250,000,000 gallons a day more is added, the other two pipes of this and the other steel pipe siphons will be laid. The length of the aqueduct from Ashokan to Peekskill creek is 56 miles.

The route is now generally south-southeast for about 2 miles, east-southeast 2 miles, and southeast 4¾ miles; and at a distance of 64¾ miles from Ashokan it passes under Croton lake about a mile above the new Croton dam. These 8¾ miles are mostly cut-and-cover, although there is a grade tunnel nearly a mile and a quarter long through a mountain of schist near Hunter brook, a shorter tunnel and two short siphons on the way.

The Croton lake siphon is a pressure tunnel which passes under the lake at an elevation of 150 feet below tide level and comes up to 354 feet above datum.

It is ten miles from the Croton siphon to Kensico reservoir. In this interval there are 7 tunnels, all through schist, aggregating about 3¾ miles, and the rest is cut-and-cover.

Kensico Reservoir

The aqueduct reaches Kensico reservoir at an elevation of

West Side of River

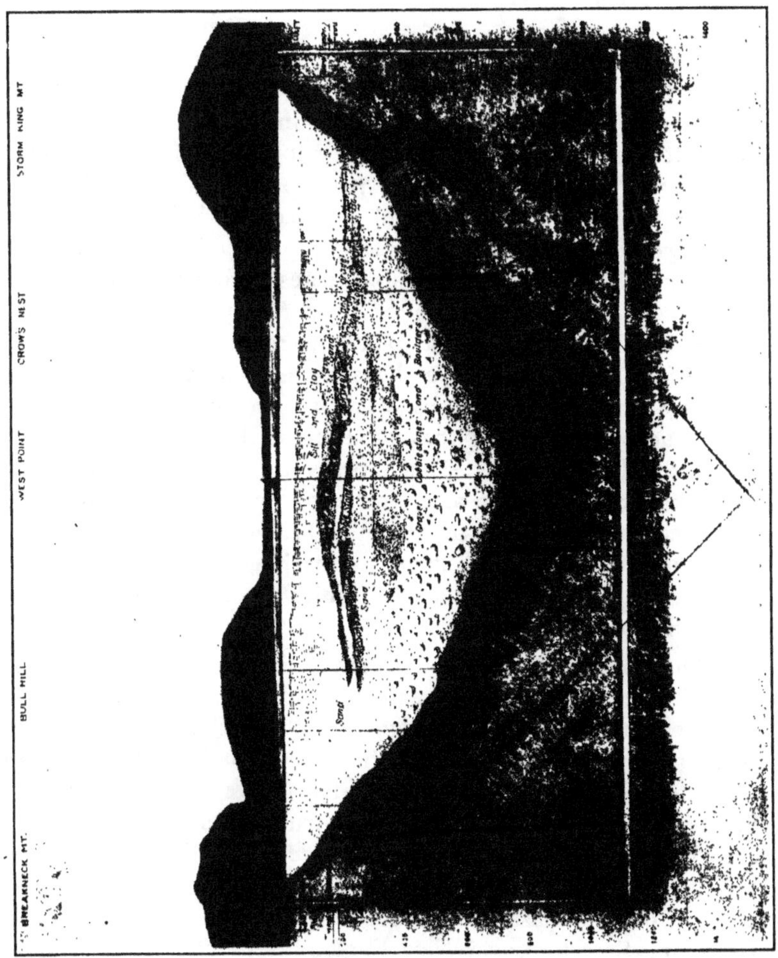

East Side of River

Crossing Under Hudson River Between Storm King and Breakneck Mountains

339 feet but the flow-line of the reservoir is 355 feet high. This reservoir is formed by a dam across the Bronx river about three miles north of White Plains, and is about one-fourth the size of the Ashokan reservoir. With its marginal strip, the reservation comprises 4,500 acres or about 7 square miles, one half of which is covered with water. The reservoir is 4 miles long, from 1 to 3 miles wide, has 40 miles of shore line, and has a total capacity of 38,000,000,000 gallons. The main object of this reservoir is to store about 50 days' water supply for the city against accident. The flow line of the reservoir includes 1,300 acres acquired by the City from the old Kensico reservoir and its auxiliary Rye ponds, and for the enlarged project 3,200 acres more were purchased. There were no villages within this area to be obliterated, and a population of only 500 persons had to be removed. Only a few burial places were disturbed. Fourteen miles of old highways were discontinued and 9 miles of new highways, including 4 bridges, were built. The most important of the new highways is the county road leading from White Plains to Mount Kisco. This crosses an arm of the reservoir on a reinforced concrete arch bridge of five spans of about 127 feet each, known as the Rye Outlet bridge. Another highway runs along the top of the dam, approaching from the east over a masonry bridge of three arches, which crosses the waste channel of the reservoir.

The dam itself is an impressive piece of masonry. It is located about 400 feet up-stream from the old dam. It is 1,825 feet long, has a maximum height of 307 feet, is 235 feet thick at the base, and 28 feet wide on the top. It is built of cyclopean concrete. The up-stream face is of concrete blocks. The profile of the down-stream face is a true hyperbola. The concealed portion of the down-stream face below the final grading was molded against concrete forms, while the exposed portion above ground consists of massive cut blocks of granite, ranging from pink Scotch to grey New England, set sufficiently far apart to produce an effective contrast of light and shade. The arrangement of the masonry of the face of the dam is quite original. For structural reasons, the dam has 22 expansion joints, thus dividing the down-stream face into 21 panels and 2 terminal structures. At each expansion joint a massive band of rusticated stone 15 feet wide projects boldly from the general surface. The intermediate panels are of roughly squared stone, surrounded by borders 3½ feet wide of dimension stone with relatively flat surface. Throughout the fields of the panels, headers of dimension stone, about 1½ feet square, set to a diamond pattern, project slightly from the general surface. See illustration.

Along the level portion of the visible base of the dam is a masonry terrace, about 30 feet broad and 10 feet above the adjacent earth. Separated from the terrace by a tree-planted plaza, is a rectangular pool with fountains, forming a fitting terminal to the Bronx river parkway.

The inflow and outflow gate houses of the reservoir, which are separated by a distance of about 2¼ miles, are connected outside the reservoir by a by-pass conduit of concrete, 11 feet in diameter, by means of which water can be conducted to the aqueduct south of the reservoir without the intermediation of the reservoir if at any time it becomes desirable.

When, as determined by analysis at the laboratory in New York City, the water in the Ashokan reservoir requires chemical treatment for purification, it receives its first treatment at Ashokan, its second, here at Kensico reservoir, and its final treatment at Hill View reservoir.

When the work in Kensico reservoir was at its height, about 1,500 men and their families lived in the camp built by the contractor a few hundred feet down-stream from the dam. There were also smaller outlying camps. The provision for the welfare of these men and their families during the years of construction was the same in kind as that described under the head of the Ashokan reservoir.

From Kensico to Hill View Reservoir

From Kensico reservoir the aqueduct runs 16 miles southward to Hill View reservoir. In this stretch there are six grade tunnels aggregating over 2½ miles, the principal one of which is the East View tunnel, over a mile long. In a portion of the East View tunnel, the rock penetrated was found, after construction, to contain acid-forming mineral; and water, percolating through this rock, became acidulated and attacked the concrete tunnel lining. This difficulty was overcome by adding an interlining of vitrified brick to this portion of the tunnel. Between

Kensico and Hill View reservoirs there are five siphons aggregating two miles, over half of which is represented by the Bryn Mawr siphon. The principal work in this section is the Yonkers pressure tunnel, 2¾ miles long. The southern end of this tunnel is about 120 feet under ground, at an elevation of 138 feet above tide-level. From this end, an up-take shaft carries the water up into Hill View reservoir.

Hill View Reservoir

Hill View reservoir is in the City of Yonkers just north of the New York City line. Its function is to equalize the differences in the use of water in the City of New York from hour to hour. The final chemical treatment of the water is given here if necessary for its purification. It is an artificial reservoir of the earth embankment type, with a depth of 36½ feet holding 900,000,000 gallons of water. It has a water surface of 90 acres at a flow line of 295 feet. Unlike the Ashokan and Kensico reservoirs, the bottom is protected by six inches of concrete. The lower portion of the inner slope of the embankment is also protected by eight inches of concrete. The reservoir is divided into two basins by a wall that contains the aqueduct, so that either basin may be used, or the reservoir may be entirely cut out, if desired, by a by-pass.

New York City Pressure Tunnel

From the Hill View reservoir the water drops through a down-take shaft 300 feet to a depth of 40 feet below tide level and enters the great city pressure tunnel. From this point onward, the aqueduct is constructed through solid rock until it reaches its terminal shafts in Brooklyn and Queens and starts to cross the Narrows. For the first 5¾ miles, from Hill View reservoir to the Harlem river, through the Borough of the Bronx, the aqueduct is about 250 feet below the surface of the ground, in Fordham gneiss. Its course through the Bronx is indicated by the location of the shafts and its depth below the surface by the length of the shafts, as follows:

Shaft—Location	Depth below surface of Ground
1. 241st street and Jerome avenue, Van Cortlandt Park	245
2. Mosholu and Jerome avenues, Van Cortlandt Park	228
3. Sedgwick avenue and Mosholu Parkway, Jerome Park Reservoir	218
4. 196th street and Jerome avenue, Jerome Park Reservoir	242
5. 183d street and Aqueduct avenue	226
6. 176th street and Aqueduct avenue	278
7. 167th street and Sedgwick avenue	352

At the Harlem river it drops to a depth of 331 feet below tide-level to pass under the Stockbridge dolomite which underlies the river to Manhattan island. Its course through Manhattan is indicated by the location of the shafts, as follows:

Shaft—Location	Depth below Surface
8. 165th street and High Bridge Park	478
9. 150th street and St. Nicholas avenue	441
10. 135th street and St. Nicholas Park	405
11. 121st street and Morningside Park	449
12. 106th street and Central Park (west side)	262
13. 93d street and Central Park (west side)	253
14. 79th street and Central Park (west side)	240
15. 65th street and Central Park (near center)	221
16. 50th street and Sixth avenue	218
17. Sixth avenue and Bryant Park	223
18. 24th street and Broadway (Madison Square)	205
19. 6th street and Fourth avenue (Cooper Square)	710
20. Delancey and Eldridge streets	749
21. Clinton and South streets	752

From a depth of 331 feet below sea-level at Harlem river, the aqueduct continues to descend in order to get under the insecure limestone (Stockbridge dolomite) which underlies the Manhattan street valley, and at Morningside Park and 121st street it is 365 feet below tide-level. It then rises abruptly until it is only about 50 feet below tide level and so continues till it reaches Cooper Square. There it drops vertically to 664 feet below tide-level preparatory to passing under the East river. In its course through Manhattan Island, the aqueduct encountered several subterranean springs, which were successfully dealt with.* Near Madison Square, a few slight cracks were caused by the compression of the rock under pressure of the water, and the

* A curious example of this is afforded by the experience of the New Netherland bank at No. 41 West Thirty-fourth street. When the bank building was erected in 1904 a never-failing spring was struck and the owners of the building had to install an automatic pump in the cellar to keep the water pumped out. When the aqueduct was driven under that building in 1914 the spring was cut off and the use of the cellar pump has been discontinued. Oppenheim, Collins & Co., next adjoining on the east at 35 West Thirty-fourth street, had a similar experience.

tunnel was made tight by adding a sheet copper lining. The yielding of the rock under pressure, the cracking of the tunnel lining and the consequent outward leakage were so slight that if they had occurred out in the country no remedy would have been required.

The aqueduct passes from Manhattan Island at Clinton and South streets to Long Island at Sands and Bridge streets, under the rotten rock of the East river, at a depth of 704 feet below sea-level and 752 feet below the surface of the ground on the Manhattan side. Shaft 21 deeper than the Woolworth building is high.

On the Brooklyn side, the aqueduct comes up to above sea-level, and continues at varying heights to Fort Greene Park by the following routes.

Shaft—Location	*Depth below surface of Ground*
22. Sands and Bridge streets	717
23. Flatbush avenue and Schermerhorn street	318
24. Fort Greene Park at Myrtle avenue	329

From Brooklyn, the water is conducted to the Boroughs of Queens and Richmond.

Crossing the Narrows

The crossing of the Narrows, from Brooklyn to Richmond (Staten Island) is accomplished in a very ingenious manner. Instead of tunneling under the Narrows, where the rock is at an unknown depth, a 36-inch flexible jointed cast iron pipe was laid in a trench dredged in the bottom of the harbor. This pipe was made in twelve-foot lengths, the joints being designed on the ball-and-socket principle, allowing for a maximum deflection of 10° 50′ more or less. The joints were filled with lead, about 300 pounds of lead being used in each. Starting from the gate chamber on the Brooklyn side, the pipe was laid from a derrick scow which moved toward Staten Island as joint after joint was added to the inboard end on the scow. The portion of the pipe between the scow and the bottom of the harbor was sustained in a curve by temporary rigging which was carried along by the scow as the work progressed. When Staten Island was reached, connection was made with the gate-house on that shore. The

Kensico Dam at Valhalla, in Westchester County

total length of this siphon is 9830 feet. Meters at each end indicate the leakage, if any. (See illustration.)

Silver Lake Reservoir

From the Staten Island end of the Narrows siphon, at the foot of Arietta street, a 48-inch cast-iron pipe is laid through Arietta street, Richmond road, etc., to Silver Lake reservoir, which is situated a mile and three-quarters southwest of St. George. The length of the aqueduct from Ashokan to this reservoir is 119 miles, to be exact, but it is called 120 miles in round numbers. The reservoir is about 2400 feet long and 1500 feet wide, and holds about 435,000,000 gallons. It is formed by natural depressions in the ground with earth embankments. The area of the water surface is 54 acres, which is surrounded by 111 acres of land. It has over a mile and a half of shore line. The water is 35 feet deep, and rises to a level at 228 feet above tide. The difference in the elevation of the surface of Silver Lake and Ashokan reservoirs, 362 feet, is due to friction.

Measuring the Water

To keep track of the amount of water passing through the aqueduct, and to detect leakage, Venturi meters have been installed at various places. Those at the big reservoirs are the largest water-meters ever built. There is one just below the Ashokan reservoir, a second just above the Kensico reservoir, and a third where the water is drawn from the Kensico reservoir. Each of these meters is 410 feet long, of reinforced concrete excepting for the bronze throat castings and the piezometer ring, which is also of cast bronze. In addition to these large meters, five gaging chambers have been built at various points along the aqueduct where the flow of water is measured by means of current meters. In the city tunnel just north of shaft 2 is a Venturi meter which measures all the Catskill water suppplied to the City, and in the connection to Jerome Park reservoir a Venturi meter measures the flow in either direction. In the city tunnel there is a Venturi meter upon each connection between the tunnel and the distribution pipes in the streets.

Cost of Construction

While the Catskill aqueduct is completed in the sense that

it is now delivering 250,000,000 gallons of water a day to the city, the constructive work of the Board of Water Supply,—which must always be distinguished from the administrative Department of Water Supply, Gas and Electricity—is not yet finished. The Catskill aqueduct has been built with the capacity to transmit 500,000,000 gallons a day, but the Esopus watershed can supply only 250,000,000 gallons. The Board of Water Supply is therefore still engaged in developing the Schoharie watershed which is to furnish the next 250,000,000 gallons a day. The Catskill aqueduct has cost about $140,000,000 thus far, and the Schoharie development will cost about $22,000,000 more.

Distribution of Water

The filling of Hill View reservoir began November 30, 1915, and Catskill water was first introduced into the distribution pipes of New York City, in the Borough of the Bronx, December 27, 1915. Manhattan Borough was first supplied November 29, 1916: Brooklyn and Queens Boroughs January 22, 1917; and the filling of Silver Lake reservoir, in the Borough of Richmond, began January 27, 1917.

The administration of the water-supply of the city is in the hands of the Department of Water Supply, Gas and Electricity, of which Commissioner William Williams is the head.

The water is distributed through 3,127 miles of city-owned water mains within Greater New York, of which 172 miles are high pressure mains. Of the latter, 128 miles are in Manhattan and 44 in Brooklyn. The distribution is controlled by 66,300 gates. There are 49,200 fire hydrants in the Greater City, of which 4,100 are on the high pressure service in Manhattan and Brooklyn.

The Catskill water will rise by gravity in lower New York to a height of about 280 feet above tide water, or to about the sixteenth story of a building. A modern fire engine can pump it to the top of the Woolworth building, which is 750 feet high. The "high pressure" service referred to is designed to do the work of the most powerful fire-engine on a larger scale. There are two high pressure stations in lower Manhattan, each forcing into the high pressure mains as much water as 40 fire-engines. There are two high pressure stations in Brooklyn. A high pressure hydrant can furnish as many streams as five ordinary fire-engines and send the water fourteen stories high; and through stand-pipes the water can be sent forty stories high. Salt water can be used in the high pressure system if needed. (See illustration.)

The city now consumes water at the rate of about 600,000,000 gallons a day, of which 40,000,000 gallons are supplied by private companies and 560,000,000 by the city. Of the latter, 250,000,000 gallons are Catskill water and the balance Croton water. The two Croton aqueducts have a combined capacity of 390,000,000 gallons a day, but for economic reasons only so much thereof as is necessary to supplement the Catskill supply is used, the remainder being held in reserve. The uses to which the Catskill and Croton supplies respectively are put are determined by their respective "heads" or pressures due to elevation of sources. The "head" of the Catskill supply is nearly two and a half times that of the Croton, sufficient to send it by gravity to all portions of the Bronx and Brooklyn and to all buildings of average height in other than the very highest portions of the three remaining boroughs. As this saves the expense of pumping, the Catskill water is the more valuable of the two.

In concluding this sketch of the Catskill aqueduct, it must again be confessed that it very inadequately conveys an idea of the magnitude of the work accomplished and of the splendid services rendered by those who encouraged, sustained and carried it out. The whole is epitomized in the significant inscription upon the commemorative medal struck by the Mayor's Catskill Aqueduct Celebration Committee, which characterizes it as

An Achievement of Civic Spirit
Scientific Genius and
Faithful Labor

Chapter VIII

An Allegorical Pageant

"The Good Gift of Water"

The pageant, as distinguished from a parade, has in recent years come to be recognized in America, as for years it has been recognized abroad, as a very effective form of educational commemoration. The historical facts and civic and moral lessons of the Catskill aqueduct are readily susceptible of expression in this form of art, and with a view to such performances, either in an unpretentious way by school-children or on a more elaborate scale by others, the following suggestions for a pageant entitled "The Good Gift of Water" were prepared. As it is possible that these suggestions may be helpful to other communities on similar occasions, they are given herewith.

The pageant consists of a Prologue, five Episodes or Allegories, and an Epilogue.

The Prologue represents man's prime need of water to sustain life, and the universal prayer which all races and creeds of all ages, from the aborigines to the present time, have lifted up to Heaven for water.

The five Allegories depict the five great uses of water. The first symbolizes the gift of water for food production, at the same time typifying the manner in which Nature gives water to man. The second symbolizes the gift of water for drink, and the curse of drunkenness. The third represents the gift of water for health; in this are included the general ideas of personal cleanliness, domestic hygiene and public sanitation. The fourth represents the use of water for fire extinguishment. And the fifth typifies the use of water for power, its use in the industries, and its function in bearing commerce.

The Epilogue represents the city sending to the mountains for water; the building of the aqueduct; Ashokan giving water to the city; and the distribution of the water to the five Boroughs; the whole concluding with a choral ascription of praise to God from whom all blessings flow.

The mechanical arrangements contemplate the erection at one end of the enclosure (called hereafter the "left") of a stage, simulating a natural elevated plateau of rocks and earth, upon which there is a throne with seats for the principal characters. The painted background in the first Allegory is simply sky and light clouds; in the other scenes it is sky and trees. On the plateau is a small fountain and basin, the overflowing water of which falls into a pool located on the ground in front of the stage. Back of the pool, under the stage, is a grotto, the abode of the Water Spirits.

At the opposite end of the enclosure (called the "right") is a mountain, the abode of Ashokan.

Midway between the stage and Mountain (called the "center") the Prologue calls for a few Indian wigwams; and the third and fourth Allegories for a cluster of cottages to represent a village.

The other mechanical requirements are suggested by the text.

The whole is susceptible of the most beautiful lighting effects, if produced at night, as, for instance, in the first Allegory in which the Clouds take on different hues. If the pageant be produced in the daytime, the references to changing lights are to be disregarded.

Prologue: The Universal Prayer

The Prologue represents in the middle ground (center) an Indian village on Manhattan Island, in the month of the Planting Moon. The inhabitants are engaged in various domestic occupations. The Sachem calls them together and announces that Planting Time has come. They take down ears of corn which hang on their wigwams, shell the corn, and soak the kernels in water. With their wooden hoes and pointed sticks they plant the corn. Then they gather and have a Rain Dance and a Corn Planting Dance, looking upward and lifting up their hands to the skies, praying for rain. When their ceremonies are over, they sit upon the ground around their camp-fires.

The action shifts to a distant elevation (the left), upon which an altar has been raised. Priests of different races. ancient and modern, in their robes of office, appear before it and pray for rain. The Babylonian priest sets up his Fish-God, symbolizing, in their ancient belief, the union of Wisdom and Water; and other priests set up their respective divinities or symbols and chant their supplications.

The Indians, hearing the distant music, steal toward it, and,

Laying 30-inch Flexible Pipe-line Across the Narrows

gathering at the foot of the eminence, join in the Universal Prayer, which all men of all ages have offered to Heaven for the Good Gift of Water to meet their Universal Need.

First Allegory: The Gift of Water for Food

The Sun, dressed in splendor, enters, riding in a golden chariot. His horses are led by the Hours; he is attended by the four Winds and is followed by the four Seasons. He rides around the earth and ascends his shining throne (left). He has heard the prayers of men for rain and sends the four Winds to bring the Clouds. The Clouds, in light flowing draperies and carrying little vases or goblets of water, come at his bidding. They dance toward him in groups, taking on various hues as they gradually approach his throne. They ascend the eminence on which he is elevated and gather around him so closely that they obscure his light and they themselves become dark.* At the signal of thunder peal and lightning flash, the Clouds break away and the Sun reappears. The Clouds go flying down to the earth, emptying their vases and growing brighter as they go. Then the Corn-Maidens and the Flower Maidens (who have been lying on the ground concealed under brown mantles) spring up, throw off their earthy coverings, and with corn-stalks and sheaves of flowers in their hands, dance in the sun-light and make glad the earth.

Second Allegory: The Gift of Water for Drink

Upon the eminence at one end of the enclosure (left) is a fountain with a background of trees. Its overflowing waters fall into a pool upon the ground below. Behind the pool is a grotto. Beside the fountain on the eminence are two Ministering Spirits. Around the pool below and in the grotto are many Water Spirits. A procession, symbolizing Humanity, slowly approaches the eminence in single file, ascends at one side, partakes of the refreshing waters, passes on and descends on the other side. In the procession is a traveller leaning heavily on his staff; a horseman leading his jaded steed; a drover leading his thirsty ox; a husbandman with scythe over his shoulder wiping his brow; a woman with babe in her arms; a man with a burden

* This effect may be produced by lessening the illumination if produced by night, or by having the outer clouds in darker draperies if represented by daylight.

on his back, etc. Some sit a moment by the fountain while the Ministering Spirits bathe their brows. All drink the water offered by the Spirits and resume their journey refreshed.

The scene shifts to the middle of the enclosure (center) and reveals a Bacchanalian orgie. The god of Strong Drink, surrounded by Satyrs, is leading slovenly-clothed men and women in a drunken revel. They dance and drink, quarrel and fight. One man strikes another down, symbolizing crime. The men and women gradually fall from exhaustion and inebriety. Bacchus and the Satyrs dance in glee around their victims.

The Water Spirits go to the rescue. They surge toward the Evil Ones, and the opposing forces sway back and forth alternately striving for the spiritual mastery. At length the Water Spirits succeed in forming a ring around the fallen ones, and the Evil Spirits, with a cry of defeat, flee into darkness. The Water Spirits bring water, bathe the brows of the fallen and give them water to drink. When the prostrate ones drink, they rise from the ground, their bad habits—typified by spoiled garments—fall away; they appear transformed; and all join in a dance of thanksgiving.

Third Allegory: The Gift of Water for Health

At one end of the enclosure (left) Hygeia, the goddess of Health, and her father Æsculapius, in white robes, sit upon an elevation by a fountain of healing waters. Around the pool and in the grotto below are Water Spirits.

At the opposite end of the enclosure (right) two cloaked and hooded figures squat upon a heap of earth: The one in the gray cloak is Disease. The one in the black cloak, whose face looks like a skull, is Death. Their cloaks are supposed to make them invisible.

Between the two extremities (center) is a little village. The villagers are indolent and negligent. The men lounge and smoke; the women gossip. Then they go to an open space somewhat apart from their cottages and have folk-dances.

While the villagers are making merry, repulsive figures, half beast and half human, representing Filth in various forms, crawl out of little hovels by the houses. Some wallow in the village street; some bespatter the houses with mud; some rummage among and overturn the waste receptacles; some crawl in windows and doors and come out again. They keep this up while the villagers are dancing and then lie down like dogs by the houses.

The villagers return but do not drive off the filthy beasts.

Then Disease and Death, in their invisible cloaks, stalk through the village, touching the door-posts, and pass out of sight.

Presently the women come out of one cottage and wring their hands and lament. Other villagers come out of their houses and join their lamentations. The wisest man of the village, he with a long beard, gives them counsel, and then goes as a messenger for Æsculapius. While he is absent, the sick on their sick-beds are brought out into the village street.

The white-robed physician leads Hygeia to the village. They are followed by the Water Spirits carrying basins of water. They kill the Filth beasts by sprinkling and the dead beasts are dragged out of the village. Then the street is sprinkled from the basins, and the Water Spirits hold the basins while the villagers bathe their faces and hands. All then form a procession and, carrying the sick-cots, go to the Pool of Health where the sick are healed and a dance of rejoicing is held.

Fourth Allegory: The Gift of Water for Protection from Fire

Around the pool at one end of the enclosure (left) the Water Spirits, carrying voluminous loose draperies of light green color, sit and stand. They sport among themselves and splash in the water.

At the opposite end of the enclosure (right) a group of Fire Fiends, dressed in red, with red bat-like wings, sit, stand and make sport around a bonfire. They play with torches and firebrands.

Between the two groups (center) is a cottage occupied by a happy family. The father labors in the field. An elder daughter spins before the door. The children play games. The mother goes in and out about her household duties, cooking the family meal. Light smoke curls from the chimney.

The chief of the Fire Fiends steals toward the cottage, beckoning to his fellows to follow. The first one fastens himself with his outspread hooked wings upon the side of the little house. The chimney smoke increases. Another Fiend approaches followed by more. The mother discovers them and gives a cry of alarm. The family try to beat off the Fiends but more come to the attack. Other villagers join in the fight but are unable to drive the enemy away. A play of lurid light seems to foretell the doom of the house.

Then some of the villagers run toward the pool calling on the Water Spirits for help. The latter rush to the rescue. The Fire Fiends and the Water Spirits surge back and forth, the latter trying to envelope the former in the folds of their loose draperies. At length, the Fiends are surrounded, completely enveloped in the green folds of Water, and are smothered. They fall dying to the ground, covered by the green mantles. The villagers rejoice at their delivery.

Fifth Allegory: The Gift of Water for Industry and Commerce

Two figures, symbolizing Industry and Commerce, sit upon a throne (left) as presiding geniuses of the scene. Bales of goods, wheels of machinery, and other objects lie at their feet.

By the pool near the throne is a mill, with a water-wheel, representing the use of water in Industry. The water-wheel turns and electric lights begin to glow in a halo above the heads of Industry and Commerce. Men go into the mill carrying burdens of materials.

The procession of Commerce enters the enclosure in four groups and approaches the mill. First is a group of Indians bearing a canoe on their shoulders. They are encircled by dancing Water Spirits, now representing Waves. The Waves carry between each other voluminous green draperies which they gently undulate. The group bears the canoe to the mill where it receives a cargo, presumably corn meal, and passes along. Next comes a group of old time sailors, bearing on their shoulders a sailing vessel. They are likewise surrounded by dancing Waves. They halt at the mill, receive their cargo, and pass along. In like manner a third group of men bearing a steamboat, and a fourth group in the uniform of the Navy bearing a warship, both surrounded by Waves, approach, receive their cargoes, and follow their predecessors. The procession circles the enclosure and gathers in the middle. Each vessel is set upon the ground, previously covered with green cloth to represent water. The Indians gather around the canoe and the sailors gather around their respective ships. The Waves form a circle around all, holding their green draperies between each other and keeping them in gentle motion. The Indians and the groups of sailors each in turn have a characteristic dance.

A fifth group of Waves now enters the enclosure, dancing and bringing Peace and Plenty in their midst. Peace, with a dove on her shoulder, carries two laurel wreathes in her hands. Plenty carries a cornucopia of abundance. As they go around the enclosure, the first four groups follow in their train and all proceed to the foot of the throne (left). Peace and Plenty ascend, the former laying wreaths on the heads of Industry and Commerce, the latter emptying her cornucopia at their feet. In the groups below, the Waves are outermost, dancing and gently waving their green draperies.

Epilogue: The Mountains Give Water to the City

Enthroned upon an elevation at one end of the enclosure (left) sit five classically draped female figures, symbolizing the five Boroughs of Greater New York.* Festoons of flowers unite them. Above them presides the Mayor, wearing a gown as Chief Magistrate of the City. A little below them, on the same elevated place, sit three Commissioners of Water Supply in conference. Near them are engineers studying maps with surveying instruments by their sides, and draftsmen with compasses and rulers drawing plans.

At the opposite end of the enclosure (right) upon a mountain, sits an Indian chief, personifying Ashokan, and typifying the Spirit of the Mountains. About him, little Brownie-like Mountain Sprites gambol. They bring him water to drink and he drinks some, but there is more than he needs and he motions them to go away.

After due deliberation by the Water Commissioners and engineers, the chief Commissioner arises and addresses the Mayor, pointing frequently toward the Mountain. The Mayor nods assent and hands him a scroll containing a command to go to the Mountain and seek Water. A procession starts for the Mountain. First go the Commissioners; next the engineers who measure the ground as they go and set up little stakes or flags to mark the route; and next a few workmen with picks and shovels on their shoulders.

* See group on the obverse of the Greater New York Medal, 1898, designed by the writer.

Mount Prospect Laboratory, Brooklyn

South Street High Pressure Fire Service Station, Manhattan

Arriving at the Mountain, the scroll is read to Ashokan. He nods his assent, claps his hands and the Mountain Sprites bring him a large Indian jar. The Sprites disappear and return with gourds or small jars of water which they empty into the large jar.

The Commissioners clap their hands and motion to the engineers and workmen to proceed with their task. The Commissioners remain with Ashokan; the engineers and workmen slowly retrace their steps toward the City, the workmen striking the ground with their picks and shovels.

As they proceed, the Aqueduct Spirits (who formerly represented the Water Spirits) come trooping into the enclosure, bringing large circlets or hoops decorated with flowers. Some roll their hoops, others skip with them. They go through various picturesque evolutions and finally form a line beginning at the Mountain and stretching toward the City. They hold their hoops in a row, forming the outline of a tube. The Commissioners, Ashokan bearing the jar of water, and the Mountain Sprites descend and pass through the Aqueduct,* to the City. Ashokan delivers the water-jar to the Mayor who, in turn, pours out five gobletfuls of water and delivers them to the five Boroughs. The Boroughs rise and drink, and all present join in the final chorale, "Praise God from whom all blessings flow."

* If preferred, the Aqueduct Spirits may carry long flexible wands instead of hoops, and, standing in double file, form an archway with their wands to represent the Aqueduct. If there are not enough figures to reach from the Mountain to the City, those who are nearest the Mountain may, after Ashokan has passed them, dance to the other end of the line and thus continually extend it until the City is reached.

Chapter IX.

The Mayor's Celebration Committee

In March, 1916, Messrs. Grosvenor Atterbury, A. B. Hepburn, John J. Kling, George Frederick Kunz, John W. Lieb, Jr., C. Grant La Farge, William M. Carroll, Cyrus C. Miller, William Fellowes Morgan, E. H. Outerbridge, Theodore Rousseau, William Jay Schieffelin, C. F. Shallcross, Bradley Stoughton and Henry R. Towne, organized into a preliminary committee, met Mayor Mitchel and requested him to appoint a citizens committee to arrange a fitting celebration of the completion of the Catskill aqueduct. On December 22, 1916, His Honor appointed for that purpose a committee of about 750 citizens, and pursuant to his invitation, the committee met in the City Hall on Wednesday afternoon, January 3, 1917, and organized. Hon. George McAneny, formerly President of the Board of Aldermen, was designated by the Mayor as Chairman; and the executive organization was effected later. The officers, Executive Committee, and Chairmen of sub-committees are as follows:

Chairman
Hon. George McAneny

Treasurer
Isaac N. Seligman

Secretary
Edward Hagaman Hall

EXECUTIVE COMMITTEE

Chairman
Arthur Williams

William C. Breed	Samuel L. Martin
William Hamlin Childs	Hon. William McCarroll
Edward Hagaman Hall, L. H. D.	Isaac N. Seligman
George Frederick Kunz, Ph. D., Sc.	Charles H. Strong
J. W. Lieb. Jr.	Henry S. Thompson
Hon. George McAneny	Henry R. Towne

Chairmen of Sub-committees

Central Park Pageantry, William J. Lee
City Hall Exercises, William Fellowes Morgan
Civic Bodies, Robert Greer Cooke
Illuminations, Nicholas F. Brady
Official Dinner, Hon. Elbert H. Gary
Official Medal, Robert W. de Forest, LL. D.
Museum Exhibits, George F. Kunz, Ph. D., Sc. D.
Music Festivals, Oswald G. Villard, Litt. D., LL. D.
Public Schools, Leo Arnstein
Religious Exercises, Rev. Walter Laidlaw, Ph. D.

The Executive Committee is acting as the Committee on Permanent Memorial.

The following are the names of the entire Mayor's Committee:

Allan Abbott
Franklin P. Adams
Hon. Herbert Adams
John Quincy Adams, L. H. D.
Hon. Robert Adamson
John G. Agar
Robert I. Aitkin
Edward F. Albee
James S. Alexander
Gen. James N. Allison
Louis Annin Ames
A. A. Anderson
Charles W. Anderson
Edwin H. Anderson, Litt. D.
Gen. Daniel Appleton
Edward A. Arnold
Leo Arnstein
Charles S. Aronstam
John Aspegren
Vincent Astor
Grosvenor Atterbury
Gordon Auchincloss
Joseph S. Auerbach
Frank L. Babbott
Robert Low Bacon
Andrew D. Baird
George F. Baker, Jr.
Stephen Baker
Hon. Otto T. Bannard
Albert S. Bard
B. Walter Barnett
Joseph Barondess
Hon. Willard Bartlett
Bernard M. Baruch
Hon. Edward M. Bassett
Benjamin L. M. Bates
Hon. George Gordon Battle
Samuel Bauman
Edmund L. Baylies
Julian B. Beaty
Hon. James M. Beck
Hon. Daniel M. Bedell
David Belasco
August Belmont
Henry Harper Benedict
Russell Benedict
Hon. John A. Bensel
Charles P. Berkey, Ph. D.
Charles L. Bernheimer
Samuel Reading Berton
Frank H. Bethell
Nicholas Biddle
Cornelius K. G. Billings
Leo Bing
Robert S. Binkerd
John V. Black
J. Stuart Blackton
Sol Bloom
S. J. Bloomingdale
Eugene Blumenthal
John Bogart, Sc. D.
Henry L. Bogert
Ernest Bohm
William E. Bohn
G. Louis Boissevain
Albert C. Bonaschi
Paul J. Bonwit
Robert H. Bosse
John McE. Bowman
Edward F. Boyle
Nicholas F. Brady
William A. Brady
John W. Brannan, M. D.
Marcus Braun
William C. Breed
Cranston Brenton
W. K. Brice
Max D. Brill
Arthur Brisbane
Nathaniel L. Britton, Ph. D., Sc. D.
J. Arthur Brooks
Elmer E. Brown, LL. D., Ph. D.
Henry Collins Brown
Samuel Brown, M. D.
Arnold W. Brunner
Henry W. Bull
Benjamin Bulmer
Cyril H. Burdett
George W. Burleigh
Charles C. Burlingham
Rev. James Burrell, D. D.
John H. Burroughs
Ellis P. Butler
Glenworth R. Butler, M. D.
Nicholas M. Butler, LL. D., Ph. D.
Wallace Buttrick, M. D.
Henry W. Cannon
William B. Cardoza
Andrew Carnegie, LL. D.
J. B. Carrington
Robert A. Carter
John J. Cavanagh
William M. Chadbourne
Frank R. Chambers
Walter Chandler, Jr.
J. Parke Channing
C. E. Chapin
M. S. Chappelle

Alexander C. Chenoweth
Beverly Chew
William Hamlin Childs
Hon. Thomas W. Churchill
Appleton L. Clark
Hon. William A. Clark
Joseph I. C. Clarke
Lewis L. Clarke
Henry Clews
Francis Wright Clinton
Frank I. Cobb
Thomas Cochran
William S. Coffin
Edward R. Cohn
Robert J. Collier
Theodore W. Compton
C. B. Comstock
Hon. Maurice E. Connelly
Joseph E. Constantine, M. D.
Vito Contessa
Patrick J. Conway
Robert Grier Cooke
John Cort
George A. Cormack
Hon. George B. Cortelyou
Clarkson Cowl
C. Ward Crampton, M. D.
Bruce Crane
Hon. Alfred Craven
John B. Creighton
Hon. John D. Crimmins
Herbert Croly
Lincoln Cromwell
William B. Crowell
Warren Cruikshank
Frederick Cunliffe-Owen
E. J. Cuozzo
Hon. Henry H. Curran
Harry A. Cushing
R. Fulton Cutting
Edward H. Daly
Walter Damrosch, Mus. D.
Anderson Dana
Thomas Darlington, M. D.
Frank E. Davidson
J. Clarence Davies
J. V. Davies
Hon. Cherardi Davis
Henry H. Davis
Hon. Vernon M. Davis
Allan Dawson
Joseph P. Day
James A. Dayton
George Debevoise
Joseph H. DeBragga
Robert W. DeForest, LL. D.
Joseph L. Delafield
Richard Delafield
Eugene Delano
Elias A. DeLima
Horace E. Deming
William C. Demorest
Alfonso DeNavarro
Hon. Chauncey M. Depew
Walter T. Diack
Prof. Frederick Dielman
Hon. A. J. Dittenhoefer
Dr. Norman E. Dittman
Cleveland H. Dodge
Henry L. Doherty
A. L. Doremus
Louis Hays Dos Passos
J. Hampden Dougherty
William H. Douglas
Hon. Frank L. Dowling
John J. Downing
Michael Dreicer
Henry Russell Drowne
Capt. Charles A. DuBois
William Butler Duncan
Harris A. Dunn
Finley Peter Dunne
John Ward Dunsmore
Knowlton Durham
Thomas F. Dwyer
Gen. George R. Dyer
Charles Jerome Edward
George Ehret, Jr.
Robert W. B. Elliott
Robert Erskine Ely
Haven Emerson, M. D.
William Emerson
Joseph H. Emery
Frank C. Erb
Abraham L. Erlanger
Leander B. Faber
Samuel W. Fairchild
William C. Fargo
William V. Farkas
Arthur Farwell
Maurice Featherson
Hon. John T. Fetherston
Haley Fiske
William E. Fitch, M. D.
Rev. E. D. Fitzgerald
Harry H. Flagler
Prof. Henry T. Fleck
Ned Arden Flood
Rube R. Fogel
James B. Ford
Edward W. Forrest
Hon. Raymond B. Fosdick
Mortimer Fouquet
Thomas P. Fowler
William Fox
Hon. Joseph N. Francolini
Hugh Frayne
William C. Freeman
Daniel C. French, Litt. D.
Hon. John J. Freschi

Michael Friedsam
Algernon S. Frissell
Algernon S. Friessell
Frank L. Frugone
Emil E. Fuchs
C. H. Fuller
George W. Fuller
Paul Fuller, Jr.
Michael Furst
Robert M. Gallaway
Col. Asa Bird Gardiner
Elbert H. Gary, LL. D.
Charles E. Gehring
Sumner Gerard
Arpad G. Gerster, M. D.
Stuart Gibboney
Eugene C. Gibney
Charles Dana Gibson
A. S. Gilbert
Cass Gilbert
W. G. Gilbert
Isaac Gimbel
J. M. Glenn
John J. Glennon
Hon. Leon G. Godley
Robert Goelet
Jacob Goldstein
James Riley Gordon
Joseph P. Grace
Rollin P. Grant
Thomas D. Green
Capt. Richard H. Greene
B. J. Greenhut
Daniel Greenwald
Rt. Rev. David H. Greer, D. D.
Herbert L. Griggs
Hon. Lloyd C. Griscom
O. J. Gude
Isaac Guggenheim
Dr. Luther H. Gulick
Herbert F. Gunnison
Charles T. Gwynne
R. M. Haan
Henry F. Haas
George Hahn
Rev. Frank O. Hall, D. D.
Edward Hagaman Hall, L. H. D.
Hon. J. J. Halleran
Francis W. Halsey
Albert Hallgarten
George M. Hard
Hon. Lamar Hardy
Duncan G. Harris
Joseph M. Hartfield
William Hartfield
Frank E. Harth
John A. Hartwell, M. D.
Ernest Harvier
Arthur M. Hatch
James A. Hawes
Hon. McDougall Hawkes
J. Noble Hayes
Rowland Haynes
Isaac B. Hazelton
A. Augustus Healy
Thomas Healy
Hon. Job E. Hedges
A. Barton Hepburn, LL. D., D. C. L.
Victor Herbert
Oswald C. Hering
Col. William Hester
Theodore Hetzler
John H. Hill
William R. Hillyer
Stephen D. Hirschman
Stuard Hirschman
James T. Hoile
Edward Holbrook
Hamilton Holt, LL. D.
Hon. John J. Hopper
William T. Hornaday, Sc. D.
Conrad Hubert
Hon. Charles E. Hughes
Chas. Warren Hunt, LL. D.
Richard H. Hunt
Hon. Raymond V. Ingersoll
Adrian Iselin, Jr.
Charles Isham
A. Jacobi, M. D., LL. D.
S. K. Jacobs
D. S. Jacobus, E. D.
Walter B. James, M. D., LL. D.
Rev. Charles E. Jefferson, D. D.
Robert U. Johnson, Ph. D., L. H. D.
Prof. Henry P. Johnston
William A. Johnston
Oscar C. Jurney
Otto H. Kahn
Leon Kamaiky
Joseph E. Kean
Albert Keller
Hon. L. Laflin Kellogg
Com. J. D. J. Kelly, U. S. N.
John T. Kelly
Thomas Kelly
Henry W. Kent
Hon. Frederick Kernochan
John J. Kindred, M. D.
Darwin P. Kingsley
Gustavus T. Kirby
Marc Klaw
S. R. Klein, M. D., Ph. D.
Jacob C. Klinck
Col. Ardolph L. Kline
John J. Kling
Frank Kneisel
John J. Knewitz
Roland F. Knoedler
Samuel Knopf, Jr.
Carl A. Koelsch

Samuel S. Koenig
Lee Kohns
Cornelius G. Kolff
Hon. Frederick J. H. Kracke
George F. Kunz, Ph. D., Sc. D.
Howard Kyle
C. Grant LaFarge
Rev. Walter Laidlaw, Ph. D.
Frederick S. Lamb
Samuel W. Lambert, M. D.
Thomas W. Lamont
Abraham Landau
Louis Lande
Abraham Landau
Frank R. Lawrence
Richard W. Lawrence
John A. Leach
G. Howland Leavitt
J. Edgar Leaycraft
Albert Ledoux, Ph. D.
Frederic G. Lee
John J. Lee
Hon. William J. Lee
Thomas L. Leeming
Herbert Lehman
Eugene Leifels
Felix F. Leifels
Henry M. Leipziger, Ph. D., LL. D.
James M. Leopold
A. Mitchell Leslie
Joseph Levenson
Benjamin W. Levitan
Isadore M. Levy
Franklin C. Lewis
Nelson P. Lewis, LL. D.
William E. Lewis
Adolph Lewisohn
Samuel Lewisohn
John W. Lieb
Charles M. Lincoln
Hon. Martin W. Littleton
Carl M. Loeb
Vincent Loeser
Gen. George B. Loud
John H. Love
James Luby
William M. Macbean
H. M. MacCracken, LL. D., D. D.
Charles R. MacDonald
Rev. J. L. Magnes
H. Van Buren Magonigle
Jeremiah T. Mahoney
Hon. Dudley Field Malone
Hon. Milo R. Maltbie
O. H. Mannes
Rev. Wm. T. Manning, D. D.
William Allen Marble
James E. March
Joseph S. Marcus
Hon. Marcus M. Marks
Don Marquis
George A. Marsh
Walton H. Marshall
Edgar L. Marston
Bradley Martin, Jr.
Samuel L. Martin
Hon. Douglas Mathewson
Hon. Julius M. Mayer
Walter E. Maynard
Hon. George McAneny
Hon. Edward E. McCall
Hon. John T. McCall
Hon. William McCarroll
George B. McClellan, LL. D.
William McClellan
William F. McCombs
Philip J. McCook
Walter L. McCorkle
John J. McCormack
James A. McDonald
Gates W. McGarrah
Lawrence McGuire
John Hall McKay
Andrew McLean
Emerson McMillin
S. C. Mead
Richard W. Meade
John Henry Mears
Daniel Meenan
Rev. Harlan G. Mendenhall, D. D.
O. J. Merkel
Hon. Herman A. Metz
Julius P. Meyer
Sidney E. Mezes, LL. D., Ph. D.
Merle Middleton
Charles R. Miller, LL. D.
Cyrus C. Miller
George N. Miller, M. D.
Hugh Gordon Miller
Ogden L. Mills
Walter S. Mills, M. D.
Henry B. Minton, M. D.
Edward P. Mitchell, LL. D.
James M. Montgomery
George T. Moon
Eugene F. Moran
Hon. Edward M. Morgan
J. P. Morgan
William Fellowes Morgan
William Forbes Morgan
Henry Morgenthau
Max Morgenthau
Robert Lee Morrell
George T. Mortimer
Henry Moskowitz, M. D.
Rev. Joseph Mulry
James J. Munro
Hon. Daniel F. Murphy
Hon. John J. Murphy
Patrick F. Murphy

Thomas Murray
Thomas E. Murray
William C. Muschenheim
George W. Naumburg
Walter Neumuller
Hon. Richard S. Newcombe
Edward T. Newell
William G. Newman
Courtlandt Nicoll
Hon. DeLancey Nicoll
John W. T. Nichols
Dr. William H. Nichols
John H. O'Brien
John P. O'Brien
Hon. Morgan J. O'Brien
Adolph S. Ochs
Rollo Ogden, L. H. D.
Col. Willis L. Ogden
Hon. James A. O'Gorman
Hon. Arthur J. O'Keeffe
Eben E. Olcott
Hon. Denis O'Leary
Frank Oliver
Harry E. Oliver
Robert Olyphant
Alfred E. Ommen
Hon. Samuel H. Ordway
Henry F. Osborn, LL. D., Sc. D.
William Church Osborn
Farley Osgood
Kano Oshima
Eugene H. Outerbridge
K. Pagenstecher
Hon. Victor H. Paltsits
Hon. Alton B. Parker
G. Elton Parks
Hon. Herbert Parsons
William Barclay Parsons
William Bowne Parsons
Hon. Thomas G. Patten
Prof. Henry Carr Pearson
W. Albert Pease, Jr.
Vincent C. Pepe
Hon. George W. Perkins
Ralph Peters
Nathaniel Phillips
Hon. N. Taylor Phillips
Gottfried Piel
James F. Pierce
John B. Pine, L. H. D.
Antonio Pisani, M. D.
Celestino Piva
Ira A. Place
George A. Plimpton, LL. D.
William M. Polk, M. D.
Walter B. Pollock
Ralph H. Pomeroy, M. D.
Rev. D. de Sola Pool
Ruel W. Poor
H. Hobart Porter
George B. Post
Dr. Woodruff L. Post
Hon. Lewis H. Pounds
Dallas B. Pratt
Frederic B. Pratt
Herbert L. Pratt
Hon. William A. Prendergast
Frank Presbrey
Charles W. Price
J. Coil Price
Joseph M. Price
Hon. Cornelius A. Pugsley
Prof. M. I. Pupin
George Haven Putnam, Litt. D.
Stanley G. Ranger
Irving E. Raymond
Leo L. Redding
Fred A. Reed
William C. Reick
Ogden Mills Reid
John F. Reis
Rev. Christian F. Reisner, D. D.
James Bronson Reynolds
Philip Rhinelander
Calvin W. Rice
Leonard Richards
Victor Ridder
Welding Ring
Francis L. Robbins, Jr.
Allan Robinson
David Robinson
Edward Robinson, LL. D., Litt. D.
Nelson Robinson
John D. Rockefeller, Jr.
G. Vernor Rogers
Saul E. Rogers
Theodore Roosevelt, Jr.
Hon. Otto Rosalsky
Walter T. Rosen
Morris Rosenwasser
Edward S. Rothschild
Theodore Rousseau
Henry E. Royce
E. A. Rumely, M. D.
Col. Jacob Ruppert, Jr.
Charles H. Sabin
Col. Henry W. Sackett
Isadore Saks
Walter J. Salomon
Col. Herbert L. Satterlee
William L. Saunders
Reginald H. Sayre, M. D.
R. J. Schaefer
Arthur F. Schermerhorn
William J. Schieffelin, Ph. D.
Jacob H. Schiff
Mortimer L. Schiff
Gustave Schirmer
Carl L. Schurz
Charles M. Schwab

Charles Scribner
Charles E. Scribner
Hon. Patrick J. Scully
Frederick C. Seabury
Hon. Samuel Seabury
Isaac N. Seligman
Lorenzo Semple
Cecil F. Shallcross
W. S. Sharpe
John M. Shaw
George R. Sheldon
Finley J. Shepard
Gen. Charles H. Sherrill
Abraham Shiman
Charles E. Sholes
Lee Shubert
Joseph Ferris Simmons
Franklin Simon
Robert E. Simon
William A. Simonson
Lewis E. Sisson
William Sloane
William Douglas Sloane
Thomas W. Slocum
Chandler Smith
Henry Clapp Smith
Jesse M. Smith
J. Gardner Smith, M. D.
Rev. Joseph F. Smith
James MacGregor Smith
Hon. R. A. C. Smith
Stephen L. Snowden
Luigi Solari
Frederick E. Sondern, M. D.
Dr. Edmund B. Southwick
Alexander H. Spencer
Nelson S. Spencer
James Speyer
Hon. Charles A. Spofford
Frank J. Sprague
Walter Stabler
Hon. Charles Steckler
Fred M. Stein
Joseph H. Steinhardt
Louis Stern
Fred Sterry
Francis Lynde Stetson
Frederick A. Stevenson
James Stillman
Hon. Henry L. Stimson
Edward W. Stitt, Ph. D.
Henry L. Stoddard
I. N. Phelps Stokes
Bradley Stoughton
Charles W. Stoughton
Charles H. Stout
Jesse Isidor Straus
Hon. Oscar S. Straus
Hon. Charles Strauss
Frank V. Strauss
Charles H. Strong
John F. Sullivan
Gerard Swope
Herbert B. Swope
Henry W. Taft
J. F. Talcott
Frederick C. Tanner
Col. James I. Taylor
John S. Thacher, M. D.
Benamin B. Thayer
Paul G. Thebaud
C. G. M. Thomas
Gustav W. Thompson
Henry S. Thompson
Jefferson D. Thompson
W. Gilman Thompson, M. D.
Charles Thorley
Joel W. Thorne
John L. Tildsley
Francesco Tocci
Hon. Calvin Tomkins
John R. Totten
Henry R. Towne
Charles H. Townsend, Sc. D.
Copeland Townsend
Harry H. Treadwell
Eliot Tuckerman
Horace S. Tuthill
William P. Tuttle, Jr.
Albert Ulmann
Theodore N. Vail, LL. D.
Guy Van Amringe
Col. Cornelius Vanderbilt
William K. Vanderbilt
F. A. Vanderlip
Hon. Calvin D. Van Name
Cortlandt S. Van Rensselaer
Addison A. Van Tine
Marion J. Verdery
Oswald G. Villard, Litt. D., LL. D.
Hon. Robert F. Volentine
Otto Von Schrenk
Hon. W. H. Wadhams
Col. Alfred Wagstaff
James M. Wakeman
Samuel Wallach
James J. Walsh, Ph. D., M. D.
Felix M. Warburg
Hon. Cabot Ward
Charles Elliott Warren
Lloyd Warren
Harry W. Watrous
Hon. Archibald R. Watson
Edward E. Watts
William Webber
F. Delano Weekes
Hon. John E. Weier
J. Alden Weir
Rev. George U. Wenner, D. D.
James E. West

Hon. John Whalen
Charles A. Whelan
Alexander M. White
Alfred T. White
Rev. Gaylord S. White
Lawrence G. White
Thomas C. Whitlock
Hon. Thomas W. Whittle
Hon. George W. Wickersham
Albert H. Wiggin
John A. Wilbur
Louis Wiley
William J. Wilgus
Hon. William G. Willcox
Hon. William R. Willcox
Arthur Williams
F. Ballard Williams
H. P. Williams
John D. Williams
Lloyd T. Williams
Talcott Williams, LL. D., L. H. D.
W. H. Williams
Hon. William Williams
George T. Wilson
Paul C. Wilson
Gen. George W. Wingate
Hon. Egerton L. Winthrop, Jr.
Henry A. Wise
Joseph H. Wise
Rev. Cornelius Woelfkin, D. D.
Walter Henry Wood
Hon. Arthur Woods
William Woodward
Frank W. Woolworth
Henry J. Wright
F. A. Wurzbach
John A. Wyeth, M. D., LL. D.
Hon. Richard Young
Dr. Paul Henry Zagat
Peter Zucker

AN EXHIBITION ILLUSTRATING THE HISTORY OF THE WATER SUPPLY OF THE CITY OF NEW YORK FROM 1639 TO 1917

HELD AT THE NEW YORK PUBLIC LIBRARY
MAY 1 TO NOVEMBER 6, 1917

SECTION OF CITY TUNNEL OF CATSKILL AQUEDUCT WITH SHAFT UNDER WORTH MONUMENT

THE NEW YORK
PUBLIC LIBRARY
1917

REPRINTED NOVEMBER 1917
FROM THE
BULLETIN OF THE NEW YORK PUBLIC LIBRARY
OF JUNE 1917

form p-96a [xi-10-17 1c]

AN EXHIBITION ILLUSTRATING THE HISTORY OF THE WATER SUPPLY OF THE CITY OF NEW YORK FROM 1639 TO 1917

SOME months ago the Mayor of New York City appointed a general committee of five hundred citizens to arrange for a celebration in observance of the virtual completion of the Catskill Aqueduct, which is to supply water for all the boroughs of the city. On account of the war it was decided to postpone this celebration, which had been planned for April or May. In order, however, that there might be some early observance of the completion of this great undertaking — which involves such remarkable feats of engineering and concerns so vitally the health of millions of people — The New York Public Library decided to carry out, in co-operation with the Mayor's committee, an exhibition previously planned. This exhibition, which opened on May 1 and will remain on view until November 6, illustrates the most striking events in the history of the development of New York City's water supply, from 1639 to the present time.

In the days of the Dutch occupation of Manhattan Island, when there were only a few hundred settlers, water was obtained from local streams, ponds, and springs. These natural water supplies are shown on a recently discovered manuscript survey, made in 1639, of the region of the present city of Greater New York and the neighboring New Jersey towns. The first recorded project for a public well, to be located in Broadway, dates back to 1658, but was not carried out. By 1660, when the houses in New Amsterdam, as shown by an original manuscript census, numbered only 342, there were a few private wells that had been dug in some of the yards. They are shown in a remarkable bird's-eye view of the city, made in that year and recently found in Italy. These wells were all south of the present Wall Street, the best known being those in the brewery yards of Oloff Stevensen Van Cortlandt and Jacob Van Couwenhoven in Brewers (now Stone) Street, and in the yard of Jacobus Kip, the first city clerk, who lived on what is now Broad Street. There was also a well in the yard of the excise collector, Paulus vander Beeck.

In 1664, an English fleet anchored before New Amsterdam and demanded its surrender. Peter Stuyvesant, after some parleying, surrendered without resistance, being forced to, he said, because there was no well within the fort and its supply of water consisted of but twenty or twenty-four barrels that had been removed from ships in the harbor. After the city had been taken by the English it was known as New York, and the new governor, Richard

Nicolls, took up his residence in the fort. Shortly after, in the summer of 1667, he had a well dug within the fort which yielded good water — much to the astonishment of the Dutch people, who had not believed such a thing possible. Later a well was dug in front of the gate of the fort, at the present Bowling Green, and the pump placed over it was the first pump recorded in the history of the city. The first stone well was made in the yard of the original City Hall, at Pearl Street and Coenties Alley, in 1671. The growth of the town made it necessary to increase the supply of water, so in 1677 the Common Council ordered a number of community wells to be dug in the middle of the streets at certain designated places.

Singularly enough, wells, pumps, and springs continued to supply all the water used in the city for more than a hundred years, though the water became insufficient in quantity and very inferior in quality. As early as November, 1748, a Swedish traveller named Peter Kalm remarked that the well-water of the city was so poor that even the horses balked at drinking it, and that the only good water was obtained from a large spring a short distance from town, which the inhabitants used for their tea and for kitchen purposes. This spring was afterwards covered with a pump, and its water conveyed in wagons and sold throughout the city. It was located at Chatham and Roosevelt Streets, and was long known as the Tea Water Pump — a prominent as well as a useful landmark of old New York. A painting in the exhibition shows the pump as it was in 1807.

The first plan for erecting a storage reservoir was undertaken in 1774–1776 by an engineer named Christopher Colles. Paper money was issued to float the project. A large well, thirty feet in diameter, was dug, and a reservoir erected with a capacity of twenty thousand hogsheads of water, on the east side of Broadway, between the present White and Pearl Streets. The water was pumped into the reservoir by a steam engine to be conveyed through the streets in wooden pipes made of pine logs. This undertaking, known as the New York Water Works, failed on account of the occupation of the city by the British army in September, 1776.

Most of the plans for an increased water supply, before the old Croton Aqueduct was settled upon, provided for taking the water from a pond known as the Collect, in the region where are now the Tombs and Criminal Court building on Centre Street. Plans of this pond are shown in the exhibition and also documents of Thomas Poppleton, a Baltimore surveyor, who came to New York in 1812 to aid a city committee in supervising the drainage of the Collect and the Lispenard Meadows, which had become unsanitary and a menace to the public health.

Aaron Burr and his friends succeeded in obtaining a charter from the legislature on April 2, 1799, which incorporated the Manhattan Company, ostensibly for the purpose of supplying wholesome drinking water, yet with a joker that gave unlimited banking privileges. The passage of the bill aroused a good deal of contention at the time, and the opposition continued for many years thereafter. The company drew water from the Collect and stored it in a reservoir on Chambers Street, whence, by means of hollow logs, it was conveyed through certain streets to the customers. In the exhibition are shown the original legislative records, the oaths of office of the first president and first cashier of the corporation, and an autograph subscription list of stockholders, containing the names of many famous old New York families, among them the Livingstons, Rutgers, Brashers, De Peysters, and Speyers, as well as such prominent men as General Horatio Gates, General Marinus Willett, and De Witt Clinton. There is also on view what is perhaps the best extant example of the wooden water main, with cut-outs and house connection. This exhibit, lent by the Engineers' Club, was dug up in June, 1915, during subway excavating.

As the city entered the second quarter of the nineteenth century, past epidemics and imminent scourges of yellow fever or cholera made evident the urgent need of a better water supply. Several water companies were chartered by the legislature, but none was successful. In 1829 the first public water works was erected at Broadway and 13th Street. It consisted of an elevated tank with a capacity of about 230,000 gallons, into which the water was pumped by a steam engine. The quality of this water deteriorated, however, and Samuel Stevens, president of the new Board of Aldermen, urged the necessity of a better supply. A report was made to the Board of Aldermen in 1831 by Judge Wright and Canvass White, and another the following year by Colonel De Witt Clinton, the latter report being a landmark in the documentary history of the city's water supply. On February 26, 1833, the legislature passed the first act authorizing a new supply, and with it begins all legislation with respect to the building of the old Croton Aqueduct. The final enabling act was passed on May 2, 1834, and in 1837 the actual construction of the Aqueduct was begun. It was built in four divisions, and connected Croton Dam with the Murray Hill distributing reservoir, now the site of the Central Building of The New York Public Library. This reservoir was completed in 1842, and the event was marked by a great civic celebration on October 14, 1842. The exhibition shows the documents in relation to this undertaking, and numerous views of the Murray Hill reservoir and the Central Park reservoir, constructed in 1857–1862, as well as of the High Bridge conduit and reservoir, finished in November, 1848. Six showcases are filled with the reports, maps, profiles, sectional drawings, and other objects, illustrative of the history of the old Croton Aqueduct, to the year 1880.

In three showcases are presented the publications bearing upon the extension of the Croton Aqueduct, beginning with the reports and plans of Chief Engineer Isaac Newton, made in 1881 and 1882. The enabling act for the new Croton Aqueduct became a law on June 1, 1883. Construction commenced in January, 1885, and water reached the Central Park reservoir in July, 1890. The Croton Dam was completed in 1907, and the Jerome Park reservoir was so far completed in 1906 that the west basin was put in service.

It soon became apparent that this new water supply could not be increased so as to keep up with the great growth of population, and there was much discussion by civic and other bodies of possible remedial measures. A private water company sought to make a contract with the city for an additional supply, and endeavored to preempt the outlying watersheds. These controversies over the Ramapo Water Company are remembered by the present generation. In 1899, Governor Roosevelt brought about the repeal of its charter, and the city was then free to look for relief in other directions. In 1897, the Manufacturers' Association of the City of Brooklyn appointed a special committee, of which Charles N. Chadwick was chairman. This committee recommended, among other things, that plans be devised "for the ultimate sources of supply for the Greater New York to contemplate a period of not less than fifty years." In 1900, John R. Freeman made to the Comptroller of the city a report which has been considered one of the most influential documents in the whole history of New York's water supply. In the same year another report was made by the Merchants' Association. A special commission appointed to take up the subject reported in 1903 to the head of the Department of Water Supply, Gas and Electricity. The growth of Brooklyn, now a part of the consolidated city, produced a shortage of water in that borough. To meet these various problems, a Board of Water Supply Commissioners was appointed by Mayor McClellan in 1905, under authority of a constitutional amendment passed in November, 1904, which exempted water supply bonds from the debt limit. This legislation cleared the way for the Catskill Aqueduct.

The printed matter relating to the Catskill Aqueduct, including the contract books, is exhibited; and also dozens of large photographs which illustrate the processes of construction of dams, tunnels, coverts, bridges, basins, river crossings, and other features, such as contractors' camps, plants, and equipment.

A large plaster cast model is shown of a section of the Kensico Dam, which is situated twenty-five miles north of New York City. This is the finest dam in the system, and is 1,843 feet long, with a maximum height of 310 feet. It is built of concrete, faced with granite; and the reservoir has a capacity of thirty-eight billion gallons.

The region traversed by the Catskill Aqueduct is shown by geological maps and profiles, which demonstrate the difficulties of carrying it through bedrock on the eighteen-mile city tunnel. These difficulties are further illustrated by an exhibit — lent by the Board of Water Supply — of actual borings of Yonkers gneiss, Inwood limestone, Fordham gneiss, Manhattan schist, Ravenswood granodiorite, and other rock formations. The Department has also lent a colored relief model map of the watersheds from the Schoharie and Esopus to Greater New York, including a portion of New Jersey. This map measures 11 feet 9 inches by 5 feet 2 inches. Its horizontal scale is a mile to an inch, and the vertical scale shows an elevation of one inch to 1,600 feet. The different watersheds are depicted by distinctive colors; the route of the Aqueduct is indicated, from its source to all parts of the city; and the connections of the Catskill Mountain watersheds, with the Croton, Bronx and Byram watersheds, and the Ridgewood system on Long Island, are shown. The Board of Water Supply has also lent a profile map of the entire Catskill water system, measuring about sixty-three feet in length.

In 1851, there was much discussion of Brooklyn's water supply problem. On June 3, 1853, the legislature passed an act which provided a water supply for the City of Brooklyn. This legislation, as well as reports of the Long Island Water Works Company, the Nassau Water Company, the Williamsburg Water Works Company, the Brooklyn Water Commissioners, and other water supply agencies before the consolidation of Greater New York, are systematically arranged in two showcases. A few publications about Queens and Richmond Boroughs are also shown, and, in a separate showcase, some general histories of New York's water supply.

The Board of Water Supply is a construction board exclusively, and has nothing to do with the administration of the finished system; this rests with another official body, the Department of Water Supply, Gas and Electricity, which made its first annual report in 1898. In two showcases are displayed all the reports of this Department.

This exhibition is of historical interest as a study of the gradual development of one of the most important of the public utilities of the City of New York. It is of additional interest and value because it enables us to understand, in some measure, how the problem of supplying great cities with adequate supplies of wholesome water is being solved by modern engineering methods.

— VICTOR HUGO PALTSITS.

PRINTED AT THE NEW YORK PUBLIC LIBRARY

THE AMERICAN GEOGRAPHICAL SOCIETY

SELECTED LIST

OF

BOOKS AND MAPS

RELATING TO THE

WATER SUPPLY OF NEW YORK CITY

BROADWAY AT 156th STREET
NEW YORK

THE AMERICAN GEOGRAPHICAL SOCIETY

SELECTED LIST

OF

BOOKS AND MAPS

RELATING TO THE

WATER SUPPLY OF NEW YORK CITY

CONTRIBUTIONS OF

THE AMERICAN GEOGRAPHICAL SOCIETY

TO THE

CATSKILL AQUEDUCT CELEBRATION

OCTOBER 12—DECEMBER 10, 1917

BROADWAY AT 156th STREET

NEW YORK

BOOKS

ANDREWS, WM. LORING (comp.). **The Bradford Map. The City of New York at the Time of the Granting of the Montgomerie Charter.** New York, 1893.

BLUNT, E. M. **Strangers' Guide to the City of New York.** New York, 1817.
[p. 38 mentions wells in streets.]

BROWN, HENRY COLLINS. **Glimpses of Old New York.** New York, 1917.

COZZENS, ISSACHER, JR. **A Geological History of Manhattan or New York Island.** New York, 1843.
[Describes location of water basin before Revolutionary War.]

—— **Documents and Plans submitted by the Water Committee of the City of Brooklyn.** 1854.

—— **Documents Relating to the Colonial History of the State of New York.** 14 vols. Albany, 1856-1887.

KING, CHARLES. **A Memoir of the Construction, Cost, and Capacity of the Croton Aqueduct Compiled from Official Documents.** New York, 1843.

KING, MOSES. **Handbook of New York City.** Boston, 1893.
[History of water supply, pp. 196-201.]

LAMB, MRS. MARTHA J. **History of the City of New York, Its Origin, Rise and Progress.** 2 vols. New York, 1877.
[Former water supply, vol. 2, pp. 728-730.]

MAC COUN, TOWNSEND. **Early New York.** (Half Moon edition.) Portfolio of 5 maps. New York, 1909.

MERCHANTS' ASSOCIATION OF NEW YORK. **An Inquiry into the Condition relating to the Water Supply of the City of New York.** New York, 1900.
[Map of water supply of New York State showing source of supply for other cities; maps of future water supply available for New York City; maps of future water supply of New York City, 1900.]

MICHAELIUS, JONAS. **Manhattan in 1628, as Described in the Recently Discovered Autograph Letter of ——, with a Review of the Letter and an Historical Sketch of New Netherland to 1628 by Dingman Versteeg.** New York, 1904.

NEW YORK CHAMBER OF COMMERCE. **Colonial Records, 1768-1784, with Historical and Biographical Sketches by John Austin Stevens.** New York, 1867.

O'CALLAGHAN, E. B. (edit.). **Documentary History of the State of New York.** 4 vols. Albany, 1850-51.

PELLETREAU, WILLIAM S. **Early New York Houses, with Historical and Genealogical Notes.** New York, 1900.
[Manhattan Water Co., and picture of water tank, p. 56.]

Phelps' Strangers' and Citizens' Guide to New York City. New York, 1857.
[History and description of Croton aqueduct, p. 50.]

PHELPS-STOKES, I. N. **Iconography of Manhattan Island, 1498, 1909.** 2 vols. New York, 1915-1916.

—— **Public Wells in Use in New York City at end of 18th Century.** *New York Sun,* March 22nd, 1911.
[A list.]

SCHRAMKE, T. **Description of the New York Croton Aqueduct in English, German and French.** New York, n. d.
[Hydrographic map of New York and vicinity, showing Croton aqueduct.]

SPENCER, JAMES C. **Report to the Aqueduct Commissioners by the President.** 1887.
[Large folding map showing location of Croton aqueduct, plans, photographs, etc.]

SMITH, THOS. E. V. **The City of New York in the year of Washington's Inaguration, 1789.** New York, 1889.

[Tea water pump, etc., described pp. 12 and 13.]

VALENTINE, D. T. **Manual of the Corporation of the City of New York, 1842-43, 1844-45, 1845-46, 1849, 1852.** New York.

VAN WINKLE, EDWARD. **Manhattan, 1624-1639.** New York, 1916.

WHITE, LAZARUS. **The Catskill Water Supply of New York City.** New York, 1913.

MAPS

The Catskill Mountains. (3 mi. to 1 in.) *Bulletin of the American Geographical Society of New York.* 1907.

A Map of the Catskill Mountains by A. Guyot. (3 mi. to 1 in.) A. Guyot, New York, 1879.

A Hydrographic Map of the Counties of New York, Westchester & Putnam, Showing the Line of the Croton Aqueduct. (3 mi. to 1 in.) D. T. Valentine, New York, 1850.

Map and Profile Showing Sources of and Manner of Obtaining an Additional Supply of Water for the City of New York. (5 mi. to 1 in.) Board of Water Supply, New York, 1907.

[With profile of Catskill Aqueduct.]

Map of the Passaic and Croton Water-Sheds, Water Courses, Storage Reservoirs, and Sources of Water Supply for the Cities, Towns, and Villages within a radius of 50 miles from the City of New York. (7/8 in. to 1 mi.) J. R. Bartlett, New York, 1888.

Topographic Map showing the Entire Water Shed of Croton River above the Croton Aqueduct Dam; also the most available sites for Storage Reservoirs, from minute surveys made during the years 1857 and 1858. (1 mi. to 1 3/16 in.) Croton Aqueduct Board, New York, 1858.

Rand-McNally Standard Map of Manhattan. (4 in. to 1 mi.) Rand-McNally & Co., New York, 1907.

[Shows aqueduct.]

Williams' Boroughs of Manhattan and Bronx. (1 mi. to 2 in.) Williams Map & Guide Co., New York, 1911.

[Shows aqueduct.]

Map of Van Cortlandt Park by Corp. Charles L. Schuettler. (1 mi. to 12 in.) 22nd. Regt. Corps of Engineers, N. Y. N. G., New York, 1914.

[Shows aqueduct.]

Home Life Publishing Co. Map of New York. (2½ in. to 1 mi.) Matthews-Northrup & Co., Buffalo, 1901-4.

[Shows aqueduct.]

A General View of the Bronx River Parkway Reservation as a Connecting Parkway between the Park System of New York City, the Croton and Catskill Watersheds and the Harriman and Palisades Interstate Parks. Bronx Parkway Commission, New York, 1915.

The Map of the Route of the New Croton Aqueduct, in Report to the Aqueduct Commission. (2 mi. to 1 in.) Aqueduct Commission, New York, 1887.

Croton Region. Page 103, 58th Annual Report, Vol. I, Bulletin 83, New York State Museum, Albany, 1906.

THE MAYOR'S CATSKILL AQUEDUCT CELEBRATION COMMITTEE

Chairman
GEORGE MCANENY

Treasurer
ISAAC N. SELIGMAN

Secretary
EDWARD HAGAMAN HALL

EXECUTIVE COMMITTEE

Chairman
ARTHUR WILLIAMS

WILLIAM C. BREED

WILLIAM HAMLIN CHILDS

EDWARD HAGAMAN HALL

GEORGE F. KUNZ

J. W. LIEB

SAMUEL L. MARTIN

GEORGE MCANENY

WILLIAM MCCARROLL

ISAAC N. SELIGMAN

CHARLES H. STRONG

HENRY R. TOWNE

THE MAYOR'S
CATSKILL AQUEDUCT CELEBRATION COMMITTEE

Sub-Committee on
Art, Scientific and Historical Exhibitions

Chairman
DR. GEORGE FREDERICK KUNZ
409 Fifth Avenue

UNIVERSITIES AND COLLEGES

Columbia University
Dr. Nicholas Murray Butler, *President*
Prof. William H. Carpenter, *Librarian*
Milton J. Davies

New York University
Dr. Elmer Ellsworth Brown, *Chancellor*

Stevens Institute of Technology
Dr. Alexander C. Humphreys, *President*

College of the City of New York
Dr. Sidney E. Mezes, *President*

LEARNED SOCIETIES AND INSTITUTIONS

American Geographical Society
John Greenough, *President*

New York Historical Society
John Abeel Weeks, *President*
Robert H. Kelby, *Librarian*

New York Genealogical and Biographical Society
Capt. Richard Henry Greene, *Representative*

Long Island Historical Society
Judge Willard Bartlett, *President*

Brooklyn Institute of Arts and Sciences
Dr. A. Augustus Healy, *President*

Staten Island Association of Arts and Sciences
Hon. Howard R. Bayne, *President*

American Numismatic Society
Edward T. Newell, *President*

Cooper Union for the Advancement of Science and Art
Miss Sarah Cooper Hewitt, *Trustee*
Miss Eleanor G. Hewitt, *Trustee*

American Scenic and Historic Preservation Society
Col. Henry W. Sackett, *1st Vice-President*

ENGINEERING SOCIETIES

United Engineering Society
Charles F. Rand, *President*
Calvin W. Rice, *Secretary*

American Institute of Mechanical Engineers
Dr. Ira N. Hollis, *President*

American Institute of Electrical Engineers
E. W. Rice, Jr., *President*

American Institute of Mining Engineers
Philip N. Moore, *President*

American Institute of Civil Engineers
E. W. H. Pegram, *President*

LIBRARIES

New York Public Library
Dr. Edwin H. Anderson, *Director*

New York Society Library
Frederic dePeyster Foster, *Chairman*

MUSEUMS

Metropolitan Musem of Art
Dr. Robert W. de Forest, *President*

Brooklyn Museum
William H. Fox, *Director*

American Museum of Natural History
Dr. Henry Fairfield Osborn, *President*

Museum of the American Indian
George G. Heye, *Founder*

Van Cortlandt Museum House (The Colonial Dames of the State of New York)
Mrs. Hamilton R. Fairfax, *President*
Mrs. Elihu Chauncey, *Chairman*

Jumel Mansion, Washington Headquarters Association (The Daughters of the American Revolution)
Mrs. George Wilson Smith, *President*
William H. Shelton, *Curator*

Fraunces' Tavern (The Sons of the Revolution)
Henry Russell Drowne, *Secretary*

CLUBS

National Arts Club
John G. Agar, *President*

City History Club of New York
Mrs. A. Barton Hepburn, *President*

PARKS AND GARDENS

Department of Parks, Manhattan and Richmond
Hon. Cabot Ward, *Commissioner*

Department of Parks, Brooklyn
Hon. Raymond W. Ingersoll, *Commissioner*

New York Botanical Garden
Dr. Nathaniel L. Britton, *Director*

New York Zoological Garden
Madison Grant, *Vice-President*

New York Aquarium
Dr. Charles H. Townsend, *Director*

Brooklyn Botanic Garden
Dr. C. Stuart Gager, *Director*

CHURCH

The Collegiate Church of St. Nicholas
Rev. Dr. Malcolm James MacLeod, *Pastor*

THE NEW-YORK HISTORICAL SOCIETY QUARTERLY BULLETIN

Vol. I — OCTOBER, 1917 — No. 3

ENTRANCE HALL SHOWING STAIRCASE LEADING TO THE LIBRARY

NEW YORK: 170 CENTRAL PARK WEST

PUBLISHED BY THE SOCIETY AND ISSUED TO MEMBERS

OFFICERS OF THE SOCIETY

Elected January 2, 1917, for Three Years ending 1920

PRESIDENT
JOHN ABEEL WEEKES

FIRST VICE-PRESIDENT
WILLIAM MILLIGAN SLOANE

SECOND VICE-PRESIDENT
WALTER LISPENARD SUYDAM

THIRD VICE-PRESIDENT
GERARD BEEKMAN

FOURTH VICE-PRESIDENT
FRANCIS ROBERT SCHELL

FOREIGN CORRESPONDING SECRETARY
ARCHER MILTON HUNTINGTON

DOMESTIC CORRESPONDING SECRETARY
JAMES BENEDICT

RECORDING SECRETARY
FANCHER NICOLL

TREASURER
FREDERIC DELANO WEEKES

LIBRARIAN
ROBERT HENDRE KELBY

NOTES OF THE SOCIETY

Free Lectures for Children

AT their last meeting the Executive Committee ordered that a series of illustrated lectures relating to the City of New York, be given for children in the Assembly Hall of the Society on Saturday afternoons during the months of November and December. The following dates and subjects have been assigned. Lectures to begin promptly at 3 o'clock. No tickets required.

November 3d—*New York Before the Revolution—1765-1775.* BY ROBERT H. KELBY.

November 10th—*Memorials of the Revolution within our Gates.* BY ALBERT ULMANN, AUTHOR OF "A LANDMARK HISTORY OF NEW YORK."

November 17th—*Our City, Past, Passing, Present.* BY JAMES W. RUTHERFORD.

November 24th—*Fires and Fire Apparatus of Old New York.* BY A. J. WALL.

December 1st—*New York During the Revolution—1775-1783.* BY ROBERT H. KELBY.

December 8th — *Curiosities of New York.* BY ALBERT ULMANN, AUTHOR OF "A LANDMARK HISTORY OF NEW YORK."

December 15th—*Progress in Transportation in New York.* BY JAMES W. RUTHERFORD.

December 22d—*Familiar Scenes of New York. Then and Now.* BY A. J. WALL.

December 29th—*New York After the Revolution—1784-1789.* BY ROBERT H. KELBY.

The Egyptian Collection

During the month Mrs. Williams resumes her work of recataloguing the Egyptian Collection. We are happy to announce, that with her co-operation and through the courtesy of Dr. Arthur Fairbanks, Director of the Museum of Fine Arts, Boston, Mass., the Society has been able to secure the services of Mr.

Paul W. Hoffmann, a skilled artisan of that museum, to take up the treatment and repair of the objects of the Egyptian Collection, that they may be speedily placed in attractive settings for the new exhibition cases now awaiting them. Mr. Hoffmann's experience in this special work covers a period of twenty-five years, insuring to the Society the best possible results. A special repair shop has been fitted up in the building for his work, which will begin on October 15th.

THE ARCHIVES OF THE SOCIETY

A card catalogue of the manuscripts in the archives of the Society was begun in 1913, and with the completion of the library staff this year rapid progress in cataloguing was possible, so that half of the alphabet of the Miscellaneous Manuscripts with numerous cross-references is completely carded, three thousand cards having been used in the past three months. The larger collections of manuscripts have all been calendared and are accessible to all.

Material for the "Collections" of the Society is drawn from the archives of the Society, such as the present volume now in press, "The Cadwallader Colden Papers." This volume, the fiftieth of the series of "Collections," is for the current year 1917. They are issued to shareholders of The John Watts dePeyster Publication Fund, of which the Society still has 151 shares for sale at $200 each, each share carrying with it the 50 volumes already issued and all future publications.

NEWSPAPERS

The valuable collection of newspapers in the Library is being collated and when completed the catalogue will be published in a separate volume.

NEW YORK STATE HISTORICAL ASSOCIATION

The New York State Historical Association will hold their Annual Meeting in the Assembly Hall of the building of this Society on the mornings of Tuesday, Wednesday and Thursday, October 2, 3 and 4, 1917, from 9.30 A.M. to 1 P.M., and on Wednesday evening, October 3rd, at 8 P.M. An interesting program of papers on historical subjects has been prepared, and the members of The New York Historical Society are cordially invited to attend the sessions.

Exhibitions

An exhibition of material relating to the introduction of Croton Water into the City of New York will be held during the month of October in connection with the Celebration on October 12th next of the completion of the Catskill Aqueduct.

During the month of November the original water color drawings of John J. Audubon, made for his great work, "Birds of America," will be placed on exhibition. Other exhibitions to follow will include the Society's collection of Old New York Photographs and its collection of out-of-town views, mostly in lithograph, and the Calver Collection of Revolutionary Military Buttons.

Meetings of the Society

The next meeting of the Society will be held on November 13th. The illustrated lecture for the evening will be delivered by Sandon Perkins, F.R.G.S., entitled: "Canada the Wonderful." On December 4th Mr. Theodoor deBooy, of the Museum of the American Indian, will deliver an illustrated lecture entitled: "Explorations in the West Indies."

The Recording Secretary of the Society, Captain Fancher Nicoll, Company L, 7th Regiment, has been called to the Colors, and is with the regiment at Camp Wadsworth, Spartanburg, South Carolina.

Necrology

Since the last meeting of the Society the following members have died:

William H. Samson, a member since 1912, died at Lake Mahopac, N. Y., June 24, 1917.

Hon. Jacob A. Geissenhainer, a member since 1881, died at Mount Pocoma, Pa., July 20, 1917, in the 78th year of his age.

George L. Rives, a life member since 1891, died August 18, 1917, at Newport, R. I., in the 69th year of his age.

Evert Jansen Wendell, a life member since 1900, died August 28, 1917, at Paris, France, in the 58th year of his age.

Henry Parish, a life member since 1901, died at Elberon, N. J., September 18, 1917, in the 88th year of his age.

CHRISTOPHER COLLES, 1738–1821
From the only known portrait of him. Painted by John Wesley Jarvis
In possession of The New-York Historical Society

AN OUTLINE HISTORY OF NEW YORK'S WATER SUPPLY

WITH the advent of the Catskill Aqueduct this year, which will be celebrated on October 12th, and the wonderful resources for supplying the great City of New York with water, the old Croton Water Aqueduct takes second place in the matter of importance and welfare to this ever-growing community. But the memory and history of that feat, the introduction of Croton water into the City of New York on October 14, 1842, still lives with old New Yorkers, and always will hold an important place in the annals of our city.

The awakening spirit for the need of a proper water supply system for the city may be traced to Christopher Colles, an engineer little known in this day and generation, but whose record in practical achievements ranks with the foremost men of this time. He was born in Ireland about 1738 and died in New York City in 1821. In 1765 he emigrated to America and in 1773 delivered a series of lectures in New York on inland lock navigation. The following year he proposed to erect a reservoir for the city and convey water through the streets in wooden pipes made of pine logs. Up to this time wells were the only source of water supply, and these produced (with but one exception) water which, as early as 1748, Peter Kalm described as "very bad." The exception being the famous "Tea water" well situated in a hollow near the junction of the present Chatham and Roosevelt Streets, which continued to supply good water for many years.

On August 1, 1774, *The New York Gazette and Weekly Mercury* published the following:

> "Last Thursday sen'night the Corporation of this City met, and agreed to Mr. Christopher Colles's Proposal for supplying this City with fresh water, by means of a Steam Engine, Reservoir, and Conduit Pipes; and in order to carry the said useful and laudable Design into immediate execution, they resolved to issue Promissory Notes as the Work shall advance.
>
> "According to this Design, the Water will be conveyed through every Street and Lane in this City, with a perpendicular Conduit Pipe, at every Hundred Yards, at which Water may be drawn at any Time of the Day or

Night, and in case of Fire, each Conduit Pipe will be so contrived as to communicate with the extinguishing Fire-Engines, whereby a speedy and plentiful supply of Water may be had in that calamitous Situation."

On September 5, 1774, the same paper published the following advertisement:

"NEW YORK WATER WORKS.

"Notice is hereby given, that a large quantity of pitch pine logs will be wanting for the New York water works. Such persons as are willing to engage to furnish the same, are desired to send their proposals, in writing, before the 20th of October next, to Christopher Colles, contractor for said works.

These logs must be of good pitch pine, straight and free from large knots, and 20 feet long; one-fourth of the number of logs to be of 12 inches diameter, exclusive of sap, at the small end; and the remaining three-fourths of 9 inches diameter, exclusive of sap, at the small end."

On October 8, 1774, the city purchased from Augustus and Frederick Van Cortlandt a site on the east side of Broadway between the present Pearl and White Streets, and the erection of the reservoir to carry out Colles' plan was there carried into effect, but the Revolutionary War and the occupation of the city by the British prevented the completion of the scheme.

On January 29, 1788, a petition to the Common Council appeared in *The New York Packet,* praying that houses might be supplied with water through pipes, viz.:

"WATER WORKS.

"The following Petition is now handling about this City in order to take the sense of the inhabitants whether they would wish the city should be furnished with a plentiful supply of fresh water, by means of water works and conduit-pipes, as proposed, (and partly executed) before the late war.

"To the Hon. the Mayor, Aldermen and Commonalty of the City of New York in Common Council convened:

"The Petition of the subscribers, inhabitants of the said city,
Respectfully sheweth,

"That as the present mode of furnishing this City and shipping with water, is in many respects subject to many inconveniences, we do hereby declare our approbation of a design for supplying the same by means of water-works and conduit-pipes, and will (as soon as the same shall be compleated) be satisfied to pay our respective proportion of a tax for the purpose, provided the same does not exceed twenty-six shillings for each house per annum, at an average.

THE CROTON WATER CELEBRATION, OCTOBER 14, 1842

"May it therefore please your honors to take the premises into consideration, and to adopt such measures for effecting the same as you shall judge most expedient, for the advantage, convenience and safety of the City.

"Calculation.

"Supposing 3200 houses in the City, at 26s of which		is	£.4160
1000 houses rated at	45 s per ann		2250
1000 ditto	26		1300
1200 ditto	10 2 d		610
			£.4160"

Nothing, however, came from this petition, and "tea water men" continued to carry water around the city in carts built for the purpose, selling the same at 3d. a hogshead of 130 gallons at the pump. The well in which this pump stood was fed from the Collect Pond, and was about twenty feet deep and four feet in diameter.

From 1789 to 1798 various propositions were made to the city for an adequate water supply, all of which named the Collect Pond for the source of supply.

On July 2, 1798, Dr. Joseph Browne proposed furnishing the city with water from the Bronx River, and with far-sightedness and good judgment argued his point in the following language:

"The large stagnating, filthy pond, commonly called the Collect, which now is, or soon will be, the centre of the City, has been looked to by some of the people as a fund from whence an adequate supply might be obtained, by means of a steam-engine, for the purposes already spoken of. I cannot undertake to say that this source would at present be incompetent to all the preceding purposes for which a supply of water is wanted; but if the quantity naturally discharged from this pond be the whole that is furnished by its springs, then I might say with propriety, it is infinitely too small for those uses. But admitting that at present it might be competent, the time will come, and that very shortly from the growth of the City, when this source will most certainly be very inadequate to the demand. And again, supposing the pond to contain and furnish enough, it is a consideration well deserving attention, whether a pond, into which the filth from Many of the streets must, without very great expense and care, be constantly discharged, and to which the contents of vaults, etc., will continually drain, is a desirable source from whence we should like to take water for drinking, cooking, etc., without taking into account its noxious qualities, medically considered; although it may be laid down as a general rule that the health of a City depends more on its water than on all the rest of the eatables and drinkables put together."

WATER GATE IN THE PIPES LAID BY THE MANHATTAN COMPANY, INCORPORATED APRIL 2, 1799

Dr. Browne's plan met with approval, and Mr. William Weston, an engineer, was engaged by the city to study the proposed plan. His report favored the tapping of the Bronx River and was adopted by the Common Council; a bill was prepared and introduced in the Legislature granting the City of New York the necessary powers for constructing water works. At this point opposition arose from such men as Alexander Hamilton and Gulian Verplank and from Aaron Burr and others who had in mind the forming of a private company, and on April 2, 1799, the Legislature passed an act "for supplying the City of New York with pure and wholesome water," and incorporated the Manhattan Company, with a capital stock not to exceed two million dollars, divided in shares of fifty dollars each, to which the city subscribed for two thousand shares. The water was to be introduced into the city within ten years of the passage of the act. Although the charter of the Manhattan Company gave them the right "to erect any dams or other works across or upon any stream or streams of water, river or rivers, or any other place or places" in order to obtain an ample supply of water for the city, it did not avail itself of the privileges granted them and only sunk a large well twenty-five feet in diameter at the corner of the present Reade and Centre Streets and pumped the water into a reservoir on Chambers Street, from which it was distributed through wooden pipes.

From this time until the construction of the Croton Reservoir, a period of over thirty years, nothing of permanent good was accomplished toward solving the question of supplying the city with pure and wholesome water in abundance, and during all these years its need was ever apparent. In 1819 Robert Macomb was granted the privilege of bringing water from the Bronx River to a reservoir on Manhattan Island, but nothing came of it. In 1821 a committee, with Mayor Stephen Allen as chairman, again considered securing water from the same source, without result. The next proposition was to construct an open canal from the Housatonic River, and another scheme suggested a canal from the Oblong River, at Sharon, Conn., to New York, a distance of fifty miles. In 1825 the New York Water-Works Company was incorporated to carry out the plan of Mr. Canvass White, who was selected in 1822 as engineer to make investigations concerning the Bronx River supply, on which he had reported favorably. This company

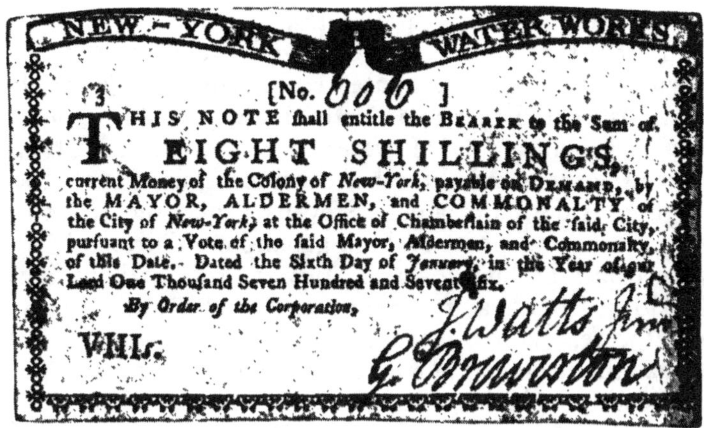

NEW-YORK WATER WORKS

[No. 606]

THIS NOTE shall entitle the BEARER to the Sum of EIGHT SHILLINGS, current Money of the Colony of *New-York*, payable on DEMAND, by the MAYOR, ALDERMEN, and COMMONALTY of the City of *New-York*, at the Office of Chamberlain of the said City, pursuant to a Vote of the said Mayor, Aldermen, and Commonalty, of this Date. Dated the Sixth Day of *January*, in the Year of our Lord One Thousand Seven Hundred and Seventy-six.

By Order of the Corporation,

VIIIs.

J. Watts Jun

G. Brewerton

PROMISSORY NOTE FOR EIGHT SHILLINGS ISSUED TO CARRY ON THE WORK OF THE "NEW YORK WATER WORKS." DATED JANUARY 6, 1776

dissolved in 1827, as its charter conflicted with those of the Sharon Canal Company and of the Manhattan Company. In 1827 the New York Wells Company was incorporated to bore wells, but soon abandoned the task, realizing that sufficient water could not be obtained from that source. Several wells were bored by Levi Disbrow, who had invented and patented improved tools for the work, but it was estimated that two hundred wells would be necessary to obtain a sufficient supply of water, and the expense of operating pumps for the same ended further consideration of that scheme.

In 1829 Alderman Samuel Stevens urged the city to build a reservoir for fire purposes on high ground on Thirteenth Street and to lay an iron pipe line down the Bowery to Chatham Square and another down Broadway to Canal Street. This was actually carried out, and the reservoir constructed on the south side of Thirteenth Street near the present Fourth Avenue, and was the first public reservoir and the beginning of the public water-works of the City of New York. It had a capacity of 233,169 gallons. Twelve-inch mains were used, with branches of ten and six inches, and by January, 1833, 34,646 feet of pipes had been laid.

It was not until 1830 that the Croton River had been mentioned as a possible source for the city's water supply, and in that year Mr. Francis B. Phelps suggested it in a memorial, as one of four sources, the others being Rye Ponds, Passaic River and wells on Manhattan Island.

On November 10, 1832, a joint committee of the Common Council on Fire and Water engaged DeWitt Clinton to examine the various sources and routes of water supply thus far suggested. His conclusions determined upon an aqueduct from the Croton Valley to the city, and on May 2, 1834, the final act for constructing the Croton Aqueduct was passed. Work was begun in 1837 and completed in 1842, when, on October 14th, a great civic celebration was held in honor of the event. The Murray Hill Reservoir was completed that year, and served as the distributing reservoir for the city. On June 1, 1883, an act was passed authorizing the construction of a new aqueduct, reservoirs and dams, for supplying the City of New York with an increased supply of pure and wholesome water. On July 15, 1890, water was turned into the new aqueduct from Croton Lake to the Central Park Reservoir. The Catskill Aqueduct was begun June 20, 1907, and completed January, 1917.

ORIGINAL DOCUMENTS FROM THE ARCHIVES OF THE SOCIETY

WASHINGTON ORDERS LEATHER BREECHES

The following is a copy of a letter written by George Washington to John Mitchell, who lived in Philadelphia, dated Newburgh, November 5, 1782, which is reproduced in fac-simile on the following pages:

Newburgh 5th Novr 1782

Dear Sir,

By Doctr Craik I send you four half Joes—£6—9—3 of which appears to be the Balle due you, allowing the Pensa. State Paper (in yr hands) at one for four.

I pray you to get me made by the Measure inclosed a pair of the neatest & best Leather Breeches.—I know not at this time who is esteemed the most celebrated workman, or I would not trouble you in so trifling a matter.—formerly there used to be a skin called I think, the Carraboas, of which very neat Breeches were made—whether they are yet to be had I know not—nor do I know the price of Leather Breeches at this day, but if the money sent is insufficient the deficiency shall be paid on demd.

I would beg to have them sent to me as soon as possible & I shall thank you for reiterating my request that they may be made roomy in the seat and not tight in the thigh.—They generally make them so strait that it is with difficulty they can be drawn on, to which I have an utter aversion.—the measure gives the size I would have them—not what they can be brought to by stretching.—My Complimts to Mrs. Mitchell.

I am—Dr Sir

Your Most Obedt Servt.

Go. WASHINGTON.

Jno Mitchell Esqr.

[The "measure" inclosed" mentioned in the letter is not in evidence, hence we are deprived of that interesting information.]

Newburgh 5th Novr 1782

Dear Sir,

By Docr Craik I send you four half Joes £6.9.3 of which appears to be the Balle due you, allowing the Penna State Paper (in yr hands) at one for four.

I pray you to get me made by the measure inclosed a pair of the neatest & best Leather Breeches. — I know not at this time who is esteemed the most celebrated Workman, or I would not trouble you in so trifling a matter. — formerly there used to be a Skin called I think, the Carrabous, of which very neat Breeches were made — whether they are yet to be had I know not — nor do I know the price of Leather Breeches at this day, but if the money sent is insufficient the deficiency shall be paid on demd.

I would beg to have them sent to me as soon as possible, & I shall thank you for reiterating my request that they may be made roomy in the seat and not tight in the thigh. — They generally make them so strait that it is with difficulty they can be drawn on, to which I have an

utter

utter aversion.—the measure gives the size I would have them—not what they can be brought to by stretching —My Complim.ts to Mr. Mitchell

I am—D.r Sir

Your Most Obed.t Serv.t

G:Washington

Jn.o Mitchell Esq.r

A NON-PROHIBITIONIST DINNER OF THE COLONIAL PERIOD

During the Colonial period in New York two important anniversaries, which were always celebrated, were the King's Birthday and the Repeal of the Stamp Act. In the evenings of those days a dinner, attended by the principal inhabitants, marked the conclusion of festivities. The itemized bill printed below and reproduced on the following page shows the cost of one of these banquets and those who did not pay their share of 17 shillings. Among 232 diners, 599 bottles of various wines, etc., were consumed, as well as 51 quarts of ale and a considerable quantity of punch, beer and toddy. Immediately after the items of what was drank on that occasion is a charge for £4 for "glass, etc., broke." Six musicians cost 1£ 4s. each, while a French horn received £5. Following the illustration is printed a partial list of those present at the dinner.

50	To Cash		49. 6.—
36	To Do.		30:12.—
24	To Do.		20: 8.—
25	To Do.		21. 4.3
38	To Do.		32: 5.—
20	To Do.		17:— —
	To Anty Rutger		3 :8.—
	To Jn° Woods		
	To Peter Merselis		174: 3 3
	To Wm. Marriner		
	To Cash		6.18.9
			181:2:0
	To John De Lancey	.0–17.—	
	D Stiles	17.—	
	T Brookman	17.—	
	F Dominick	17.—	
	T V Schaak	17.—	
	Tho Jones Doctor	17.—	
	David Knolt	17.—	
	James Sloan	17.—	
	John Scantlen	17.—	
	Andries Lucum pd to Mr. Laight	17.—	
		8–10.—	

By 527 Bottles Wine	4/		105: 8. —
30 Do Clarret	5/		7.10 —
26 Do Cider	1/		1. 6 —
6 Do Porter	2/		—12 —
10 Do Mead	6d		— 5 —
51 Quarts Ale	6d		1. 5:6
Punch Bear & Toddy			12 19:6
Glass &c broke			4: 0: —
232 Dinner	3/		34:16. —
Pd Farrel & Burger	16—		£168 2..—
6 musicks at 24/		7. 4 —	
French Horn		5: 0:—	
			13:0: —
Pd by E Bancker			181:2: —
To John Dally (Pd Totten)		1 6 6	
To St Croux		11.—	
To Hardenbrook		10.—	
			£2:6:6
			£183:8:6

50	To Cash	49.6.–
36	To D^o	30:12.–
24	To D^o	20:8.–
25	To D^o	21.4.3
38	To D^o	32:5.–
20	To D^o	.17:–
	To Ant^y Rutger	
	To Jno Woods	3:8.–
	To Peter Merceles	174:3:3
	To Wm Marriner	
	To Cash	6.18.9
		181:2:0

To John DeLancey	0-17–
D Stiles	17–
S Brookman	17–
H Dominick	17–
P V Schaak	17–
Th^o Jones Doctor	17–
David Knolt	17–
James Sloan	17–
John Scantlery	17–
andrus Lecum p^r to McLaight	17–
	8-10–

By 527 Bottles Wine	4/		105:8.–
30 d^o Clarret	5/		7.10–
26 d^o Cider	1/		1.6–
6 d^o Porter	2/2		12–
10 d^o Mead	6½		5–
51 Quarts Ale	6		1.5:6
Punch Bear & Toddy			12 19:6
Glass &c brake			4:0..–
232 Dinner	3/		£34:16.–
			£168 2..–
p^r Farrel & Burger	16		
6 Musicks @ 24/	7.4–		
French Horn	5:0:–		13:0:–
p^d by L Bancker			181:2..–
To John Dally (St Totten)	1 6 6		
To St Croux	11.–		
To Hardenbrook	10.–	£	2:6:6
		£	183:8:6

A NON-PROHIBITIONIST DINNER OF THE COLONIAL PERIOD

A Partial List of Those Present at the Dinner

John De Lancey Esqr
David Johnston
Andrew Barclay
John Alsop
George Berks
Phillip Kusick
James Armstrong
John Lockhead or
Lockhart
Thomas Hyat
Anthony Rutgers
Oliver De Lancey Esqr
Peter Brower
Nicholas Governeur
Agustes Van Horne
G. J. Van Courtland
Isaac Low
James Van Courtland
John De Noyelle Esqr
Fred De Peyster
Wm Vredenbergh
Geo. Bruerton Junr
John Tuder
James Bennet
George Ball
Thomas W. Moore
Gerard Walton
Alexr Wallace
Wm Jaunsey
Jas Jauncey Junr
Walter Cozine
Thos Walton
Geo. Hopson
M. Jones
Leo Lespnard Junr
Jas Beekman
John Schuyler
John Thurman
F. Phillipse Esqr
Jeremus Alstyne
Peter Majier
Rem Rapelie
Jonathen Nash
Coenradt Ham
Baltus Van Kleek
Jacob Walton Esqr
James Willmot
Mr. Humphrys
David Beekman
Vinsent Tilyow
Thos Brookman
Jonathan Lawrence
Thomas Lawrence
Frances Domenick
James Jauncey Esqr
John Clarke Senr
Wm Nixon
Abraham Lynson
James Wells
Peter Barton
G. G. Beekman
Daniel Stiles
Wm McAddams
J. H. Crugar
Doctor McKinsey
Jacob Bruerton
Miles Sheerbrook
John Woods
Isaac Heron
Thos Jones Esqr
Theops Beache
Wm Winterton
Samuel Van Plank
John Scantline
Leo Lespnard Senr
John Saunders
Sylvenus Delenham
Capn Turner
G. Wm Beekman
Robert Waddell
Peter Van Scaick Esqr
Thos Jones (Doctor
Harmen Governeur
John Marston
Wm Butler
Thos Pettet
Mervine Perry
Wm Marriner
Geo. Foliot
John Kelly
Cap Chambers
James Slone
Peter Merselis
Cap Finglas
Benja Stuot
Dan McCormack
Peter Scarmehorne
John Dykeman
David Knolt
Wendel Dubois
Alexander Fink
Thos Cheseman
Wm Miller
James Harris
Isaac Guion
John Clarke Junr
Andries Lucum
Fred Shunard
James Barclay
Oliver Middleburgh
John Clerk
Wm Loughead
H. Peckwell
——— De Groot
——— De LeMatre
P. Cockran

RECORDS OF THE FRENCH CHURCH AT NEW ROCHELLE, N. Y.

The following marriages and baptisms of the French Church at New Rochelle, N. Y., were performed by Rev. Daniel Bondet, 1703-1712. The translations from the French were made by A. J. Wall from the original manuscript in possession of this Society, and now published for the first time. The spellings of the names are printed just as they appear, and in some instances vary somewhat from the present-day form.

Marriages

1703 May 3—Guillaume Le Conte and Marguerte Manhomay, by license of his Excellency Lord Cornbury. Married at New Rochelle.

1703 June 6—Jean Boyer and Catherine Ariane after the publication of three announcements. Married in the church.

1703 June 25—William Pingney and Thamax Pell, attended by their relatives and friends. Married in the church.

1703 November 13—Jaques Flandreaw of Chataignerai, Poitou, France, and Elizabeth Boderit of Rye, England.

1705 May 20—Pierre Bertin of Mortagne, Province of St. Onge, France, and Anne Borron of Rye, England. The said Bertin was attended by his mother and Theophite Forche, his stepfather, and Anne Boron was attended by the young Anne Gion. Married in the church.

1705 May 20—Jean Jun of Cherveu [Cherveux], Poitou, France, and Jeane Bouquet of Soubise, St. Onge, France. Attended by Isaac Quantin. Married in the church.

1705 June 10—Andre Naudin and Susanne Devaux. Andre Naudin was attended by his father, Andre Naudin, and Susanne Deveaux by her father and mother, Frederic and Ester Deveaux. Married in the church.

1709 October 19—Alexandre Reseg [Resseguire] and Sara Bondecou, and Daniel Bondecou and Mariane Machet. By license of Lieut. Gov. Richard Englodby. Married at New Rochelle in the presence of their relatives and other company.

1709 November 23—Pierre Martin and Jeane Bouchet. Jean Jun presented the bride in the presence of her mother and other relatives and friends. Married in the church.

1709 December 13—Jonatan Roger and Sibille Sands. By license of Lieutenant Engoldsbe, attended by their relatives, in the presence of several other witnesses.

1709/10 February 7—Elie Peltreau and Jeane Many, at the house of the bride, in the presence of several relatives and friends. By license.

1710 December 9—Jean Sorin and Jeane Forche. Married in the church. Theophie Forche presented his daughter to Jean Sorin in the presence of several persons assembled in the church.

1711 January 1—Samuel Readen and Sara Schurman. Married in the church in the presence of their relatives and other company, announcements having been made on three consecutive Sundays.

Baptisms

1702/3 March 9—Henri Streing, son of Daniel Streing and Charlote Streing, born Feb. 27, 1702/3. Sponsors, Jean David Jr., and Clorinde Streing.

1702/3 March 14—Judith Lauran, daughter of Jean and Marie Lauran, born March 10, 1702/3. Sponsors, Pierre Ladou and Judith Renau.

1703 March 28—Abraham Frehet, son of Isaac Frehet and Mercy [Blomer], born Feb. 21, 1702/3. Sponsors, Guillaume Le Conti and —— Maho [Mahault].

1703 April 11—Jeane Magdelaine Many, daughter of Jean and Jeane Many, born March, 1702/3. Sponsors, Jacques Balereau and Madelene Fillieux. Baptized in the church.

1703 April 15—Jeane Bonet, daughter of Daniel and Jeane Bonet, born April 9, 1703. Sponsors, Estiene Lavigne and Isabelle Lavigne. Baptized at home because of illness.

1703 May 2—Jaques Perot, son of Jaques and Marie Perot, born April 15, 1703. Sponsors, father and mother. Baptized in the church.

1703 May 2—Isabelle Simon, daughter of Pierre Simon, born the 12th of ———. Sponsors, Pierre Parcot and ——— Gion. Baptized in the church.

1703 June 13—Thomas Smith, son of Jean and Guierke Smith, born May 31, 1703. Sponsors, Daniel Sicar and Catherine Sicar. Baptized in the church.

1703 July 26—Elizabeth Ogtden, daughter of ——— and Elizabeth Ogtden, born January 3, 1702/3. Sponsors, father and mother. Baptized in the church.

1703 July 26—Frederic Schurman, son of Jean Schurman and Anne Schurman, born June 6, 1703. Sponsors, father and mother. Baptized in the church.

1703 August 1—Catherine Mebe, daughter of Gaspar and Elizabeth Mebe, born June 14, 1703. Sponsors, Gaspar Mebe, his father, and Marie Simon. Baptized in the church.

1703 ——— 29—Bellequie, daughter of William and Bellequie Kerk, born June 28, 1703.

1703 October 25—Esther, daughter of Jacques and Jeanne Berjeau, born October 18, 1703. Sponsors, Daniel Giraud and Thomasse Guyon.

1703 December 28—Susanne Marie, daughter of Pierre and Jeane Valeau, born December 2, 1703. Sponsors, Josia Le Vilain and Susanne Valeau. Baptized in the church.

1703/4 January 23—Susanne Sicart, daughter of Jaques and Anne Sicart, born January 14, 1703/4. Sponsors, Jean Coutan and Jeane Sicart. Baptized in the church.

1703/4 January 30—Elizabeth Cantin, daughter of Isaac and Francoise Cantin, born January 17, 1703/4. Sponsors, Daniel Sanson and Elizabeth Lavigne. Baptized in the church.

1703/4 January 30—Marthe Ladou, daughter of Pierre and Marthe Ladou, born January 18, 1703/4. Sponsors, Jean Lauran and Francoise Parcot. Baptized in the church.

1704 April 2—Marthe, daughter of Elie de Bonrepos, born February 4 last. Sponsors, Col. Caleb Heatcote and Mad. Heatcote.

1704 May 21—Zacharie, son of Zazarie and Marye Langevin, born March 13. Sponsors, father and mother.

1704 June 18—Madelaine Parcot, daughter of Pierre and Francoise Parcot, born May 15, 1704. Sponsors, Jean Vincent and Jeane Gendron.

1704 September 17—Marie Willam, aged about 25 years, baptized in the church, before the congregation after the first service.

1704 September 17—Anne Lounsbery, wife of Jean Lounsberi, living in the parish of Rye, aged about 26 years, also a child Isaac, aged eleven months. Sponsors, the father and Thomasse Gion. Baptized in the church.

1704 December 3—Mariane Sicart, daughter of Ambroise and Jeane Sicart, born October 4, 1704. Sponsors, Jean Neuville and Anne Sicart. Baptized in the church.

1704 December 10—Pierre, son of Guillaume and Marguerit LeConte, born July 25 last. Sponsors, Philipe Cazier and Marie Vergeraud.

1704 December 10—Marie Elizabeth, daughter of Pierre and Marie Vergeraud, born April 7 last. Sponsors, Guillaume LeConte and Elizabeth LeBerton.

1704/5 January 1—Catherine Sicard, daughter of Daniel and Catherine Sicard, born October 10 last. Sponsors, Daniel Giraud and Suzanne Coutant.

1704/5 February 4—Jean, son of Jean and Catherine Bouyer, born January 23. Sponsors, Louis Guion and Marie Fourestier.

1704/5 February 12—Jeane Gougeon, daughter of Gregoire and Renee Gougeon, born December 29, 1704. Sponsors, Pierre Valeau and Jeane LeVilain. Baptized in the church.

1705 April 15—Elizabeth Madelaine Flandreau, daughter of Jaques and Elizabeth Flandreu, inhabitants of New Rochelle, born February 26, 1705. Sponsors, Isaac Mercier and Madlaine Bondet. Baptized in the church.

1705 May 3—Susanne, daughter of Daniel and Madelaine Sanson, living in New Rochelle, born April 17, 1705. Sponsors, Isaak Cantin and Jeane Giraud.

1705 May 6—The following were received as Elders of the church: Pierre Valeau, Ambroise Sicart and Daniel Giraud.

1705 May 20—Anne Guerin, daughter of Etiene and Susanne Guerin, born April 24, 1705. Sponsors, Daniel Sicart and Anne Martin.

1705 August 30—Ambrose Ladou, son of Pierre and Marthe Ladou, born August 10. Baptized at the house of his parents in the presence of several witnesses. Sponsors, Ambrose and Jeane Sicard. The sponsors are to take the child to the church on the 4th of September and have him enrolled after the lecture of the evening.

1709 November 6—Susanne Cantin, daughter of Isaak and Francoise Cantin, born October 20, 1709. Sponsors, Daniel Blondeau and Judith Lamouraux. Baptized in the church.

1709/10 January 8—Jean Bonet, son of Daniel and Jeane Bonet, born December 11, 1709. Baptized in the church.

1709/10 February 7—A young negro [torn], Doctor Neufville, aged about 5 years. He has been named Jaques.

1709/10 February 19—Anne Martin, daughter of Pierre and Jeanne Martin, born February 4, 1709/10. Sponsors, Pierre Bretain and Anne Bretin.

1710 April 16—Susanne Bertin, daughter of Pierre and Anne Bertin, born March 15, 1710. Sponsors, Daniel Blonde[au] and Madelaine Bertin.

1710 December 22—In the house of Daniel Sicart, a sick child, aged about 3 weeks, named Isaak. Sponsors, Daniel and Caterine Sicart, father and mother.

1710/11 March 4—Mariane Cantin, daughter of Isaak and Francoise Cantin of New Rochelle, born the 7th F[ebruary?], 1710/11. Sponsors, Josias Neufville and Mariane Marchant.

1710/11 March 18—William Palmer, son of Obadia and Anna Marguerit Palmer, born September 12, 1710. Sponsors, Elias and Ester Debonrepos. Baptized in the church.

1711 March 25—Having been called by Marie Broun, seriously ill, for consolation, I baptized her at her request. I also baptized at the same time three of six children—Lidie, aged about 11 years; Jacob, aged about 5 years, and Thomas, aged 7 months. Her husband died about 8 months ago. The said Marie Broun died the 27th of the same month and year above and was buried in our Cemetery the 28th. We also buried the same day Pierre Boisseau.

1711 April 29—Susanne Martin, daughter of Pierre and Jeane Martin, born April 8, 1711. Sponsors, Jean Jun and Susanne Colier. Baptized in the church.

1712 September 21—Elizabeth Naudin, daughter of Andre and Susanne Naudin, born August 17, 1712. Sponsors, Josiah Neufville and Marguerit Angevin. Baptized in the church.

1712 August 15—Jean Valeau, son of Pierre and Magdalaine Valeau, born August 14, 1712. Sponsors, Esaie Valeau and Elizabeth Fau [torn]. I was called for the baptism by the relatives on account of the weakness of the child.

PRINCIPAL LIBRARY ACCESSIONS

GENEALOGY

The Beville Family of Virginia, Georgia and Florida. By Agnes B. V. Tedcastle. Privately printed. Boston, 1917.

The Nowlin-Stone Genealogy. By James E. Nowlin. Salt Lake City, Utah (1916).

A Genealogical Record of the Descendants of John Edwards. By Llewellyn N. Edwards. Toronto, Ont., 1916.

Genealogy of Thomas Pope (1608-1683) and His Descendants. By Mrs. Dora P. Worden, Prof. Wm. F. Langworthy and Mrs. Blanche P. Burch. Hamilton, N. Y., 1917.

A Genealogical Table and History of the Springer Family in Europe and America. Vol. 1. By M. C. Springer. Amesbury, Mass., 1917.

The English Ancestry of Peter Talbot of Dorchester, Mass. Compiled for Emily Talbot Walker by J. Gardner Bartlett. Privately printed. Boston, 1917. Gift from Mrs. Cyrus Walker.

Genealogical Records. Transcript Entries of Births, Deaths and Marriages, taken from Family Bibles, 1581-1917. Edited by Jeannie F. J. Robison and Henrietta C. Bartlett. New York, 1917. Published by the Colonial Dames, State of New York.

GENERAL

The Story of the Pullman Car. By Joseph Husband. Chicago, 1917. Gift from Samuel V. Hoffman.

American State Trials. By John D. Lawson. Volume 8. St. Louis, 1917.

The History of Early Relations Between the United States and China, 1784-1844. By Kenneth Scott Latourette. (Transactions of the Connecticut Academy of Arts and Sciences, Vol. 22, pp. 1-209.) New Haven, 1917. Gift from the Author.

History of the Sinn Fein Movement and the Irish Rebellion of 1916. By Francis P. Jones. New York, 1917. Gift from Samuel V. Hoffman.

A Social History of the American Family, from Colonial Times to the Present. By Arthur W. Calhoun. Volume 1. Cleveland, 1917.

History of Transportation in the United States before 1860. Prepared under the direction of Balthasar H. Meyer. By Caroline E. MacGill and others. Washington, 1917. (Published by the Carnegie Institution of Washington.)

LOCAL AND STATE

Typewritten Copy of the Records of the First Presbyterian Church in the City of Albany, N. Y. Transcribed by the N. Y. Genealogical and Biographical Society. New York, 1917.

"Bedford Corners, Brooklyn." Prepared by the Division of Archives and History, University State of New York. Albany, 1917. Gift from the University State of New York, Division of Archives and History.

History of Chelmsford, Mass. By the Rev. Wilson Waters. Lowell, Mass., 1917.

History of Conway (Massachusetts), 1767-1917. By the People of Conway. Rev. Charles S. Pease, Editor. Springfield, Mass., 1917.

Typewritten Copy of the Records of the Reformed Protestant Dutch Church in Easton, N. Y. Transcribed by the N. Y. Genealogical and Biographical Society. New York, 1917.

Typewritten Copy of the Records of the Reformed Protestant Dutch Church at Fonda, New York. Transcribed by the N. Y. Genealogical and Biographical Society. 2 vols. New York, 1917.

Vital Records of Gloucester, Mass., to the End of the Year 1849. Vol. 1—Births. Topsfield, Mass., 1917.

Personal Reminiscences of Men and Things on Long Island. By Daniel M. Tredwell. Part 2. Brooklyn, 1917. Gift from Charles A. Ditmas.

Journal of the Honorable House of Representatives of the Colony of the Massachusetts-Bay in New England. Began and Held at the Meeting-House in Watertown in the County of Middlesex, on 29th day of May, Anno Domini 1776. Boston, 1777. (Photographic reproduction from the original in the American Antiquarian Society.)

The Story of New Amsterdam. By William R. Shepherd. New York, 1917. (Reprinted from the Year Book of the Holland Society of New York, 1917.)

"New York of To-Day." By Henry Collins Brown. New York, 1917.

Vital Records of New Haven, Conn., 1649-1850. Part 1. Hartford, 1917.

Encyclopedia of Biography of New York (State). By Charles E. Fitch. Vols. 1 to 4. New York, 1916.

Representative Families of Northampton, Mass. (By Charles F. Warner.) Vol. 1. Northampton, 1917.

National Bank of Commerce in New York. An Introduction to the Character and Service of a Great American Commercial Bank. New York, 1917. Gift from Samuel V. Hoffman.

Chronicles of Pennsylvania. From the English Revolution to the Peace of Aix-La-Chapelle, 1688-1748. By Charles P. Keith. 2 vols. Philadelphia, 1917.

The History of the Jews of Richmond (Va.) from 1769 to 1917. By Herbert T. Ezekiel and Gaston Lichtenstein. Richmond, Va., 1917.

History of the Town of Wellesley, Mass. By the late Hon. Joseph E. Fiske. Edited and enlarged by Ellen Ware Fiske. Boston, 1917.

TRAVELS

Cruise of the U. S. Brig *Argus* in 1813. Journal of Surgeon James Inderwick. Edited from the original manuscript in the New York Public Library, with an Introduction and Notes by Victor Hugo Paltsits. New York, 1917. Gift from the Editor.

MANUSCRIPTS

Grant of Land issued by and signed by Gov. Francis Lovelace, dated October 16, 1671; Ten Mayor's Court Pleas, 1789-1800; and thirty-one pieces of miscellaneous manuscripts. Gift from Samuel V. Hoffman.

MAPS

Four maps of the battlefield of Shiloh (War of 1861-65) and one map of Fort Sumter from South-west angle, Dec. 9, 1863. (Prepared by Col. Alexander R. Chisolm, for his "Account of the Battle of Shiloh.") Gift from Richard S. Chisolm.

Map of Central Park, n.d. Gift from Dr. Wm. S. Thomas.

NEWSPAPERS

Seventy-four numbers of miscellaneous newspapers, 1799-1833, including a rare copy of the *Ulster County Gazette,* May 4, 1799. Gift from Samuel V. Hoffman.

PHOTOGRAPHS

Two autographed photographs of Hon. Theodore Roosevelt and Hon. William H. Taft. Gift from Samuel V. Hoffman.

The New York Historical Society founded in the year 1804, and incorporated in 1809, was organized for the purpose of discovering, procuring and preserving whatever may relate to the natural, civil, literary and ecclesiastical history of the United States in general and of this State in particular. Also to establish and maintain collections in Art and Archaeology.

The building of the Society on Central Park West 76th to 77th Streets was erected by subscriptions and the generous donation of our late benefactor Henry Dexter. It is maintained by endowment funds and membership fees without the aid of City or State.

The Art Galleries and Museum are open to the Public daily from 9 A.M. to 5 P.M. Sundays excepted. Library hours, 9 A.M. to 6 P.M. Open on Holidays from 1 to 5 P.M., excepting Christmas, New Year and July 4th. Closed during August for cleaning and repairs.

MEMBERSHIP

Members, on their election, pay an initiation fee of Twenty Dollars, which includes dues for the current year, and annually thereafter Ten Dollars as dues; or a life-membership fee of One Hundred Dollars, in lieu of all other dues and fees.

The contribution of Five Thousand Dollars to the funds of the Society shall entitle the person giving the same to be elected a Patron of the Society in perpetuity.

The contribution of One Thousand Dollars shall entitle the person giving the same to be elected a Fellow for life.

Members have the privilege of introducing visitors to the rooms of the Society by their card or a note, and of bringing two persons with them to the monthly meetings.

Nominations are to be sent by members to the Recording Secretary, 170 Central Park West, N. Y. City.

PUBLICATIONS OF THE SOCIETY

Collections of the Society, Vols. I-V; second series, Vols. I-IV, 1811-1859. 10 Volumes. (Out of print.)

Proceedings, 1843-1849. 6 Volumes. (Out of print.)

The John Watts de Peyster Publication Fund originally designated as the "Publication Fund" in 1858 for publishing Collections of the Society is limited to 1000 shares of which 849 have been sold up to the present time. The remaining 151 shares are for sale at $200.00 per share, each certificate of stock carries with it the 49 volumes of "Collections," 1868–1916 published consisting of original material relating to American History. A descriptive list of this series may be had at the Library.

The John Divine Jones Fund founded by John Divine Jones of New York in 1879, for the publication and sale by the Society of works relating to the early history of New York and other American Provinces. In accordance with the terms of this trust, the Society has published the following volumes, which relate to the Loyalists of the War of the Revolution, copies of which may be had at the Library.

I. "History of New York During the Revolutionary War," by Thomas Jones; edited by Edward F. de Lancey. With Notes, Contemporary Documents, Maps and Portraits. 8vo, two volumes. New York, 1879. Price $15.00.

II. "The Journal of a Voyage from Charlestown, S. C., to London, Undertaken During the American Revolution," by a Daughter of an Eminent American Loyalist (Louisa Susannah Wells). 8vo, pp. 132. Portrait and Facsimile. New York, 1906. Price, $2.00.

III. Orderly Book of De Lancey's Brigade British Army, 1776–8. With a list of New York Loyalists during the War of the Revolution, by Willlam Kelby, late Librarian of the Society. New York, 1917. Price, $2.50.

Catalogue of the Gallery of Art (Illustrated) on sale at the Society, 50 cents.

Catalogue of the Abbott Collection of Egyptian Antiquities, 25 cents.

A Bibliography of the Publications of the Society up to 1904, was published in the appendix of the history of "The New York Historical Society, 1804–1904. By Robert Hendre Kelby, Librarian of the Society, New York, 1905." Copies of this volume will be forwarded to members upon application to the Librarian enclosing six cents in stamps to cover delivery. The balance of the edition numbers about three hundred copies for distribution.

EXECUTIVE COMMITTEE

FIRST CLASS—FOR ONE YEAR, ENDING 1918

JAMES BENEDICT
RICHARD HENRY GREENE
ARCHER M. HUNTINGTON

SECOND CLASS—FOR TWO YEARS, ENDING 1919

J. ARCHIBALD MURRAY
B. W. B. BROWN
EDWIN W. ORVIS

THIRD CLASS—FOR THREE YEARS, ENDING 1920

STANLEY W. DEXTER
HENRY F. DE PUY
FREDERICK TREVOR HILL

FOURTH CLASS—FOR FOUR YEARS, ENDING 1921

PAUL R. TOWNE
LANGDON GREENWOOD
R. HORACE GALLATIN

JAMES BENEDICT, *Chairman*
ROBERT H. KELBY, *Secretary*

[The President, Vice-Presidents, Recording Secretary, Treasurer, and Librarian are members of the Executive Committee.]

STANDING COMMITTEES

COMMITTEE ON FINANCE

RICHARD HENRY GREENE
F. DELANO WEEKES
JAMES BENEDICT

COMMITTEE ON LECTURES

B. W. B. BROWN
STANLEY W. DEXTER
FREDERICK TREVOR HILL

COMMITTEE ON LIBRARY

HENRY F. DE PUY
ROBERT H. KELBY
PAUL R. TOWNE

COMMITTEE ON PUBLICATIONS

GERARD BEEKMAN
R. HORACE GALLATIN
ROBERT H. KELBY

COMMITTEE ON ANNIVERSARY

ARCHER M. HUNTINGTON
WILLIAM M. SLOANE
J. ARCHIBALD MURRAY

COMMITTEE ON BUILDING

FANCHER NICOLL
F. ROBERT SCHELL
EDWIN W. ORVIS

COMMITTEE ON FINE ARTS

JAMES BENEDICT
WALTER L. SUYDAM
LANGDON GREENWOOD

COMMITTEE ON PLAN AND SCOPE

HENRY F. DE PUY
WALTER L. SUYDAM
PAUL R. TOWNE

TRUSTEES OF NEW BUILDING

JOHN ABEEL WEEKES, *Chairman*
ARCHER MILTON HUNTINGTON, *Vice-Chairman*

ROBERT HENDRE KELBY
WALTER L. SUYDAM
FREDERIC DELANO WEEKES

EXHIBITION

OF THE

City History Club of New York

105 West 40th Street (Room 709)

10-12, 3-5, DAILY; SATURDAYS, 10-12

Contributed to the Catskill Aqueduct Celebration, in co-operation with the work of the Art, Scientific and Historical Exhibitions Committee.

GENERAL COMMITTEE

Chairman

GEORGE MCANENY

EXECUTIVE COMMITTEE

Chairman

ARTHUR WILLIAMS

WILLIAM C. BREED
WILLIAM HAMLIN CHILDS
GEORGE FREDERICK KUNZ
J. W. LIEB
SAMUEL L. MARTIN
GEORGE MCANENY
WILLIAM MCCARROLL
HENRY S. THOMPSON
CHARLES H. STRONG
HENRY R. TOWNE

Secretary

EDWARD HAGAMAN HALL

MUSEUM EXHIBITS COMMITTEE

Chairman

GEORGE FREDERICK KUNZ

The Mayor of New York's Catskill Aqueduct Celebration Committee

Sub-Committee on Art, Scientific and Historical Exhibitions

Chairman
Dr. George Frederick Kunz
409 Fifth Avenue

UNIVERSITIES AND COLLEGES

Columbia University
Dr. Nicholas Murray Butler, *President*
Prof. William H. Carpenter, *Librarian*
Milton J. Davies

New York University
Dr. Elmer Ellsworth Brown, *Chancellor*

Stevens Institute of Technology
Dr. Alexander C. Humphreys, *President*

College of the City of New York
Dr. Sidney E. Mezes, *President*

LEARNED SOCIETIES AND INSTITUTIONS

American Geographical Society
John Greenough, *President*

New York Historical Society
John Abeel Weeks, *President*
Robert H. Kelby, *Librarian*

New York Genealogical and Biographical Society
Capt. Richard Henry Greene, *Representative*

Long Island Historical Society
Judge Willard Bartlett, *President*

Brooklyn Institute of Arts and Sciences
Dr. A. Augustus Healy, *President*

Staten Island Association of Arts and Sciences
Hon. Howard R. Bayne, *President*

American Numismatic Society
Edward T. Newell, *President*

Cooper Union for the Advancement of Science and Art
Miss Sarah Cooper Hewitt, *Trustee*
Miss Eleanor G. Hewitt, *Trustee*

American Scenic and Historic Preservation Society
Col. Henry W. Sackett, *1st Vice-President*

ENGINEERING SOCIETIES

United Engineering Society
Charles F. Rand, *President*
Calvin W. Rice, *Secretary*

American Institute of Mechanical Engineers
Dr. Ira N. Hollis, *President*

American Institute of Electrical Engineers
E. W. Rice, Jr., *President*

American Institute of Mining Engineers
Philip N. Moore, *President*

American Institute of Civil Engineers
E. W. H. Pegram, *President*

LIBRARIES

New York Public Library
Dr. Edwin H. Anderson, *Director*

New York Society Library
Frederic dePeyster Foster, *Chairman*

MUSEUMS

Metropolitan Museum of Art
Dr. Robert W. de Forest, *President*

Brooklyn Museum
William H. Fox, *Director*

American Museum of Natural History
Dr. Henry Fairfield Osborn, *President*

Museum of the American Indian
George G. Heye, *Founder*

Van Cortlandt Museum House
(The Colonial Dames of the State of New York)
Mrs. Hamilton R. Fairfax, *President*
Mrs. Elihu Chauncey, *Chairman*

Jumel Mansion, Washington Headquarters Association
(The Daughters of the American Revolution)
Mrs. George Wilson Smith, *President*
William H. Shelton, *Curator*

Fraunces' Tavern
(The Sons of the Revolution)
Henry Russell Drowne, *Secretary*

CLUBS

National Arts Club
John G. Agar, *President*

City History Club of New York
Mrs. A. Barton Hepburn, *President*

PARKS AND GARDENS

Department of Parks, Manhattan and Richmond
Hon. Cabot Ward, *Commissioner*

Department of Parks, Brooklyn
Hon. Raymond W. Ingersoll, *Commissioner*

New York Botanical Garden
Dr. Nathaniel L. Britton, *Director*

New York Zoological Garden
Madison Grant, *Vice-President*

New York Aquarium
Dr. Charles H. Townsend, *Director*

Brooklyn Botanic Garden
Dr. C. Stuart Gager, *Director*

CHURCH

The Collegiate Church of St. Nicholas
Rev. Dr. Malcolm James MacLeod, *Pastor*

EXHIBITION

OF THE

City History Club of New York

105 West 40th Street (Room 709)

HISTORICAL SCRAP BOOKS

I. City Hall to Wall Street (3 Books)
II. Greenwich Village and Lispenard Meadows (2 Books)
III. The Bowery and East Side (2 Books)
IV. Central Park to Kingsbridge (3 Books)
V. The Nineteenth Century City; Tenth to One Hundred and Twenty-fifth Street (2 Books)
VI. Fraunces Tavern
VII. New York City, South of Wall Street (2 Books)
VIII. Historic Brooklyn
IX. Historic Bronx
X. Historic Richmond
XI. Historic Queens
XII. Historic Brooklyn
The Milestones and the Old Post Road
Islands of East River and the Bay
Miscellaneous Landmarks of the City
Landmarks in Suburban New York
Upper New Jersey Landmarks (3 Books)
New York City's Battle Fields
Literary Landmarks
General Historical Articles

Original Photographs made to illustrate historic landmarks are arranged to correspond with these scrap books.

MAPS

Map of Original Grants of village lots from the Dutch West India Company to the inhabitants, 1642

Plan of New Amsterdam (Innes) 1644

Plan of New Amsterdam " 1655

Fisscher's Map of New Netherland, 1655

Map of Country Seats in English Period 1765

Plan of the City of New York, 1770

Plan of the City of New York, 1804

Historic Traces in Upper Manhattan

Maps used in work with clubs

Maps used by the Teacher to show landmarks

Modern large scale section maps published for the Borough Presidents

LECTURE SUBJECTS ILLUSTRATED WITH CLUB SLIDES

(Over 2,500 slides made for the Club or for the City and the Citizens Union)

I. DESCRIPTIVE AND FOREIGN

1. Holland and the Dutch War with Spain for Independence.
2. Modern Holland and the Coronation of Wilhelmina.
3. York, England (or Old York and New York).

II. GENERAL HISTORY

4. The Evolution of the Greater New York (including Physical and Political Geography).
5. The Discovery and Settlement of New York (including Indian Traces).
6. New York under Father Knickerbocker (or the Dutch Period).
7. New York during the English Period.
8. New York during the American Revolution.
9. New York during the Federal Period.

III. HISTORIC TRACES IN NEW YORK TODAY

10. Historic Traces in New York Today (most important points in Manhattan).
11. Historic Traces below Wall Street.
12. Historic Traces: City Hall Park and the English City.
13. Old Greenwich Village.
14. The Bowery and the East Side.
15. Central Manhattan: Union, Madison and Bryant Squares; Chelsea and Bloomingdale.
16. Upper Manhattan, 110th Street to Kings Bridge.

IV. SPECIAL BOROUGH STUDIES

17. The Historic Bronx (may be two lectures—East and West Bronx).
18. Historic Brooklyn (2 lectures).
19. Historic Queens Borough (2 lectures).
20. Historic Richmond.

V. CIVICS LECTURES

21. Graphic Views of Government—(comparison of National, State and City Governments).
22. History of the Development of Local Government in New York City.
23. City Departments in Action—Separate lectures for Departments of Police, Fire, Street Cleaning, Correction, Charity, Docks and Ferries, Education, etc.

PATRIOTIC LECTURE

24. New York in Wars for Self-Defense.

WHAT IS THE CITY HISTORY CLUB?

IT is a self-supporting society which includes among its members New Yorkers of all ages, of all conditions in life and of all the nationalities that our great city welcomes.

Its aim is to foster *Good Citizenship.*

Its method is to awaken a love for the city, and an active, personal interest in its welfare by spreading a knowledge of its picturesque history and of the lives and deeds of its worthy sons and daughters. The Club employs competent teachers of local history and organizes recreational meetings and excursions to sites and environs of historical interest. It also gives instruction in civics and in matters relating to the present and future conditions and needs of the city.

It appeals to all kinds and classes of our people, but especially to our School Children. "Just as the twig is bent the tree's inclined." Will you help to turn the mind of the New Yorker in the direction of conscientious effort for the welfare of our city?

HISTORICAL SKETCH

On the little height south of Harlem Mere in Central Park an old cannon and a rusty mortar lay neglected for years. Seen daily by many, they yet aroused no particular interest except when some mischievous boys rolled them to the edge of the cliff and gleefully watched their quick descent into the quiet lake below. From this watery grave they were rescued and laboriously hauled back into their former position by the park attendants whom tradition had told that the height was known during the War of 1812 as Fort Fish. We, however, have learned that it was called Fort Clinton; that the breastwork to be seen to-day was thrown up in 1814 by volunteers to protect the city against a possible attack by the British and that the height is also the site of a British earthwork of Revolutionary days.

In the autumn of 1895 a well-known surgeon was walking with his wife through this part of the Park. Spying the old guns and knowing his wife's interest in old New York, he turned to her and asked if she could tell him anything concerning their origin. She confessed her ignorance and both agreed that it would be a good point to investigate, with the idea of marking the relics so that the children of the neighborhood might learn their story.

The couple were Dr. and Mrs. Robert Abbe, and on this spot first took definite shape Mrs. Abbe's desire to have local history taught to the children of New York City, in order that, while learning to revere the old landmarks, they might become more loyal citizens. (The two guns have since been suitably mounted and a bronze tablet explaining their history placed on the pedestal.)

A few months later, Mrs. Abbe asked some friends to meet at her home and plans were made to organize City History classes in several centers.

The lack of available printed material on the history of the city made it necessary for the new organization to publish bibliographies, handbooks of Club methods of teaching and organization, historical illustrations and twelve "Excursion Leaflets" of from twelve to forty pages each, carefully mapped and illustrated and finally collected within the covers of an attractive volume of over five hundred pages, "The Historical Guide to the City of New York." See list of Publications, page 8.

Mrs. Abbe's home remained the headquarters of the Club until the fall of 1898, when desk room was engaged with the League for Political Education. For two years the City History Club was in close affiliation with the League. In 1909, the alliance was dissolved and the Club engaged a room on the ground floor of the Berkeley Lyceum, from which it moved in 1912 to its present quarters in the Tilden Building at 105 West 40th Street.

HISTORIC LANDMARKS

Restored by the City History Club of New York

CANNON

No. I, at McGown's Pass, northern end of Central Park, a Revolutionary cannon and mortar, mounted with the co-operation of the Park Department, November 25, 1906.

The tablet reads:

THIS EMINENCE COMMANDING
McGOWN'S PASS
WAS OCCUPIED BY BRITISH TROOPS SEPT. 15, 1776
AND EVACUATED NOVEMBER 21, 1783.
HERE, BEGINNING AUG. 18, 1814, THE CITIZENS OF NEW YORK
BUILT FORT CLINTON TO PROTECT THE CITY
IN THE SECOND WAR WITH GREAT BRITAIN.
THIS TABLET IS ERECTED BY THE CHILDREN OF
THE CITY HISTORY CLUB OF NEW YORK, A. D. 1906.

No. 2, in Battery Park, on the site of the flag pole of Colonial days, the Revolutionary cannon formerly at 55 Broadway.

The tablet reads:

THIS ANCIENT CANNON WAS EXHUMED IN 1892 ON
THE SITE OF NO. 55 BROADWAY, ON THE CORNER OF EXCHANGE
ALLEY OR "THE HIGHWAY LEADING TO THE FORTIFICATION
CALLED OYSTER PASTY" (1695-1783).
PRESENTED TO THE CITY OF NEW YORK
BY
WILLIAM HENRY MAIRS.
PLACED HERE BY THE CHILDREN OF
THE CITY HISTORY CLUB
1914.

MILESTONES

Manhattan

No. I, at Bowery and Rivington Street, reset and marked in 1915, as follows:

I MILE
CITY HALL
NEW YORK
ON THE OLD
BOSTON ROAD.
THIS TABLET PLACED, 1915
CITY HISTORY CLUB.

No. VII restored and reset in 1917 on St. Nicholas Avenue and 116th Street.

No. XI removed to Roger Morris Park, 1911; in 1912 marked by The City History Club of New York; the inscription reads:

11 MILES
FROM
N. YORK.
IN 1769 AT 159TH ST.
IN 1819 AT 170TH ST.
THE CITY HISTORY CLUB
1912.

No. XII, at Isham Park, 1915, marked by plate set in wall above it, as follows:

"12 MILES
FROM
N. YORK."
ON THE KINGSBRIDGE ROAD
1769.
PRESERVED BY WILLIAM B. ISHAM.
PLACED HERE, 1912, BY
THE CITY HISTORY CLUB.

Bronx

No. XV, on Albany Avenue, just north of the subway terminal, 242d Street, reset in cement in 1904. This was recently removed by a friend who has agreed to safeguard it until the avenue is relocated and improved.

Brooklyn

At Van Pelt Manor House, New Utrecht, in 1917, in co-operation with Mrs. Townsend Cortelyou Van Pelt and the Park Department of Brooklyn; the inscription is as follows:

14
MILES TO
N. YORK
FERRY.
THIS ROAD
TO DENYSS
FERRY
2½ MILES.

10½
MILES TO
N. YORK
FERRY.
THIS ROAD
TO JAMAICA
15 MILES.

Nos. II, IV, V, on Jackson Avenue, reset in co-operation with the Borough President of Queens on June 10, 1916.

PUBLICATIONS OF THE CITY HISTORY CLUB

(105 West 40th Street)

HISTORICAL EXCURSION LEAFLETS

* No. I.—City Hall to Wall Street, 20 pp., 2 cuts, 4 maps; 10 cents.
* No. II.—Greenwich Village and Lispenard's Meadows, 20 pp., 4 maps, 10 cents.
* No. III.—The Bowery and East Side, 16 pp., 3 maps; 5 cents.
* No. IV.—Central Park to Kingsbridge, 36 pp., 7 maps; 2 cuts; 10 cents.
* No. V.—The 19th Century City; 10th Street to 125th Street; 36 pp., 5 maps; 10 cents.
* No. VI.—Fraunces' Tavern, 12 pp., 1 map, 3 cuts; 5 cents.
* No. VII.—South of Wall Street, 32 pp., 4 maps, 6 cuts; 10 cents.
* No. VIII.—Historic Brooklyn, Part I, 32 pp., 7 maps, 8 cuts; 10 cents.
* No. IX.—Historic Bronx, 44 pp., 9 maps, 3 cuts; 10 cents.
* No. X.—Historic Richmond, 24 pp., 3 maps; 10 cents.
* No. XI.—Historic Queens, 36 pp., 5 maps; 10 cents.
* No. XII.—Historic Brooklyn, Part II, 16 pp., 5 maps; 10 cents.

Milestones and the Old Post Road, 12 pp., 5 cuts; 10 cents.

*HISTORICAL GUIDE TO THE CITY OF NEW YORK

Includes the above Excursion Leaflets, several appendices and an alphabetical index; 450 pp., 70 maps and 46 illustrations. Cloth, small 12mo, $1.50 net; postpaid, $1.60. Revised 1913.

---

* **Teachers' Handbook:** Outlines of a Course of Study in Local Geography and History (revised, 1908); 25 cents.

* **Graphic Views of Government:** to illustrate the relations of our National, State and City Governments; 16 pp., 6 plates; 10 cents.

N. Y. City Government Leaflets: 10 cents each. No. 1. Municipal Government in N. Y. State.

* **Hudson-Fulton Leaflet:** containing part of the log of Robert Juet: price 10 cents.

Historical Souvenir Postals: 10 cents per set of five.

Club Game—(revised 1909); an historical game of cards, containing many facts about New York City History (played like the game of Authors), 25 cents.

* **City History Illustrations:** 68 pictures of the famous men, buildings and events of local history: 35 cents per set.

* **Civics Hand Book:** Local Civics for Club Leaders; 15 cents.

---

* **Public School Teachers** are advised that they can secure the above starred publications for themselves and their classes through the Supply List of the Board of Education (7402-15; 7996).

THE HALF MOON SERIES

Papers on Historic New York, 24 Monographs on Local History, published in the interest of the City History Club of New York. Edited by Maud Wilder Goodwin, Alice Carrington Royce, and Ruth Putnam; 10 cents each.

CLASS MATERIALS

These consist of loose leaf note books, set of 68 pictures, outline and colored maps to illustrate local history and the connection of New York with world trade.

THE CATSKILL AQUEDUCT EXHIBITION

IN THE MUSEUM AT WASHINGTON'S HEADQUARTERS
(JUMEL MANSION) IN THE CHARGE OF

THE WASHINGTON HEADQUARTERS ASSOCIATION

FOUNDED BY

Daughters of the American Revolution

Organizer, MRS. SAMUEL J. KRAMER

President
Mrs. GEORGE WILSON SMITH

Honorary Presidents
Mrs. WILLIAM R. STEWART
Mrs. N. TAYLOR PHILLIPS

Vice-Presidents
Mrs. STANLEY LYMAN OTIS
Mrs. WILLIAM ARROWSMITH
Mrs. SIMON BARUCH

Honorary Vice-President
Mrs. H. CROSWELL TUTTLE

Recording Secretary
Mrs. MALCOLM McLEAN

Corresponding Secretary
Mrs. OVIEDO M. BOSTWICK

Treasurer
Mrs. JOSEPH KENDRICK BUTLER

Enrolling Secretary
Mrs. GEORGE D. BANGS

Historian
Mrs. PERCY HAMILTON GOODSELL

OCTOBER 12th to NOVEMBER 12th

NEW YORK

1917

THE MAYOR OF NEW YORK'S CATSKILL AQUEDUCT CELEBRATION COMMITTEE

GEORGE McANENY, *Chairman* ISAAC N. SELIGMAN, *Treasurer* EDWARD HAGAMAN HALL, *Secretary*

Executive Committee

ARTHUR WILLIAMS, *Chairman*

WILLIAM C. BREED
WILLIAM HAMLIN CHILDS
EDWARD HAGAMAN HALL
GEORGE FREDERICK KUNZ
J. W. LIEB
SAMUEL L. MARTIN
GEORGE McANENY
WILLIAM McCARROLL
ISAAC N. SELIGMAN
CHARLES H. STRONG
HENRY R. TOWNE

SUB-COMMITTEE ON ART, SCIENTIFIC AND HISTORICAL EXHIBITIONS

DR. GEORGE FREDERICK KUNZ, *Chairman*
409 FIFTH AVENUE

Universities and Colleges

Columbia University
Dr. Nicholas Murray Butler, *President*
Prof. William H. Carpenter, *Librarian*
Milton J. Davies

New York University
Dr. Elmer Ellsworth Brown, *Chancellor*

Stevens Institute of Technology
Dr. Alexander C. Humphreys, *President*

College of the City of New York
Dr. Sidney E. Mezes, *President*

Learned Societies and Institutions

American Geographical Society
John Greenough, *President*

New York Historical Society
John Abeel Weeks, *President*
Robert H. Kelby, *Librarian*

New York Genealogical and Biographical Society
Capt. Richard Henry Greene, *Representative*

Long Island Historical Society
Judge Willard Bartlett, *President*

Brooklyn Institute of Arts and Sciences
Dr, A. Augustus Healy, *President*

Staten Island Association of Arts and Sciences
Hon. Howard R. Bayne, *President*

American Numismatic Society
Edward T. Newell, *President*

Cooper Union for the Advancement of Science and Art
Miss Sarah Cooper Hewitt, *Trustee*
Miss Eleanor G. Hewitt, *Trustee*

American Scenic and Historic Preservation Society
Col. Henry W. Sackett, *1st Vice-President*

Engineering Societies

United Engineering Society
Charles F. Rand, *President*
Calvin W. Rice, *Secretary*

American Institute of Mechanical Engineers
Dr. Ira N. Hollis, *President*

American Institute of Electrical Engineers
E. W. Rice, Jr., *President*

American Institute of Mining Engineers
Philip N. Moore, *President*

American Institute of Civil Engineers
B. W. H. Pegram, *President*

Libraries

New York Public Library
Dr. Edwin H. Anderson, *Director*

New York Society Library
Frederic dePeyster Foster, *Chairman*

Museums

Metropolitan Museum of Art
Dr. Robert W. de Forest, *President*

Brooklyn Museum
William H. Fox, *Director*

American Museum of Natural History
Dr. Henry Fairfield Osborn, *President*

Museum of the American Indian
George G. Heye, *Founder*

Van Cortlandt Museum House (The Colonial Dames of the State of New York)
Mrs. Hamilton R. Fairfax, *President*
Mrs. Elihu Chauncey, *Chairman*

Jumel Mansion, The Washington Headquarters Association (Daughters of the American Revolution)
Mrs. George Wilson Smith, *President*
William H. Shelton, *Curator*

Fraunces' Tavern (The Sons of the Revolution)
Henry Russell Drowne, *Secretary*

Clubs

National Arts Club
John G. Agar, *President*

City History Club of New York
Mrs. A. Barton Hepburn, *President*

Parks and Gardens

Department of Parks, Manhattan and Richmond
Hon. Cabot Ward, *Commissioner*

Department of Parks, Brooklyn
Hon. Raymond W. Ingersoll, *Commissioner*

New York Botanical Garden
Dr. Nathaniel L. Briton, *Director*

New York Zoological Garden
Madison Grant, *Vice-President*

New York Aquarium
Dr. Charles H. Townsend, *Director*

Brooklyn Botanic Garden
Dr. C. Stuart Gager, *Director*

Church

The Collegiate Church of St. Nicholas
Rev. Dr. Malcolm James MacLeod, *Pastor*

EXHIBITION

in the museum at Washington's Headquarters (Jumel Mansion) in charge of the Daughters of the American Revolution (Mrs. George Wilson Smith, President) in co-operation with the Art, Scientific and Historical collections of the Mayor's Catskill Aqueduct Celebration Committee, and in celebration of the completion of the Aqueduct.

This exhibition in Jumel Mansion, at this time, relating to the early movements to supply the City of New York with water, is peculiarly interesting to this museum, because the west end of the Old Croton Aqueduct, which brought the first water to the city, landed on the Jumel property. Supreme Court records of one of the famous Jumel lawsuits, deposited in the Congressional Library at Washington, state that the site for the reservoir at High Bridge and for the pumping tower, was sold to the City of New York by Madame Jumel for the sum of forty thousand dollars.

Furthermore, at about the same time, the city bought from the same property the plot of ground known as High Bridge park for one hundred and twenty-five thousand dollars.

For many years thereafter the "Aqueduct Path," a lane above the pipe line leading south towards the Forty-second Street Reservoir, as it crossed the Jumel lands, between One Hundred and Sixtieth Street and High Bridge, including the slope to the Harlem River, was a popular suburban resort, which, after the opening of the Elevated Road, was abandoned—the attractions and the crowd moving on to Fort George.

The case of special exhibits contains the following articles:

1. A section of the wooden pipe laid by the Manhattan Company, whose charter, obtained by Aaron Burr, empowered it to

supply the city of New York with water. Gift of Mr. J. B. Rutherford; also framed historical sketch of the Manhattan Company.

2. Framed picture of the old water tank building at Lafayette and Reade Streets and historical description. Property of the museum.

3. Woodcut of the "Croton Water Celebration, 1842," and

4. Woodcut of the water gate in the pipes laid by the Manhattan Company, incorporated April 2, 1790 (from a recent publication by the New York Historical Society).

5. A portrait of Aaron Burr, who procured the charter for the first water supply to the City of New York.

6. A full length silhouette of Madame Jumel, by August Edouart, cut in 1843, while the High Bridge Aqueduct was under construction. Gift of Louis V. Bell.

7. Card stating the terms of the purchase by the city from Madame Jumel of the site for the High Bridge Reservoir.

8. Card relating to the purchase of the site for High Bridge Park.

Additional exhibits in the museum, interesting in connection with the Catskill Aqueduct Celebration.

9. A colored engraving from original drawing by William Burgess, published in the London Magazine, 1761, "The South Prospect of the City of New York, in North America," then under the pump and well system, with key to the principal buildings and vessels in the harbor, including "No. 22, Colonel Morris's 'Fancy,' turning to windward with a sloop of common mould."

10. One of the original Augsburg prints, "Representation du Feu Terrible a Nouvelle Yorck," showing the burning of New York City on the night of September nineteenth, 1776, when the water was passed from the pumps in buckets, and when one-fifth of the city was destroyed. This fire was watched from the windows and the balcony of the Roger Morris House by Washington and his staff until the spire of Trinity Church fell into the ruins.

11. Old Print, "The great fire of the City of New York, 16 December, 1835," showing a hand engine worked by volunteer firemen and twenty-one prominent citizens and firemen, numbered and named on the key to the picture. Gift of Mrs. George D. Bangs.

12. Two of the old rubber fire buckets of that period, lent by the late Alexander W. Drake.

OLD PRINTS

13. "La Destruction de la Statue Royale a Nouville Yorck, 1776."

14. "New York about 1790. Presented to D. T. Valentine by Edw. Crommelin, 195 Prince St., New York."

15. "The Government House, erected 1790, at the foot of Broadway, facing Bowling Green. Originally designed for the residence of General Washington." Drawn by C. Milbourne, 1777."

16. "Federal Hall, on site of the present Treasury Building, Wall Street, opposite Broad, New York, where Washington was inaugurated April 30th, 1789."

17. "A View of Fort George with the City of New York from the S. W., 1740."

18. "Battery and Bowling Green, New York, as it appeared during the Revolution."

19. "A Topographical Map of the North Part of New York Island, exhibiting the plan of Fort Washington, now Fort Knyphausen, and Col. Morris's House, by Claude Joseph Sauthier."

20. "A Plan of the Operation of the King's Army under the Command of General Sr. William Howe, in New York and East New Jersey, 1776."

21. View of the New York Post Office, 1845.

22. "North Interior View of the New York Post Office, located by authority of the Hon. Charles A. Wickliffe, Post Master General, and arranged by John Lorimer Graham, Esq., Post Master."

23. "The British surrendering their Arms to General Washington after their defeat at Yorktown in Virginia, October, 1781."

24. "The Apotheosis of Washington."

25. "Le General Lafayette." Old Mezzotint of Lafayette on the deck of his ship, coming to America, surrounded by the shades of his former friends, and

26. "Conclusion de la Campagne de 1781 en Virginie—Le Marquis de La Fayette."

(These two Lafayette prints came out of Paris one week before the war began. Gift of Mr. J. Sanford Saltus.)

The museum at the Jumel Mansion includes several special collections.

The William Lanier Washington Collection of Washingtonia consisting of more than 600 exhibits.

The Reginald Pelham Bolton Collection of relics dug up on the old battle fields and camp sites of the Revolution on Harlem Heights.

The Louis V. Bell Collection of Jumel furnishings, including the life size family group, painted by Alcide Ercole at Rome in 1854.

The Mrs. Louis Bennet Collection of colonial furniture.

A portrait of Washington, aged about 45, owned by the Association, painted by John Trumbull on a panel, 8 x 10 inches in size, and signed with the initials "J. T."

An important exhibit is the carriage clock of Napoleon Bonaparte, obtained by the Jumels at Rochefort on July 14th, 1815, together with his traveling carriage and trunk.

VAN CORTLANDT HOUSE MUSEUM

A SPECIAL EXHIBITION

IN CONNECTION WITH

THE MAYOR'S CATSKILL AQUEDUCT CELEBRATION

THE COLONIAL DAMES
OF THE STATE OF NEW YORK
OCTOBER MCMXVII

VAN CORTLANDT HOUSE MUSEUM

A small exhibition has been arranged in commemoration of the completion of the Catskill Aqueduct, at the request of the chairman of the sub-committee of the Mayor's Committee of Art, Scientific and Historical Exhibitions.

The educational value of such an exhibit to the school children of the vicinity, who visit the Museum in ever increasing numbers, appealed strongly to the President of the Colonial Dames and the Chairman of Van Cortlandt, and as the ancestors of the former owners of Van Cortlandt were in close touch with the early water supply of New Amsterdam it became almost obligatory that this representative Museum of Colonial days should do its part in the general observance of the celebration.

While in the days of the Dutch occupation of Manhattan Island water was obtained from local streams, ponds and springs, the first recorded project for a public well to be located in Broadway, dates back to 1658.

By 1660 a few private wells had been dug in some of the yards —as we learn from the Bulletin of the New York Public Library, whose exhibition illustrates the history of the water supply of the City of New York from 1639-1917.

These wells are shown in a remarkable bird's-eye view of the City made in that year (1660) and recently found in Italy. They were all south of the present Wall Street—the best known were those in the brewery yards of Olaff Stevenson Van Cortlandt and Jacob Van Couwenhoven in Brewers (now Stone) Street, and in the yard of Jacobus Kip, the first City Clerk, who lived on what is now Broad Street. There was also a well in the yard of the Excise Commissioner, Paulus Vander Beeck.

In 1774 the City purchased from Augustus and Frederick Van Cortlandt a site on the east side of Broadway between the present Pearl and White Streets, for the erection of the reservoir planned by Colles.

Among the articles of the four showcases in the Museum Room of Special Exhibits is a work entitled "Reminiscences of Christopher Colles," by John M. Francis, 1867, wherein is a "copy of a proposal of Christopher Colles for furnishing the City of New York with a constant supply of Fresh Water."

Lent by William Loring Andrews.

Christopher Colles, an engineer little known in this day and generation, but whose record in practical achievements ranks with the foremost men of this time. He was born in Ireland about 1738 and died in New York City in 1821. In 1765 he emigrated to America, and in 1773 delivered a series of lectures in New York on inland lock navigation. The following year he proposed to erect a reservoir for the City and convey water through the streets in wooden pipes made of pine logs.

Up to this time wells were the only source of water supply, and these produced (without exception) water which as early as 1748 Peter Kalm described as "very bad."

Taken from the New York Historical Society
Quarterly Bulletin, October, 1917.

A polished piece of the original wooden watermain.

Lent by the Bank of Manhattan.

A similar piece presented to the Museum by Miss Angelica Church, descendant of Benjamin Church, one of the original subscribers of the Manhattan Co.

Eight views from Valentine's Manuals are distributed through two of the showcases.

The Collect Pond,
Map of Kalch Brook, 1782,
Reservoir of Manhattan Water Works, Chamber Street, 1825,
Washington Institute and City Reservoir,
Street Pumps, 1796,
Water Chronology of 1774-1853, BY THEO. R. DE FOREST

Croton water pipes laid for supply of water during 1856.

Old Tea Water Pump.

Peter Stuyvesant's surrender of New Amsterdam without resistance was due, we are told, to the lack of water within the fort—later in 1667 a well was dug there and the good water caused astonishment to the Dutch people. Still later a well was dug in front of the gate of the port at the present Bowling

Green and the pump placed over it was the first pump recorded in the history of the City. In 1677 the Common Council ordered a number of community wells to be dug in the middle of the streets at certain designated places.

Wells, pumps, and springs continued to supply all the water used in the city for more than one hundred years.

In 1748 the Swedish traveler, Peter Kalm, remarked that the well water of the city was so poor even the horses balked at drinking it, and that the only good water was obtained from a large spring a short distance from town which the inhabitants used for their tea and for kitchen purposes. This spring afterward was covered with a pump and its water conveyed in wagons and sold throughout the city. Located at Chatham and Roosevelt Streets and long known as the Tea Water Pump.

Taken from the New York Historical Society Bulletin, October, 1917.

A plan of the City of New York from an actual survey made by James Lyne, 1731. Painted by Wm. Bradford, first New York Printer. The valuable original of this photograph is owned by William Loring Andrews, to whom we are indebted for the present use of photograph.

Spring water versus river water for supplying the City of New York. By Mathew Hale.

Marsle & Harrison, Printers, 5 Eldridge St., 1835. Beautifully bound.

Lent by William Loring Andrews.

Pamphlet—Bank of the Manhattan Company, Origin—History—Progress, 40 Wall St., New York. Chartered, 1799.

Oath of the first President, Daniel Ludlow. First meeting of the Directors held at the house of Edward Barden, Innkeeper, on April 18, 1799, the following Directors were present:

Daniel Ludlow, John Watts, John B. Church, Brockholst Livingston, William Laight, Pascal N. Smith, Samuel Osgood, John Stevens, John B. Coles, John Broome, Aaron Burr, Richard Harrison. Only absentee being William Edgar.

Old wooden watermains.

The Bank of Manhattan Water Co., 1829.

From Pelletran's Early New York Homes.

"The Sick Patient," 1833.

Original the Property of the Bank of Manhattan.

Croton Water Celebration, 1842.

By S. F. Atwell.

Lent by Mrs. Charles Warren Hunt.

Paper money issued by New York Water Works.

Printed by H. Gaine.

Eight small prints relating to the opening of the old Croton Water Works.

1 Croton Aqueduct at Mill River.
Drawn for D. T. V. M. 1850.

2 Croton Aqueduct at Harlem River.
Drawn for D. T. V. M. 1850.

3 Hydrographic map of the counties of New York, Westchester and Putnam, also showing line of the Croton Aqueduct.

4 South Gate House, new reservoir during construction.
For D. T. V. M. 1862.

5 High Bridge during construction of the large main viewed from the West Gate House, looking east. 1862.

6 High Bridge during construction of the large main viewed from Westchester side, looking north.
For D. T. V. M. 1862.

7 View of High Bridge, New York, 1861.

8 Bird's-eye view of Lake Manhattan and old reservoir, Central Park. *Lent by Messrs. Fred'k Keppel & Co.*

Nine engravings or lithographs.

1 View of McComb's Mills on the River Harlem near Kingsbridge.

T. Milbert.

2 Front view, the fortifications at Harlem.

3 Spiten Devils Creek.

T. Milbert.

4 McComb's Bridge Avenue.

T. Milbert.

5 McComb's House on the River Harlem.

6 View of the Fall on Bronx River, Lydick's Mill, West Farms.

7 View of the Tavern, on the road to Kingsbridge near Fort Washington.

8 Bridge on the Croton forty miles north of New York.

9 View of Lydick's Mill and House on Bronx River, West Farms.

Lent by Harris D. Colt.

Copy of the will of Lawrence Vanderhoff, dated 1797, with Great Seal of New York attached.

Portrait, Henry Rutgers Remsen, first cashier of the Manhattan Co., took oath Sept. 11th, 1799.

Lent by Mrs. J. Todhunter Thompson.

Early piece of wooden watermain in its natural condition used in the service of the Manhattan Co. and dug up in Centre Street about 1910.

Lent by Mrs. Charles Warren Hunt.

An old oil painting representing Peter Stuyvesant and his army.

View of the City and Harbor of New York taken from Mount Pitt, the seat of John R. Livingston, Esq. An original by St. Memin. 18th Century.

Map of the original grants of village lots from the Dutch West India Company to the inhabitants of New Amsterdam (now New York) lying below the present line of Wall Street. Grants commencing A. D. 1642.

Painted tray, view of Hudson River.

Lent by Norman M. Isham.

An old engraving. View in Hudson's River of Pakepsey and the Catts-kill Mountains. From Sopos Island in Hudson River.

Lent by Mrs. Charles Henry Roberts,
Miss Grace van Buren Roberts,
Laura A. Dayton, Highland, N. Y.

Novum Amsterodamum, 1671. Montanu's celebrated View.

Lent by Harris D. Colt.

Engravings, No. 2 Wall Street, looking down, 1831.

State Security—Pure Manhattan and Manhattan Security.

Heads of Wall Street—with famous dog—who saw each clerk to his desk on his arrival for work in the morning.

Wall Street, New York.

Lent by the Bank of Manhattan.

The old landmarks of New York. Spuyten Duyvel Creek.

The Audubon estate on the banks of the Hudson, foot of 156th Street, at Carmansville.

For D. T. Valentine's Manual, 1865.

Origin of steam navigation. "Honor to whom honor is due." A view of Collect Pond and its vicinity in the City of New York, 1793.

By John Hatchways,

Original on View in New York Public Library.

Map, Danckers. Entitled, "Novi Belgii Novaeque Anglia Nec Non Pennsylvaniae et Partis Virginiae tabula."

Topographical Map of the North part of New York Island exhibiting the plan of Fort Washington, now Fort Kuyphausen, with the Rebels' lines to the Southward which were forced by the Troops under the command of the Rt. Honble Earl Percy on the 16th Nov., 1776, and surveyed immediately after by order of his lordship.

By Claude Joseph Sauthier.

To which is added the attack made to the north by the Hessians. Surveyed by the order of Lieut. Gen. Kuyphausen.

Published by Permission of the Rt. Honble
Commissioners of Trade and Plantations,
by Wm. Faden, 1777.

Map of the Oriskany patent.

Map of North and South America.

"L'Amerique Septentrionale et Meridionale divisee en ses principales parties, on sont distingues les nes des autres les Estats suivant qu'ils appartienment presentement aux Francois, Castellans, Portugais, Anglais, Suedois, Danois, Hollandois, etc.

"Dresse sur les memoires les plus Nouveaux par G. Valck." Gerard Valck, a celebrated portrait painter, 1626-1720, Father-in-law and business partner of Peter Schenck. Copy.

A small print portrait of A. Willett, Rev. Andrew Willett, born in Ely, 1562, Father of Capt. Thomas Willett, First Mayor of New York.

Corner cupboard, early 18th century. Chinese porcelain, part of a dinner set marked with monogram belonging to Governor De Witt Clinton; presented to him while mayor, by the citizens of New York.

Silver bowl, formerly owned by Col. Henry Rutgers, born 1745, one of the promoters of the First Water Co. of New York. Marked Adrian Bancker, A^{C}B. Born 1703, Died 1761.

Lent by Mrs. Mary Crosby Brown.

A study of Van Cortlandt, by Norman Morrison Isham, F. A. I. A., is so contemporaneous with the times of the water supply of New York that it seems eminently proper to include it in this catalogue.

The Dutch Room referred to has only recently been opened to the public.

J. F - J. R.

A STUDY OF VAN CORTLANDT HOUSE

By Norman Morrison Isham, F. A. I. A.

The taking of the Dutch Colony by the English in 1666 marked the beginning of a change in the architecture of the New Netherlands. This change seems, however, to have been of exceedingly slow development, and, in the remoter settlements, of almost no effect. The farmers and the village people generally would have little to say to the English fashions. The mercantile class would be the first to show the effect of the new style, and even this was probably very slow to take up with it. The commercial supremacy of England, as the eighteenth century grew older, began, however, to show itself in the buildings of the wealthier classes, at any rate in the large towns, which show dwellings like the Van Rensselaer and the Schuyler house at Albany. Another instance of the English character of even the later country dwelling built when the wealth of the family had increased, is the new mansion erected on the banks of the Mosholu Brook by Frederick Van Cortlandt in 1748.

Yet the Van Cortlandt mansion is not thoroughly English. It has an English dress, indeed, for the State apartments are quite in the new manner, but some of the more domestic rooms show stronger Dutch influence, till we come to the kitchen which is the most Dutch of all.

The plan of the building has the L-shape which, whether it was built at one time, or was the result of additions, was beloved of the Dutch craftsmen.

Neither wing of the "L" is more than one room deep. In the main block, which faces about south, are two rooms, an East Parlor and a West Parlor, which have each a chimney, and which are separated by an entry or passage containing the principal stairs. The fireplace of the West Parlor is on the outer wall of the house, and that of the East Parlor is on the same wall which is continued eastward along the south side of the passage which, with a second staircase, separates this East Parlor from what was probably the original Dining Room.

Both these stairs are carried up into the garret. There is a little Dutch feeling in the main flight, but it is not obtrusive. The strongest touch of it is in the balusters of the last run of the north flight. These are sawed out of boards and not turned, but the profile is quite Netherlandish.

The West Parlor has now a late mantel of 1835 thrust into the old panelling, while the fireplace which it surrounds has been built into the older and larger one. The whole end of the room is panelled, with a closet in each side of the chimney, and this work is probably contemporary with the house. It seems to be entirely English in its character, and shows that this room was originally meant to be the finest in the house.

If the East Parlor was originally panelled like the West Parlor that panelling was soon taken out and a mantel put in which is a beautiful example of the later Georgian manner, and which may have been imported. It seems certain, however, that this was not the principal room, that it had no panelling at all and that the mantel was put in only when it was thought proper, after fashion had changed, to finish up the room, so as to make it the chief room of the house. Our ancestors did much more of this piecemeal finishing than we have yet given them credit for. Indeed, we are learning something new about their building methods almost continually.

At some later time the room was done over in the style of the Greek Revival, with a plaster cornice.

In restoring this room it was determined, without disturbing the mantel of course, to panel it as it might have been panelled from floor to ceiling, on all four sides, with the raised and bevelled panels which succeeded those with the heavy bolection mouldings so much liked by Wren.

The "L" was not occupied by the Kitchen, as it would have been in a colonial house of the English type, but by the Dining Room in which the present woodwork is later than 1800. The Dutch tradition prevailed and the Kitchen, in many ways the most interesting room in the house, was put in the Cellar. Its fireplace, with an oven at one side, is a veritable cavern, though it is small compared to some of the seventeenth century specimens. There is no manteltree, but a bent iron bar sustains the very flat elliptical arch which spans the opening. The ceiling is not plastered and the beams of the floor above, 5x10 nearly, and about 11 inches apart are plainly to be seen with all the marks of the broad-axes of the old workmen. It is a mistake to call these old cuts adz marks. The adze was a tool for use when the surface to be cut was horizontal and could not be turned to a vertical position, and thus could not be attacked with the axe. It is more a shipwright's than a housewright's tool.

In the chambers the west room is panelled on the fireplace end with considerable elaboration, while the East Room is quite plain, showing indeed, only a mantel, a fact which supports the theory that the East Parlor below it was originally a very plain room and that the mantel, one of the best on the seaboard, was added later. The North Chamber is more elaborate again than the East Room, though not so much so as the West Room, which was evidently the State Sleeping Apartment. It is this North Room which has been fitted up as the principal apartment of a prosperous Dutchman of the late seventeenth century. The transition from the negative type to that which came in during the eighteenth century, under the English rule, can thus be very clearly seen within this one building.

In the garret of the front block are two rooms, one of which has been fitted up with New England panelling. In the "L" garret there are several rooms which probably do not go back to the original house. The Dutch flavor here, however, is more pronounced. There are two doors and some hardware which are strongly of that character. Perhaps the doors were brought from the story below, for it is not certain that the present roof and garret are original, even if there were rooms in the third story at the beginning. A hip roof was to be expected, as in the Glenn-Sanders house at Scotia, and the pitch of the roof is what we should look for.

It has been the general intention to keep the house furnished as it would have been in its prime—the time from the date of its building to the Revolution. The Dutch Room, of course, is a thing by itself, and some fine seventeenth century pieces have been displayed for their educational value. Now and then, also, a late piece of exceptional merit has been used.

In the East Parlor a fine secretary of about 1760 stands between the windows on the eastern wall. It once belonged to Mr. Canfield and is very probably an early piece by John Goddard, of Newport, one of the finest of our Colonial cabinet makers. It is the eighth of his secretaries known to be in existence.

The lowboy between the southern windows was made by William Savery, of Philadelphia, another noted Colonial craftsman, whose advertisement is pasted in the top drawer.

All Sorts of Chairs and
Joiners Work
Made and Sold by
WILLIAM SAVERY
At the Sign of the
Chair, a little be-
low the Market, in
Second Street.
PHILADELPHIA

Over this piece is a fine gilt mirror of Chippendale type.

Two other Chippendale pieces are the elegant sofa against the west wall, north of the door, and the delicately beautiful Pembroke table in the corner next to the chimney.

The middle of the room is occupied by two wonderful Chippendale seats and a magnificent tripod or tip table with a pie-crust and claw-and-ball feet—an astonishing specimen—a present from General Nathaniel Greene, of Rhode Island, to Madam Van Vechten, of Finderne, New Jersey, at whose house he stayed in the winter of Valley Forge. From the Misses Frelinghuysen, descendants of Madam Van Vechten, the table came to Mrs. Margaret Elmendorf Sloan, whose children gave it to the Society of Colonial Dames in memory of their Mother.

In the center of the Dining Room, the old West Parlor, is an American gate-legged or "thousand-legged" table with an oval top. It has beside it two very fine walnut chairs, one with cane seat and back, of about 1700, the other with a banister-back, of a little later date.

Another seventeenth century American piece is the fine oak chest with one drawer. This stands between the southern windows and has beside it still another early example in the very interesting butterfly table on the west wall. On the other side is a Turkey work chair that can hardly be excelled.

On the east wall is an extremely good six-legged highboy with a cushion-front drawer just under its flat top.

In the East Parlor Chamber there is, on the door to the north stair hall, a very curious bolt which, by means of a cord, could be released by a person in bed without getting up, so that the servant could come in to make the wood fire in the morning.

On the south wall of this room is a fine block front dressing table of mahogany, while the walnut period is represented by the highboy with its curved broken pediment. Near by is a notable "wing" or easy chair with claw-and-ball feet.

The Dining Room Chamber—once the West Parlor Chamber—contains a bed of the early eighteenth century with hangings covering all its posts, as was the fashion at that date.

Over the mantel is a mirror of 1680. Near the bed is an excellent example of a couch or day-bed, the precursor of the couch of the present time, and against the wall stands an inlaid lowboy.

The Dutch Room has a very fine painted Kas cupboard, and a most interesting model of a Dutch sloop. This model, which dates from 1705, came from the counting room of an old ship-building firm after the last member had died. It was wont to be taken out and blessed whenever the real vessel which it represented put out to sea.

The sleigh is Dutch also, that is, Holland Dutch, and was brought over by the first Van Rensselaer who came to this country.

In the further left-hand or northwest corner is an excellent example of a ship's treasure chest of painted iron—one of the kind which figures in the fabled burials of money by Captain Kidd. Above it is a very noteworthy Dutch china cupboard with a curving, well carved, and with glazed doors.

On the floor is a real Dutch rug or carpet.

A beautiful maple desk and a wagon chair, as it was called, are notable exhibits in the Southeast Chamber of the Garret.

Perhaps the most interesting piece in the Southwest Garret is the Doll's House made for a member of the Homans family, of Boston, in 1744. It is now being filled with furniture which reproduces in miniature that in the Van Cortlandt House itself.

There are also some remarkable early toys in this room, a cradle covered with leather and a very good gate-legged table.

The preservation of this house means far more than the maintaining of a museum, and thus of an object lesson in the domestic life of our fathers. Such a house is not a mere landmark in our social or military history, it is a monument in the history of our architecture as well. Even with the restorations which have been made for the purpose of showing special periods in the manner of a museum, the house is practically undisturbed and forms, just as a fabric, just as a matter of design and construction, a most important and valuable example of the Georgian or English type of Colonial house, tinged in the most interesting way with the Dutch influence of the former New Amsterdam.

NORMAN MORRISON ISHAM.

THE DANCEY-DAVIS PRESS
NEW YORK

Celebration *of* the Completion of the Catskill Aqueduct *and* the Seventy-fifth Anniversary of the bringing of Croton Water into the City of New York, A. D. 1917

Exhibit

of the

(Collegiate)
Reformed Protestant Dutch Church
of the City of New York

(Organized A. D. 1628)

✠

October 12th *to* October 20th, 1917

In the Chapel of the Collegiate Church of St. Nicholas
Fifth Avenue and Forty-eighth Street

OPEN FROM 9 A. M. TO 6 P. M.

Exhibit

of the

(Collegiate)
Reformed Protestant Dutch Church
of the City of New York

(Organized A. D. 1628)

✠

FRAME (40 x 28), SHOWING PHOTOGRAPH OF LETTER OF DOMINE JONAS MICHAELIUS (first Minister), dated Manhattan (now New York), 11th August, 1628, describing the organization of the Church.

FRAME (37 x 28), PHOTOGRAPH OF THE CHARTER, granted A. D. 1696, by William III., King of England, etc. (William and Mary). This was the first ecclesiastical charter granted in the Middle Colonies.

FRAME (30 x 50), SHOWING PHOTOGRAPHS OF TEN CHURCHES erected from 1642 to 1892.

TILE PIECE (22 x 48), DELFT TILES, mounted, showing New Amsterdam A. D. 1656 (now New York), the Stone Church in the Fort, erected 1642, being a prominent object.

FRAME (22 x 26), PHOTOGRAPH OF MURAL TABLETS erected in the Middle Church, Second Avenue and Seventh Street, in 1900 to perpetuate the memory of the illustrious men who laid the foundation of both Church and State in the metropolis of the Nation. (Rev. Jonas Michaelius, First Minister; Peter Minuit, First Colonial Governor, Jan Huyck and Sebastian Jansen Krol, Krankenbesoekers. These four comprised the First Consistory.)

TILE PIECE (37 x 32), DELFT TILES, mounted, showing Middle Dutch Church, Nassau, Cedar and Liberty Streets, erected 1729, altered 1764; desecrated by the British during the War of the Revolution, 1776-1783; re-dedicated July 4, 1790. Occupied by the United States Government, 1844. Building removed 1882.

FRAME (27 x 20), METALLIC PLATE, which constituted the cornerstone of the North Church, William and Fulton Streets, 1769-1875. This edifice was the first one erected for service in the English language. The plate is a memorial of the great transition the community made from the tongue of Grotius and William the Silent to that of Milton and Hooker.

PANEL (37 x 30), EMBLEM OF THE REFORMED CHURCH IN AMERICA, based on the coat of arms of William I. (the Silent), Prince of Orange. Done in burnt wood in the original colors.

PANEL (37 x 30), A SYMBOL OF THE CHURCH— "The Lily among the Thorns." This was the pathetic symbol of the Reformed Church in the Netherlands during the eighty years of bloody struggle in the sixteenth century, when she gave herself the name of "The Church under the Cross." This is a companion to the coat of arms mentioned next above, and the panel also is in colors.

COAT-OF-ARMS OF JOHN HARPENDINCK, from whom the Church received a devise of land. This object hung for 106 years in the North Dutch Church (1769-1875), and now adorns the walls of the Middle Church, at Second Avenue and Seventh Street.

THE OLD CHURCH CHEST. This chest is believed to have been in use as early as 1724 for the preservation of the papers and plate of the Church. The following action is recorded on the minutes of the Consistory, July 2d, 1724:

> "All Church papers which shall be deemed of importance shall be put in a roll in order and be placed in the Church Chest at the house of Do. DuBois, the key of which shall remain in the Church room; and nothing shall be taken out of it but by direction of the Consistory. And in the Chest there shall be a book, in which whoever takes anything out of the Chest shall record the fact.
>
> "Likewise, when anything is deposited, that also shall be noted therein."

DOMINE SELYNS' LIST OF MEMBERS, A. D. 1686. This volume was prepared by the Rev. Henricus Selyns to direct him in the course of his family visitations. The whole number of members is five hundred and sixty. The book lies open at the name of Lady Judith, widow of De Heer Petrus Stuyvesant (Governor's Bouwerie). This book has been extensively copied by historical societies and affords the only basis of the directory of those days.

THE FIRST ENGLISH PSALM BOOK. Published by Consistory in A. D. 1767, "they having by reason of the declension of the Dutch language found it necessary to have Divine Service performed in their Church in English." The versification of the Psalms into English from the Dutch book then in use was made by Mr. Francis Hopkinson, afterward one of the signers of the Declaration of Independence.

ACCOUNT BOOK BELONGING TO THE DIACONATE OF THE CHURCH. Begun in the eighteenth century, and still in use.

CARVINGS, NORTH DUTCH CHURCH (A. D. 1769-1875). Each of the ten Corinthian pillars which supported the ceiling bore at the top the carved and gilded initials of a contributor to the erection of the edifice. (North Church, Fulton and William Streets.)

CURIOUS CHART. Prepared about 1835 by Theodore R. De Forest, M.D., a devoted member of the Collegiate Church.

ANCIENT SILVER COMMUNION PLATE—still in use by the Collegiate Church.

MINIATURE SILVER COMMUNION PLATE, for the administration of the Lord's Supper to the Sick (A. D. 1893).

ANCIENT BAPTISMAL BASIN, A. D. 1744. Translation of the inscription:

"To inherit eternal life, in after life, O man,
Be cleansed in Christ's blood, and thus before death die.
Who in God's Son does live, life everlasting has,
And lives through the truth faith, who in that love does live."

ANCIENT BAPTISMAL BASIN, A. D. 1796. This bears the inscription:

"The North Church —— 1796."

(North Church, Fulton and William Streets.)

SEVEN SILVER COLLECTION PLATES, A. D. 1792. Gifts of eminent parishioners, whose names are inscribed on them; two being gifts of ancestors of our ex-President Theodore Roosevelt.

CANE, made out of wood from the old Middle Church, Nassau Street, erected A. D. 1729; building removed A. D. 1882.

CANE, made out of wood from the old North Church, Fulton and William Streets, erected A. D. 1769; building removed A. D. 1875.

THE BELL in the tower of this Church (Church of St. Nicholas, Fifth Avenue and 48th St.) was cast in Amsterdam in A. D. 1731 and presented to the Church Corporation by Col. Abraham De Peyster, a prominent citizen of New York at that time, for the use of the old Middle Dutch Church, which stood at Nassau and Cedar Streets. It bears the following inscription:

ME FECERUNT DE GRAVOE ET N. MULLER, AMSTERDAM, ANNO 1731.

ABRAHAM DE PEYSTER, GEBOREN (Born) DEN 8 JULY, 1657, GESTORVEN (Died) DEN 8 AUGUSTUS, 1728.

EEN LEGAAT AAN DE NEDERDUYTSCHE KERKE, NEIUW YORK. (A Legacy to the Low Dutch Church at New York.)

Among the many public occasions on which this bell has done service may be noted the dates of July 9, 1776, at the time when the Declaration of Independence was read at the head of each brigade of Washington's Army then stationed in the city. Also on July 4, 1790, that being the day of the re-opening of the Middle Church for divine service after its desecration during the Revolutionary War. The bell was tolled on the occasion of the funerals of Washington, Lincoln, Grant, McKinley and Cleveland.

PORTRAITS in oil of the Ministers in succession, from Domine Gualterus DuBois (ninth Minister), who in A. D. 1699 began his ministry in the "Church in the Fort," adorn the walls of the Consistory Room. (Church of St. Nicholas, Fifth Avenue and 48th St.)

The Rev. William Linn, S.T.D. (1785-1805), whose portrait is included, was Chaplain of the House of Representatives in the First Congress under the Federal Constitution (1789).

MEMENTO made from one of the banisters of the pulpit of the Middle Dutch Church, Nassau, Cedar and Liberty Streets (1729-1882).

THE FIRST SERMON (manuscript) **PREACHED IN ENGLISH IN THE REFORMED DUTCH CHURCH IN AMERICA.** This sermon was delivered by the Rev. Archibald Laidlie, D.D., in the Middle Dutch Church, Nassau, Cedar and Liberty Streets, on April 15th, 1764, from the text "Knowing therefore the terror of the Lord, we persuade men." (II Corinthians v:ii.) Dr. Laidlie was the thirteenth minister in succession of the Collegiate Church (1764-1779).

"THE TRUE SPIRITUAL RELIGION." A treatise by the Rev. Lambertus De Ronde, published 1767. Mr. De Ronde was the twelfth minister in succession of the Collegiate Church (1751-1784).

A FUNERAL EULOGY OCCASIONED BY THE DEATH OF GENERAL WASHINGTON, delivered February 22nd, 1800, before the New York State Society of the Cincinnati, by William Linn, D.D. Dr. Linn was the fifteenth minister in succession of the Collegiate Church (1785-1805). Washington died December 14th, 1799, and this Eulogy was delivered on the first anniversary of his birth thereafter. At a meeting of the Society of the Cincinnati held the same day it was unanimously resolved that Dr. Linn "be hereby admitted an honorable member of this Society."

OLD TESTAMENT IN DUTCH, A. D. 1477. One of the earliest translations made into any vernacular tongue in modern Europe.

HEIDELBERG CATECHISM IN DUTCH, A. D. 1563. This is believed to be the only copy now extant of the first translation of the Catechism into the Dutch language. Occasional references have been made to it, but its existence has often been denied. It is therefore of exceptional interest.

ACTS OF THE STATES GENERAL relating to the Church since 1579.

ARCHIVES OF THE DUTCH CHURCH IN LONDON for about three centuries.

HISTORY IN ENGLISH OF THE SAME CHURCH, with full lists of baptisms, marriages, and burials of the Dutch in London for the same period.

ACTS OF THE SYNODS FROM 1572 TO 1620.

GENERAL CATALOGUE OF THE UNIVERSITY OF LEYDEN for three hundred years, containing many names of our early ministers.

A SIMILAR CATALOGUE OF THE UNIVERSITY OF UTRECHT.

WAGENAAR'S HISTORY OF HOLLAND, IN 21 VOLUMES.

VOSE'S HISTORY OF THE CHURCH OF THE FATHERLAND.

THE PUBLICATIONS OF THE MARNIX UNION.

The Mayor's Catskill Aqueduct Celebration Committee

GENERAL COMMITTEE

Chairman

George McAneny

EXECUTIVE COMMITTEE

Arthur Williams, *Chairman*

Edward Hagaman Hall, *Secretary*

William C. Breed
William Hamlin Childs
George Frederick Kunz
J. W. Lieb
Samuel L. Martin
George McAneny
William McCarroll
Charles H. Strong
Henry S. Thompson
Henry R. Towne

Museum Exhibits Committee

Dr. George Frederick Kunz, *Chairman*

409 Fifth Avenue

[Members and Institutions Participating]

UNIVERSITIES AND COLLEGES

Columbia University
Dr. Nicholas Murray Butler, *President;* Prof. William H. Carpenter, *Librarian;* Milton J. Davies.

New York University
Dr. Elmer Ellsworth Brown, *Chancellor.*

Stevens Institute of Technology
Dr. Alexander C. Humphreys, *President*

College of the City of New York
Dr. Sidney E. Mezes, *President*

LEARNED SOCIETIES AND INSTITUTIONS

American Geographical Society
John Greenough, *President*

New York Historical Society
John Abeel Weeks, *President;* Robert H. Kelby, *Librarian*

New York Genealogical and Biographical Society
Capt. Richard Henry Greene, *Representative*

Long Island Historical Society
Judge Willard Bartlett, *President*

Brooklyn Institute of Arts and Sciences
Dr. A. Augustus Healy, *President*

Staten Island Association of Arts and Sciences
Hon. Howard R. Bayne, *President*

American Numismatic Society
Edward T. Newell, *President*

Cooper Union for the Advancement of Science and Art
Miss Sarah Cooper Hewitt, *Trustee;* Miss Eleanor G. Hewitt, *Trustee*

American Scenic and Historic Preservation Society
Col. Henry W. Sackett, 1*st Vice-President*

ENGINEERING SOCIETIES

United Engineering Society
Charles F. Rand, *President;* Calvin W. Rice, *Secretary*

American Institute of Mechanical Engineers
Dr. Ira N. Hollis, *President*

American Institute of Electrical Engineers
E. W. Rice, Jr., *President*

American Institute of Mining Engineers
Philip N. Moore, *President*

American Institute of Civil Engineers
E. W. H. Pegram, *President*

LIBRARIES

New York Public Library
Dr. Edwin H. Anderson, *Director*

New York Society Library
Frederic dePeyster Foster, *Chairman*

MUSEUMS

Metropolitan Museum of Art
Dr. Robert W. de Forest, *President*

Brooklyn Museum
William H. Fox, *Director*

American Museum of Natural History
Dr. Henry Fairfield Osborn, *President*

Museum of the American Indian
George G. Heye, *Founder*

Van Cortlandt Museum House
(The Colonial Dames of the State of New York)
Mrs. Hamilton R. Fairfax, *President;* Mrs. Elihu Chauncey, *Chairman*

Jumel Mansion, Washington Headquarters Association
(The Daughters of the American Revolution)
Mrs. George Wilson Smith, *President;* William H. Shelton, *Curator*

Fraunces' Tavern
(The Sons of the Revolution)
Henry Russell Drowne, *Secretary*

CLUBS

National Arts Club
John G. Agar, *President*

City History Club of New York
Mrs. A. Barton Hepburn, *President*

PARKS AND GARDENS

Department of Parks, Manhattan and Richmond
Hon. Cabot Ward, *Commissioner*

Department of Parks, Brooklyn
Hon. Raymond W. Ingersoll, *Commissioner*

New York Botanical Garden
Dr. Nathaniel L. Britton, *Director*

New York Zoological Garden
Madison Grant, *Vice-President*

New York Aquarium
Dr. Charles H. Townsend, *Director*

Brooklyn Botanic Garden
Dr. C. Stuart Gager, *Director*

CHURCH

The Collegiate Church of New York
(Exhibition at the Church of St. Nicholas)
Rev. Dr. Malcolm James MacLeod, *Pastor*

CATSKILLS AQUEDUCT CELEBRATION NUMBER (October 12—15,1917)

BROOKLYN BOTANIC GARDEN

LEAFLETS

THE BROOKLYN INSTITUTE OF ARTS AND SCIENCES

SERIES V   BROOKLYN, N. Y., OCTOBER 10, 1917   NOS. 12 and 13

FOREST PROBLEMS OF THE ASHOKAN WATERSHED

One of the most important problems in the administration of a great city like New York is the water supply. At least three things are essential: 1. A continuous and abundant source of water; 2. A reservoir of adequate size and elevation whence the water can be distributed; 3. The maintenance of the water and the watershed in a condition of as perfect sanitation as possible.

For an adequate supply of water it is necessary, not only to have a suitable amount of precipitation, but to insure the conservation of as much of the rainfall as possible to the run-off draining into the reservoir. If the fallen rain evaporates too fast from the watershed, the reservoir is inadequately supplied. It is also desirable that the drainage into the reservoir be as evenly distributed throughout the year as possible, otherwise the water may get too low at certain seasons of comparative drought.

The principal factor in realizing these two needs is the vegetation, and especially the trees of the watershed. The old supposition that trees increase the amount of rainfall has been conclusively shown to be fallacious. It has been shown with equal or greater certainty that forests increase the humidity and thus decrease the rate of evaporation; and it is also known that the run-off from a forested area is more gradual and more evenly distributed through a given period of time than from an area devoid of trees.

For these and other reasons it is highly essential to maintain proper forest conditions on the watershed of any municipal water supply system. Thus, after the rainfall is assured, and the reservoir and aqueduct are constructed, there still remains one of the most important problems of all, namely, to secure and to maintain a forest on the watershed. This involves at least three things: 1. Planting the trees; 2. Giving them adequate care; 3. Removals and replacements, or, in other words, scientific forest management.

After the kind of trees is decided upon, suited to the given climate, the planting is comparatively easy; but from that time on problems arise which require the constant oversight of a trained forester, and of a specialist in the treatment of tree diseases. Unfortunately these last needs, of a forester and a plant pathologist, are too frequently overlooked or ignored.

The land controlled by New York City on the Ashokan watershed comprises a total of over 15,000 acres. Less than half of this area bears a native forest of second growth white oak, red oak, red maple, sugar maple, hemlock and white pine. Chestnut trees were plentiful until the chestnut bark disease began, about ten years ago, to kill the trees, and there are few of them left. The dead and dying ones are being cut down and should, of course, be replaced with other species.

The City has already planted on this watershed about one and a half million cone-bearing (evergreen) trees, more than one million of which include six species of pine. The present value of the trees is probably not far from one million dollars, and is increasing each year. They are also becoming annually more and more important conservators of the city's water supply.

Every one of these species is subject either to insect ravages or to diseases caused by parasitic fungi. Within three or four years there has been imported into this country, from Europe, a rapidly spreading disease that is destructive to certain species of pines. This disease has already reached the area of the Ashokan watershed, and, up to the present time, no effective treatment is known. Infected trees should at once be cut down and burned. This disease is cited merely as an illustration. It threatens to destroy every one of the million or more trees planted by the City at large expense, and vital to its water supply. It has long since been too late to save the chestnuts, as no remedy for chestnut bark disease is known. The public is fairly familiar with the forest ravages of insects.

It is the purpose of these few paragraphs merely to call attention to these facts, and to urge, with all possible emphasis, the necessity of the City appointing a competent plant pathologist, whose business should be not alone to act as a practicing physician of trees, diagnosing, and applying remedies worked out by others, but devoting much of his time and energies to scientific research into the nature and causes of tree diseases, so that he may be able to contribute toward the solution of the problem of their control. He should have a laboratory properly equipped tor the most thorough scientific research, and a suitable staff of trained assistants.

Hundreds of thousands, possibly in the course of time, millions of dollars worth of City property, as well as the proper protection of the water supply, may be insured by the comparatively small annual cost of maintaining such a laboratory.

Moreover, for its own best interests, the forest-to-be on this watershed will not only need continual removals and replacements, but this process may and should become, by judicious forest management, a source of income to the city, much more than sufficient to meet the entire cost of upkeep of both forest and reservoir. For this work a thoroughly trained and experienced forester is necessary, with a corps of assistants.

The City has no more important problem in connection with its new water supply, for here lies one of the indispensable conditions to maintaining not only the abundance but the purity of the drinking water of over five million human beings.

C. STUART GAGER.

PLANTS OF THE CATSKILL AQUEDUCT REGION

From near sea-level to the highest mountains within 100 miles of the City stretches the Catskill Water system, and this diversity of elevation suggests at once a division of the plant life of the area into the mountain and low-land types of vegetation. This may not be such an artificial division as at first sight appears when it is remembered that many of our local wild flowers are found only on the mountain-tops of the Catskills or at elevations in excess of 1,500 feet. Others, again, common enough near the mouth of the Hudson, seem to creep rather sparingly up the Valley, perhaps as far as the Highlands, only to find these hills a barrier to a more northerly journey.

There are many striking illustrations of these well marked tendencies of plant distribution in the region. For instance, near the mouth of the Croton River there is a tree of the yellow pine (*Pinus echinata*), more than fifty miles north of its usual home, near the pine-barrens of New Jersey. And on the Palisades, opposite Yonkers, there grew, until quite recently, large masses of the native yew (*Taxus canadensis*), otherwise at home in the highland region northward. Near Peekskill Bay and just below it on Verplanks Point are many specimens of the ninebark (*Physocarpus opulifolius*), which, while it is common enough northward, is rare or wanting below this in the Valley. Near Judge Parker's estate at Esopus is an island, without name, upon which occur the most southerly specimens of the arbor vitae (*Thuja occidentalis*) in the Aqueduct region. Near Piermont, just below Nyack, are large quantities of marsh fleabane (*Pluchea camphorata*), on what are locally called the "Flats". This plant is obviously an intruder from the salt marshes of the Long Island and New Jersey coasts.

Scores more of these exceptions could be cited to prove the general rule that the flora of the Catskill Aqueduct region is of two types. It is true that they intergrade somewhat, but on the whole the Highlands seem to act as a barrier to many of our wild plants, particularly to the mountain species, some of which have never been known to occur in the valley south of Storm King or Anthony's Nose. It is through the former that the aqueduct takes the great plunge under the Hudson to the east bank of the river.

THE MOUNTAIN PLANTS

No real alpine conditions are found in the Catskills, the highest peak being scarcely over 4,000 feet. But there are many peaks that are over 2,000 feet, and toward the summit of these, and on the top of Slide Mountain, there occurs a group of plants that are found practically nowhere else in the Aqueduct tract. Some of the more conspicuous of them are:

Braun's Polystichum (*Polystichum Braunii*), a strong growing fern, growing in rocky woods.

Balsam Fir (*Abies balsamea*), the tree of fragrant memory, common enough near the head-waters of Esopus Creek, unknown in the low-lands.

Wood Reed Grass (*Cinna latifotia*); besides the Catskills it has been found at Pine Plains, Dutchess county.

Several species of sedge, which are plants with the general aspect of grass, notably *Carex novae-angliae.*

Mountain Yellow-eyed Grass (*Xyris montana*), known only from the highest regions of the Catskills, in our area.

Mountain Strawberry (*Fragaria canadensis*), and its relative *Fragaria terra-novae*, both isolated on the highest peaks in the watershed of the Ashokan Reservoir.

Mountain Ash (*Pyrus sitchensis*), differing from the common mountain ash in its short-pointed leaves. The latter is common in many places in the valley, but *P. sitchensis* is found only at the highest elevations.

Violet (*Viola Selkirkii*), known, in the Catskill region, only from near mountain summits, and usually only above 2,500 feet where another species, peculiar to high elevations, *Viola renifolia*, is also found.

One-flowered Wintergreen (*Moneses uniflora*), with small white flowers in June. Found in the Adirondacks and nearly to the Arctic Circle, but reaching nearest to New York City in the Catskills.

Canadian Blueberry (*Vaccinium canadense*), a low bush not over eighteen inches tall, with leaves bright green on both sides, and nearly evergreen.

Adoxa (*Adoxa Moschatellina*), remarkable because it is found in New York State only near Arkville, Delaware county, on mountains that drain into the upper portion of Ashokan reservoir.

Large-leaved Golden-rod (*Solidago macrophylla*), reaching its most southerly distribution point on the highest peaks of the Catskills, and found far northward in the Hudson Bay region.

There are a few others of these essentially far-northern species that find their most southerly outposts in the higher elevations of the water system of Ashokan, bringing such species nearer to the City than anywhere else the plants occur. It would be a fitting permament memorial of the completion of the water system if the City could acquire some tract near the Ashokan reservoir containing these rare plants and thus preserve them.

At somewhat lower elevations, in fact nearly throughout the Catskills and in the higher elevations of the Hudson Highlands, are many other species that are rare or wanting along the lower stretches of the Hudson nearer sea-level. Among the most beautiful of these are:

Clintonia (*Clintonia borealis*), with yellow flowers and glossy basal leaves.

Green Orchis (*Habenaria hyperborea*), with spurred, irregular, greenish-white flowers.

Showy-fringed Orchid (*Habenaria grandiflora*), with very striking purple-fringed flowers in July.

White Adders-Mouth (*Microstyles monophyllos*), a small orchid with whitish flowers.

Coral-root (*Corallorhiza trifida*), a slender saprophytic orchid with whitish stems and flowers, but no leaves.

Northern Stitchwort (*Stellaria borealis*), a white-flowered chickweed-like herb found on wet rocks and flowering in summer.

Mountain Sandwort (*Arenaria groenlandica*), making small tufts in rocky places. Flowers white, in summer.

Foam Flower (*Tiarella cordifolia*), with beautiful white flowers in May and June, so plentiful as to suggest its common name. Found very sparingly below Peekskill, if at all.

Purple or White Avens (*Geum rivale*), with not very numerous flowers, and tassel-like, silky fruits.

Barren Strawberry (*Waldsteinia fragarioides*), a strawberry-like plant with white flowers, and dry fruits. Leaves nearly evergreen.

Ginseng (*Panax quinquefolium*), known only from Haverstraw Bay northward. Formerly much collected for its supposed medicinal qualities, and now nearly extinct in the region.

Labrador Tea (*Ledum groenlandicum*), a low bog shrub with russet foliage and white flowers. Known only from Dutchess county northward.

Three-leaved Solomon's Seal (*Smilacina trifolia*), very rare in the Hudson Valley in Dutchess county; unknown south of it.

Twisted-Stalk (*Streptopus amplexifolius*), with greenish-white flowers and leaves bluish beneath. Known only from the Catskills.

Showy Ladies' Slipper (*Cypripedium reginae*), the finest of all the ladies' slippers. Flowers white, variegated with crimson stripes. From Dutchess county and northward.

Round-leaved Orchis (*Habenaria orbiculata*), has two large, nearly round leaves, flat on the ground. They are silvery beneath.

Rattlesnake Plantain (*Epipactis tesselata*), a small orchid with variegated leaves and whitish flowers on slender spikes.

Golden Seal (*Hydrastis canadensis*), now known only from near West Point and northward; very rare. Formerly much collected for its medicinal roots.

Anemone (*Anemone riparia*), known only from Dutchess county in our area.

Hepatica (*Hepatica acutiloba*), a pointed-leaved form of this common wild flower in the Aqueduct region only from the Catskills.

Three-toothed Cinquefoil (*Potentilla tridentata*), a white-flowered herb with a woody base, the leaflets toothed at the end. Found only from Dutchess county and the Catskills.

Seneca Snakeroot (*Polygala Senega*), sometimes called mountain flax. Flowers in long, slender spikes; white, tinged with green.

Giant St. John's Wort (*Hypericum Ascyron*), almost a shrub, with large yellow flowers. Grows in moist places, only in the Catskills in the Hudson Valley region.

Dwarf Cornel (*Cornus canadense*), its greenish-white bloom, suggestive of minature dogwood, is borne at the end of the stems which are scarcely over four inches tall. Known now only from the Highlands northward.

Ague-weed (*Gentiana quinquefolia*), somewhat like the common fringed gentian but without the fringe. Rare in northern Westchester county, and increasing northward through the Highlands to the Catskills.

Bugle-weed (*Lycopus membranaceus*), with the aspect of mint, but without the mint odor. Known only from the Catskill area.

Hobble-bush (*Viburnum alnifolium*), a shrub with showy white flowers and red fruits. Common north of the Highlands at moderate elevations and in the Catskills.

Swamp Laurel (*Kalmia polifolia*), a small relative of the

mountain laurel which is scattered all along the water system. *K. polifolia* is a bog shrub with two-edged twigs and known only from Dutchess county northward.

Wild Rosemary (*Andromeda glaucophylla*), a low bog shrub with white drooping flowers and whitish foliage, known in the region only from Orange and Putnam counties northward.

Van Brunt's Jacob's-Ladder (*Polemonium Van Bruntiae*), a blue showy herb found in the Catskills, but scarcely south of them in the water system.

Oswego Tea (*Monarda didyma*), commonly cultivated but apparently wild only in the Catskills, so far as our region is concerned. Flower scarlet and showy.

Twin-flower (*Linnaea borealis*), a low-carpeting plant with twin-flowers. Rare or wanting now south of the Highlands, although there are old records of it from Long and Staten Islands.

Wood Valerian (*Valeriana uliginosa*), a pink or white flowered herb known only from the northern end of the Highlands northward.

Scores more of these northern species of plants could be cited, but space forbids more support of the general thesis that the Catskill water system cuts through two distinct floral regions. Many trees, such as the spruce, larch, and bur oak and a considerable number of shrubs follow the same general distributional tendency as the herbs, their occurrence south of Peekskill being very rare or unknown. The few exceptions mentioned earlier only serve to prove the rule.

THE LOWLAND PLANTS

Of the 2,038 native flowering plants found wild within 100 miles of the City, about 1,600 are found in the Hudson Valley and Catskill regions.

Deducting those that we have seen to be of northern tendencies, there remain a large number of species that make up the great bulk of vegetation of these regions. These generally distributed plants are too numerous to mention here. Wherever the vegetation has been undisturbed, as through the Highlands, it is still a forest region with a wealth of wild flowers and ferns and shrubs as undergrowth. In spite of the wealth of plants, there appears to be no species endemic there, i. e., found nowhere else.

As illustrating the tendency of many essentially lowland plants not to grow north of the Highlands the sweet-gum (*Liquidambar Styraciflua*), sour gum (*Nyssa sylvatica*), and tulip tree (*Liriodendron tulipifera*) are interesting. All are common near the City and south of it. The first has never been recorded north of Peekskill, *Nyssa* is very rare north of the Highlands, while the Tulip Tree is unknown as a wild tree in the Catskills.

Perhaps the most beautiful of all the shrubs of the Catskill aqueduct system is the mountain laurel (*Kalmia latifolia*), whose white or pinkish flowers color great areas in the Highlands and at some other places, usually about Memorial Day. Among the trees, the dogwood (*Cornus florida*), with its white showy bloom, is among the commonest in the wilder parts of the country.

NORMAN TAYLOR

NOTICES

The Garden is open free to the public daily, from 8 a. m. until sunset; on Sundays and holidays at 10 a. m. The Laboratory Building, containing the library, herbarium, and offices, is open daily, from 9 a. m. until 5 p. m. The Conservatories are open April 1-October 1, 10 a. m.-4:30 p. m.; October 1-April 1, 10 a. m.-4 p. m.

The Garden may be reached by Flatbush Ave. trolley to Malbone St.; Franklin Ave., Lorimer St., and Tompkins Ave. trolleys to Washington Ave.; St. John's Place and Rogers Ave. trolleys to Sterling Place; Vanderbilt Ave., Sixteenth Ave., Union St., Greenpoint, and Smith St. trolleys to Prospect Park Plaza and Union St., and Brighton Beach elevated to Consumers' Park Station. (The elevated trains stop only when the conductor is notified in advance.)

A docent will meet parties by appointment and conduct them through the Garden. This service is free to members of the Botanic Garden and to teachers with classes; to others there is a nominal charge of 25 cents an hour for parties of less than three, and 10 cents a person per hour for parties of three or more.

Current numbers of LEAFLETS are free to all who wish them. Back series, complete, 50c. each; single numbers, 5c. each.

The LEAFLETS are published weekly or biweekly from April to June, and September to October, inclusive, by The Brooklyn Institute of Arts and Sciences, at Washington Avenue and Montgomery Street, Brooklyn, N. Y.

Telephone: 6173 Prospect.

Mail address: Brooklyn Botanic Garden, Brooklyn, N. Y.

Catalogue

An Historical Exhibition of Paintings

to celebrate the opening of the

Catskill Aqueduct

BROOKLYN MUSEUM

November First to November Twenty-ninth

Nineteen Seventeen

THE BROOKLYN INSTITUTE OF ARTS AND SCIENCES

BROOKLYN MUSEUM

Eastern Parkway Brooklyn, N. Y.

TO REACH THE MUSEUM: From Manhattan, Subway Express to Atlantic Avenue; thence by St. John's Place car to Sterling Place, or by Flatbush Avenue car to Prospect Park and Eastern Parkway.

THE BROOKLYN INSTITUTE OF ARTS AND SCIENCES

BROOKLYN MUSEUM

A Special Historical Exhibition
to celebrate the opening of the
Catskill Aqueduct

Works of American Painters
1860-1885

In the American Gallery of the Museum

November First to November Twenty-ninth
1917

The Mayor of New York's Catskill Aqueduct Celebration Committee

Sub-Committee on Art, Scientific and Historical Exhibitions

Chairman
Dr. George Frederick Kunz
409 Fifth Avenue

Universities and Colleges

Columbia University
Dr. Nicholas Murray Butler, *President*
Prof. William H. Carpenter, *Librarian*
Milton J. Davies

New York University
Dr. Elmer Ellsworth Brown, *Chancellor*

Stevens Institute of Technology
Dr. Alexander C. Humphreys, *President*

College of the City of New York
Dr. Sidney E. Mezes, *President*

Learned Societies and Institutions

American Geographical Society
John Greenough, *President*

New York Historical Society
John Abeel Weeks, *President*
Robert H. Kelby, *Librarian*

New York Genealogical and Biographical Society
Capt. Richard Henry Greene, *Representative*

Long Island Historical Society
Judge Willard Bartlett, *President*

Brooklyn Institute of Arts and Sciences
Hon. A. Augustus Healy, *President*

Staten Island Association of Arts and Sciences
Hon. Howard R. Bayne, *President*

American Numismatic Society
Edward T. Newell, *President*

Cooper Union for the Advancement of Science and Art
Miss Sarah Cooper Hewitt, *Trustee*
Miss Eleanor G. Hewitt, *Trustee*

American Scenic and Historic Preservation Society
Col. Henry W. Sackett, *1st Vice-President*

Engineering Societies

United Engineering Society
Charles F. Rand, *President*
Calvin W. Rice, *Secretary*

American Institute of Mechanical Engineers
Dr. Ira N. Hollis, *President*

American Institute of Electrical Engineers
E. W. Rice, Jr., *President*

American Institute of Mining Engineers
Philip N. Moore, *President*

American Institute of Civil Engineers
E. W. H. Pegram, *President*

Libraries

New York Public Library
Dr. Edwin H. Anderson, *Director*

New York Society Library
Frederic dePeyster Foster, *Chairman*

Museums

Metropolitan Museum of Art
Dr. Robert W. de Forest, *President*

Museums (continued)

Brooklyn Museum
William H. Fox, *Director*

American Museum of Natural History
Dr. Henry Fairfield Osborn, *President*

Museum of the American Indian
George G. Heye, *Founder*

Van Cortlandt Museum House
(The Colonial Dames of the State of New York)
Mrs. Hamilton R. Fairfax, *President*
Mrs. Elihu Chauncey, *Chairman*

Jumel Mansion, Washington Headquarters Association
(The Daughters of the American Revolution)
Mrs. George Wilson Smith, *President*
William H. Shelton, *Curator*

Fraunces' Tavern
(The Sons of the Revolution)
Henry Russell Drowne, *Secretary*

Clubs

National Arts Club
John G. Agar, *President*

City History Club of New York
Mrs. A. Barton Hepburn, *President*

Parks and Gardens

Department of Parks, Manhattan and Richmond
Hon. Cabot Ward, *Commissioner*

Department of Parks, Brooklyn
Hon. Raymond W. Ingersoll, *Commissioner*

New York Botanical Garden
Dr. Nathaniel L. Britton, *Director*

New York Zoological Garden
Madison Grant, *Vice-President*

New York Aquarium
Dr. Charles H. Townsend, *Director*

Brooklyn Botanic Garden
Dr. C. Stuart Gager, *Director*

Church

The Collegiate Church of St. Nicholas
Rev. Dr. Malcolm James MacLeod, *Pastor*

Portrait of Abraham Lincoln — Artist Unknown

Introduction

THE period marked by the beginning of the modern water supply of the city of New York in the opening of the first Croton Aqueduct in 1851 to the recent opening of the Catskill Aqueduct, is a period of uncommon activity in the art history of the country. It began with the rise and popularity of the Hudson River School of American landscape painters. This group is strikingly represented in the current exhibition at the Metropolitan Museum of Art and as a pendant, the Brooklyn Museum offers as its contribution to the celebration of the Aqueduct opening a special exhibition made up of the works of painters who might be said to succeed the Hudson River School and who were especially prominent in the quarter of a century which followed the outbreak of the Civil War.

It is a difficult matter to affix rigid frontiers to the work of the various artistic coteries as the careers of their members over-lap one another, both in years and in the popularity of their work. There are those who painted with the Hudson River School happily still at work, and some survive who have been in touch with the contemporaries of Gilbert Stuart. Thomas Sully lived to paint portraits to within a year or so of his death in 1872. Nevertheless as seen in retrospect the work of certain artists related to each other through their common interest in the same class of subjects and to a certain extent in their resemblance in methods of work, are to be remembered as a cohesive body and filling a fixed period to the exclusion of others not in sympathy with them. There is no doubt that with the opening of the Civil War a new group of painters distracted public attention from the placid and poetic dreamers of the Hudson River School. They were a disorganized class of rugged and free individualists who seemed to be reaching out into new fields unknown to their predecessors. They were characterized by little of the solidarity of the earlier group. Everyone for himself was their slogan. That at least is the impression produced by a survey of the works of this period which lasted until the time when American artists began to feel the overpowering influence of French Impressionism under Claude Monet, about 1885. In a measure the artist reflected the kaleidoscopic changes that were taking place—the abolition of slavery, the opening of the West, the shortening of communication between communities and individuals through the electric telegraph and the development of railroads, the rising tide of business, speculation and wealth, the rich rewards for enterprise and personal initiative—all this impelled these highly individualized artists, filled with the new spirit of courage and energy, to disregard tradition and the work of their neighbors and strike out for themselves.

If any common influence was felt at this period it was exerted upon the comparatively few who had studied at the Düsseldorf Academy and their works are far too naturalistic and obvious to have any relation to the Hudson River School. It would seem almost that the drift was away from landscape; it was man and his works and not inanimate nature which now seemed to appeal to the artistic imagination. But in truth it was simply that the art of the period was heterogeneous almost to the limit of chaos. The artist experimented in all forms of expression. Genre in all its phases flourished. Winslow Homer began his career as a war illustrator. The tremendous conflict of the first four years immensely stirred the patriotism of the generation and caused a revival of historical painting as one sees in the works of Huntington, Buchanan Read, Leutze and Rothermel. This period also has the honor of having produced the poetic yet virile school of nature lovers and interpreters of which George Inness was the dean and which is the great glory of American art. It is the real golden age of landscape painting in this country. The collection will be found to contain characteristic examples of the works of its leading men.

It is specially gratifying too that the revival in American historical painting is represented in the exhibition by the great work of Huntington—"Lady Washington's Reception"—known to the past generation by the engraving by A. H. Ritchie which was a common possession of many American households. This painting, the property of the Hamilton Club of Brooklyn, has been out of public view for many years.

To the officers and members of the Club, therefore, who have recognized the appropriateness of this occasion to permit the painting again to be placed before the eyes of the public and to the possessors of other paintings exhibited, the Governing Committee of the Museum and the Cooperating Committee in charge of the Aqueduct Celebration offer their sincere thanks.

The attention of the visitors is directed to the arrangement of the collection. At the west of the gallery will be found paintings of the early and older American school, including works of the Hudson River painters, while to balance them, at the eastern end hang a selection of the Museum's paintings of the present day. Between the two are placed the "Works of American Painters 1860-1885." Thus the opportunity is afforded to study, side by side, the characteristics of the main American art periods.

W. H. F.

Madonna and Child — Robert L. Newman

Catalogue

BABCOCK, W. A. (1826-1899)

An intimate friend of Jean Francois Millet. "W. A. Babcock spent nearly all his life at Barbizon, and was a sympathetic and poetic painter of nudes and costumed figures." (From Sadakichi Hartmann's History of American Art)

1. THE OPEN BOOK. Property of the Brooklyn Museum.

BELLOWS, ALBERT F. (1829-1883)

Born at Milford, Mass. At sixteen he entered the office of an architect of Boston, but finally turned his attention to painting. Studied in Paris and Antwerp, A. N. A., 1859; N. A., 1861. He painted landscapes and genre scenes.

2. SPRINGTIME. Loaned by Mr. William J. Smith.

3. VILLAGE SCENE. Property of the Brooklyn Museum.

BIERSTADT, ALBERT (1830-1902)

Born in Germany, he was brought to America when an infant. He went to Düsseldorf in 1853 to study in the Academy and also went to Rome. He became member of the National Academy of Design in 1860. "The same careful finish of details, skillful management of light, and eye for picturesque possibilities which made Bierstadt's Old-World subjects so impressive and suggestive, have rendered his studies of American scenery full of bold and true magnificence." (From Tuckerman's Book of the Artists)

4. THE MORTERATSCHE GLACIER, UPPER ENGADINE, PONTRESINA. Property of the Brooklyn Museum.

BOUGHTON, GEORGE H. (1834-1905)

Born in England. He was brought to Albany, N. Y., by his parents in 1837. He went to London in 1853 to improve his knowledge of art which he had already studied in America and after a few years returned to New York where he opened a studio. He was made National Academician in 1871. He was also a member of the Royal Academy of London.

5. OLIVIA. Property of the Brooklyn Museum.

BRADFORD, WILLIAM (1830-1892)

Born in New Bedford, Mass. Toward the middle of his life he began painting ships in the harbor of Lynn, Mass., and along the coast as far north as Nova Scotia and Labrador. He made several trips to the ice regions of the North American coast with Dr. Hayes and other Arctic explorers.

6. A Whaler Off the Coast of Greenland.
Property of the Brooklyn Museum.

CHASE, WILLIAM MERRIT (1849-1916)

Born in Franklin Township, Indiana, he began his art studies in 1868 under B. F. Hayes, the portrait painter. He came to New York in 1869 where he spent a year in the schools of the National Academy. In 1872 he went to Munich, studied in the Royal Academy there and gained three medals. He returned to the United States in 1878 and was elected National Academician in 1890.

7. The Antiquary's Shop.

8. In the Studio.

9. Still Life. Property of the Brooklyn Museum.

COLEMAN, CHARLES CARYL (born 1840)

"His most characteristic works are studies of blossoming branches of apple or plum, and where the flowers, studied directly from nature, are yet arranged with such a balancing of mass, such a delicate choice of color in the background and accessories, and so firm an accentuation of their outline, that the canvas has a charm of decorative unity. Coleman has not made his permanent quarters at Rome, but has lived elsewhere, and even at one time had a studio in London; but of late years his home has been in a villa at Capri, never to be forgotten by its guests, with its orange trees, its vine-clad terraces, and its white walls leaning against the steep hill." (From Samuel Isham's "History of American Painting")

10. Twenty-two Studies in Pastel of Vesuvius, Capri and Vicinity, Venice and Mont Blanc.
Loaned by the artist.

DE HAAS, MAURICE FREDERICK HENDRICK (1832-1895).

Born in Holland. He studied in the Academy of Fine Arts of Rotterdam, and later went to London. In 1859 he settled in New York and was elected National Academician in 1867. He was essentially a marine painter.

11. Marine. Property of the Brooklyn Museum.

DURAND, ASHER B. (1796-1886)

Born in New Jersey, he studied engraving with his father who was a watchmaker. Later he was apprenticed to the engraver Peter Maverick, whose partner he became in 1817. He was one of the original members of the National Academy of Design, organized in 1826, of which he became president at the resignation of S. F. B. Morse in 1845.

12. LANDSCAPE.

13. THE FIRST HARVEST. Property of the Brooklyn Museum.

DUVENECK, FRANK (born 1848)

Studied in Munich for a number of years where he was a pupil of Dietz and one of his best followers. He obtained an Honorable Mention in Paris in 1895 and a special gold medal for his services to American art at the Panama-Pacific Exposition in 1915.

14. HEAD OF A MAN. Property of the Brooklyn Museum.

ELLIOTT, CHARLES LORING (1812-1868)

Also spelled Elliot; he was born in Scipio, New York; the son of an architect, and died in Albany, New York. Starting as a clerk in Syracuse, he went to New York in 1834, where he became a pupil of Trumbull. Eminently a portrait painter (he is said to have painted more than seven hundred of his contemporaries) he was made A. N. A. in 1845, and N. A. in 1846. His portrait of Fletcher Harper was shown in Paris at the exhibition in 1867.

15. PORTRAIT OF GENERAL JOHN C. FREMONT (THE "PATHFINDER") Loaned by Mr. William S. Hughes.

GIFFORD, R. SWAIN (1840-1905)

Spent the early part of his life in New Bedford and in 1864 he opened a studio in Boston. Settled permanently in New York in 1866. He was a pupil of Albert van Beest, the Dutch marine painter. He became National Academician in 1878.

16. NEAR THE MARSH.

17. TREES AND MEADOW. Property of the Brooklyn Museum.

GIFFORD, SANDFORD ROBINSON (1823-1880)

Born in Saratoga County, N. Y., he studied painting with John R. Smith in New York City. In 1850 he went abroad visiting London and Paris, and in 1860 he made a more extensive trip on the continent and in Egypt. He was elected National Academician in 1854.

18. SUNSET IN THE SHAWANGUNK MOUNTAINS.
Loaned by Mr. H. H. Knox.

Rome, Representative of the Arts — Elihu Vedder

GIGNOUX, REGIS (1816-1882)

Born in Lyons, France. He was a pupil of Paul Delaroche and of the École des Beaux-Arts in Paris. He came to America in 1844 and was elected a member of the Academy of Design in 1851. He was the first president of the Brooklyn Art Academy.

19. The Hudson River in Autumn.

20. Winter Scene. Property of the Brooklyn Museum.

HART, JAMES M. (1828-1901)

Brother of William Hart; he was born in Scotland, and was brought to America as a child by his parents. In 1851 he went to Düsseldorf where he studied under Schirmer. In 1856 he opened a studio in New York and was elected National Academician in 1859.

21. On the Way Home. Property of the Brooklyn Museum.

HART, WILLIAM (1822-1894)

Brother of James M. Hart; he was born in Scotland and was brought to the United States in childhood. Self-taught. He became National Academician in 1858.

22. Landscape—Lake George.
Loaned by Mrs. George Silas Coleman.

23. Near Hurley, Ulster Co., N. Y.
Property of the Brooklyn Museum.

HOMER, WINSLOW (1836-1910)

Born in Boston; pupil of National Academy of Design and F. Rondel, but mainly self-taught. At nineteen he was a lithographer in Boston; settled in New York in 1859. During the Civil War he contributed a number of war pictures to "Harper's Weekly." He was elected National Academician in 1865.

24. The Unruly Calf.

25. Children On the Beach.

Property of the Brooklyn Museum.

(In addition there are thirty-eight water colors by this artist on exhibition in the galleries.)

HUNTINGTON, DANIEL (1816-1906)

Born in New York. He was a pupil of S. F. B. Morse and Henry Inman. In 1839 and in 1844 he went to Italy. In 1850 an exhibition of his works in New York attracted considerable attention. He was the third president of the National Academy of Design (1862).

26. Lady Washington's Reception.
Original Sketch.

Engraving of the subject by A. H. Ritchie.

Key to above.

Loaned by the Hamilton Club, Brooklyn.

The Morteratsche Glacier, Upper Engadine, Pontresina
Albert Bierstadt

INNESS, GEORGE (1825-1894)

Born in Newburg, N. Y. Studied art in Newark, N. J., and engraving in New York, which by reason of ill-health he was forced to abandon. In 1846 he began the practice of his profession as a landscape painter, passing a few months in the studio of Regis Gignoux. He made several visits to Europe for the purpose of observation and study, remaining in Italy from 1871 to 1875. He was made National Academician in 1868.

27. THE GLOW.

28. INDIAN SUMMER.

29. JUNE.

30. SUNRISE.

31. THE ROMAN CAMPAGNA.
Loaned by Mr. Herbert H. Knox.

32. THE OLD ROADWAY.
Loaned by the L. I. Historical Society.

33. ON THE DELAWARE RIVER.

34. ROYAL BEECH IN LYNDHURST FOREST.

35. A SUMMER MORNING.

36. THE OLD FARM. Property of the Brooklyn Museum.

JEFFERSON, JOSEPH (1829-1905)

Born in Philadelphia. He was an eminent actor who devoted much of his leisure to the study of landscape painting.

37. IN THE BIRCH WOODS. Property of the Brooklyn Museum.

JOHNSON, EASTMAN (1824-1906)

Born in Lovell, Maine. He studied in Düsseldorf, Rome, Paris and The Hague. He had a studio in New York. He was made a member of the National Academy in 1860.

38. THE SAVOYARD BOY. Property of the Brooklyn Museum.

KENSETT, JOHN FREDERICK (1818-1872)

Born in Connecticut. After studying engraving under Dagget, he went abroad where he studied painting for seven years. He first exhibited at the Royal Academy, London, in 1845. Elected National Academician in 1849.

39. AN ISLAND POND, NEAR NEWPORT, R. I.
Loaned by Mr. John Hill Morgan.

40. MOUNT LAFAYETTE, N. H.
Loaned by Mr. Herbert L. Pratt.

LA FARGE, JOHN (1835-1910)

Figure, flower and landscape painter, eminent also as a mural painter and as a designer of stained glass windows. He occupied a studio in New York for some years and was elected a member of the National Academy in 1869.

41. Adoration.

42. Adoration.

43. Angel of the Sun.

44. Female Centaur.

45. Head of the Angel of the Annunciation.

Property of the Brooklyn Museum.

MARTIN, HOMER D. (1836-1897)

Native of Albany, N. Y. With the exception of a few weeks study under William Hart, early in his career, he was entirely self-taught as an artist. For many years he had a studio in New York City. He became a National Academician in 1875.

46. Ontario Sand Dunes.

47. Normandy Coast. Property of the Brooklyn Museum.

48. Sunset. Loaned by Mrs. Henry L. Quick.

MIGNOT, LOUIS R. (1831-1871)

Born in South Carolina. He spent some years in study in Holland; upon his return lived in New York, and was made a member of the National Academy in 1859. Upon the secession of his native state from the Federal Union in 1861 he removed to London, where he spent the rest of his life.

49. Niagara. Loaned by Mr. Arthur S. Fairchild.

MILLER, CHARLES H. (born 1842)

Born in New York. Studied medicine, and graduated in 1863. During his medical course he painted occasional pictures, and first exhibited at the National Academy in 1860, "The Challenge Accepted." In 1864 he went to Europe, and again in 1867, visiting the art centers, and finally settling in Munich, where he remained three years, and became a student of Professor Lier and of the Bavarian Royal Academy. He made frequent excursions to Dresden, Vienna and Berlin. He became National Academician in 1875.

50. Sunset at East Hampton. Loaned by the artist.

Female Centaur — John La Farge

MINOR, ROBERT C. (1840-1904)

Born in New York; studied art in Paris under Diaz, and in Antwerp under Van Luppen, Boulanger and others, traveling through Germany and Italy for some time. His studio was in New York, and he exhibited at the National Academy, in Brooklyn, Chicago, and elsewhere in America.

51. On the Upper Thames, Conn.
52. The Creel. Property of the Brooklyn Museum.

NEWMAN, ROBERT L. (1827-1911)

" . . . is a colourist in the sense of the old masters. He excels in richness and satiety of separate tones, and is clever in bringing them into proper relationship. His Madonnas, Red Riding-Hoods, reading girls, classical figures with animals, 'Christ walking on the Sea,' etc., are colour dreams pure and simple." (From Sadakichi Hartmann's History of American Art)

53. Madonna and Child. Property of the Brooklyn Museum.
54. Landscape with Woman and Child.
55. Christ Saving Peter.
56. Two Girls with Dolls.
57. Mother and Child and Two Children Presenting a Lily.
58. Head of a Girl.
59. Girls Reading.
60. Children Playing.
61. The Fortune Teller.

Loaned by Mr. Nestor Sanborn.

PARTON, ARTHUR (1842-1914)

Born at Hudson, N. Y.; studied under William T. Richards of Philadelphia, spending his professional life in the City of New York. He went to Europe in 1869, and returned to America the next year; he was elected an Associate of the National Academy in 1872.

62. Misty Morning. Coast of Maine.

Property of the Brooklyn Museum.

RICHARDS, WILLIAM T. (1833-1905)

Born in Philadelphia; in 1835 he went to Europe, spending a year in study and observation in Florence, Rome and Paris. In 1856 he opened a studio in Philadelphia, and in 1866 returned to Europe for a short visit. He was an Honorary Member of the National Academy of Design and an Associate Member of the Water-Color Society.

63. On the Coast of New England.

Property of the Brooklyn Museum.

ROTHERMEL, PETER F. (1817-1895)

"He was brought up as a surveyor, and did not devote himself to the study of art until he was twenty-one years of age. In 1840 he began the active practice of his profession by the painting of portraits. In 1856 he went to Europe, spending some time in the art centers of the Continent, painting his first historical picture, and later making that class of subjects a specialty. He was commended for excellence in historical painting." (From Clement and Hutton's "Artists of the Nineteenth Century," Vol. II.) His "Battle of Gettysburg" is now in the Pennsylvania State Capital.

64. The Martyrdom of St. Agnes.
Loaned by Mrs. William H. Fox.

RYDER, ALBERT P. (1847-1917)

" . . . This effect is heightened in Ryder's works by his execution, by his manipulations of paint and varnish as substances capable of being made beautiful in themselves, as well as in pattern and color. Some of them suggest the lacquer work of Korin, as when a red stag flees through dark depths of varnish beneath a streak of yellow sky, or patches of silvery, moon-lit cloud spot against the deep blue behind a brown tree." (From Samuel Isham's History of American Painting)

65. Autumn's Golden Pathway.
66. Evening Glow, The Old Red Cow.
67. The Grazing Horse.
68. Moonrise.
69. The Sheepfold.
70. The Shepherdess.
71. Summer's Fruitful Pasture.
72. The Waste of Waters is Their Field.
Property of the Brooklyn Museum.
73. Horse in Stall. Loaned by Mr. A. Augustus Healy.

SHIELDS, THOMAS W. (born 1849)

A Canadian painter in the United States. Born at St. John's, New Brunswick, of English parents; resident of Brooklyn; devoted to historical and classical subjects; pupil for three years of the N. A. D. under Prof. Wilmarth. He studied ten years abroad under Gérome, Carolus-Duran, Jukes Lefebvre and others.

74. Mozart's Requiem. Loaned by the artist.

TILTON, JOHN ROLLIN (born 1833)

Born in London, N. H. He has been a close student of the Venetian school of painting, especially of Titian, but is a graduate of no art academy, and has studied under no master. His professional life has been spent in Italy, chiefly in Rome.

75. PAESTUM. Property of the Brooklyn Museum.

ULRICH, CHARLES FREDERIC (1858-1908)

" . . . is known for his conscientious studies of the labouring class of our manufacturing era, like his 'Glass Blowers,' and his ambitious 'Promised Land,' representing immigrants arriving at Castle Garden, treated with all the strength and skill of the best German art of this kind, though rather restless in colour." (From Sadakichi Hartmann's "History of American Art," Vol. II)

76. HEAD OF AN OLD MAN. Property of the Brooklyn Museum.

VAN ELTEN, KRUSEMAN (1829-1904)

Born in Alkmar, Holland; Associate of the National Academy, New York; and member of the American Society of Painters in Water-Colors. Medals at Amsterdam in 1860, and at Philadelphia in 1876. He was instructed in drawing in his native town, and in 1844 went to Haarlem and studied painting under C. Lieste and other masters. His professional life has been spent in Haarlem, Amsterdam, Brussels, and New York, and he has made sketches in Germany, Austria, Switzerland, France, and England.

77. LANDSCAPE. Property of the Brooklyn Museum.

VEDDER, ELIHU (born 1836)

Born in New York; became a pupil of T. H. Matteson at Sherbourne, N. Y. After some years spent in Italy he opened a studio in New York for a short time, but has remained in Italy the greater part of his life, where he still resides.

78. AN ENIGMA OF THE SEA. Loaned by Mr. S. S. Cummins

79. ROME, REPRESENTATIVE OF THE ARTS.

(Design for Lunette in Bowdoin College)

Property of the Brooklyn Museum.

WYANT, ALEXANDER H. (1836-1892)

Born in Ohio; began his professional career as a landscape painter in Cincinnati. He spent some years in Düsseldorf, where he studied under Hans Gude;subsequently he studied in London, and rturned to America, settling in New York in 1864 or '65. His first picture, exhibited in New York, "A View of the Valley of the Ohio River," was at the National Academy in 1865.

80. A Grey Day. Loaned by Mr. William A. Putnam.

81. Keene Valley.

82. Moonlight and Frost. Property of the Brooklyn Museum.

UNKNOWN ARTIST.

83. Portrait of Abraham Lincoln.

This portrait is supposed to have been painted by a French artist visiting the United States during the Civil War. The original owner was a French resident of Washington, D. C.

Property of the Brooklyn Museum.

Children on the Beach — Winslow Homer

BROOKLYN MUSEUM

Eastern Parkway — Brooklyn, N. Y.

The Museum is open from 9 A. M. to 6 P. M., Monday to Saturday (inclusive). Thursday evening, from 7:30 to 9:45. Sunday afternoon, from 2 to 6. The Museum is free to the public, except on Monday and Tuesday, when the admission is 25 cents for adults and 10 cents for children under 16 years. Free on all Holidays even when these fall on Monday or Tuesday; free to teachers with their classes at all times, including pay days.

The collections of the Museum comprise Exhibits in the Fine Arts, in Natural Science and in Ethnology.

The services of the Docent are available by appointment to persons desiring guidance in visiting the Museum. Address the Docent also for information relating to special privileges extended to teachers, pupils, and art students; for the use of classrooms, and of the Museum's collection of lantern slides.

The Museum Library containing more than 22,000 volumes is open for reference daily from 9 A. M. to 5 P. M., on Sunday from 2 to 6 P. M., and Thursday evening from 7:30 to 9:45.

The publications of the Museum comprise the Museum Quarterly Review, the Annual Report, Memoirs of Art and Archæology, Memoirs of Natural Science, Science Bulletins, and Catalogues and Guides relating to the collections on exhibition.

Staten Island Association of Arts and Sciences

Hon. Howard R. Bayne, *President* Charles W. Leng, *Secretary*
Arthur Hollick, Ph.D., *Director of the Museum*

Catalog of Staten Island Exhibits
Catskill Aqueduct Celebration Exhibit

prepared in co-operation with

The Sub-Committee on Art, Scientific and Historical Exhibitions
of
The Mayor's Catskill Aqueduct Celebration Committee

General Committee
George McAneny, *Chairman*

Executive Committee

Arthur Williams, *Chairman*
William C. Breed
George Frederick Kunz
Samuel L. Martin
William McCarroll
Charles H. Strong
Edward Hagaman Hall, *Secretary*
William Hamlin Childs.
J. W. Lieb
George McAneny
Henry S. Thompson
Henry R. Towne

Museum Exhibits Committee
George Frederick Kunz, *Chairman*

Public Museum
Saint George, Staten Island
Borough of Richmond, New York City
October 11, 1917

Catalog of Exhibits

1. Wooden water main, made by boring out the center of a log.

This specimen was part of the piping of the public water supply system in use in lower Manhattan during the period from 1800 to 1835, prior to the introduction of the Croton water.

The water was obtained from a well located at Reade and Center streets and was pumped to a reservoir on Chambers street, from whence it was distributed through the wooden mains.

A piece of wood, submitted for examination to Prof. Edward C. Jeffrey of Harvard University, was identified as white pine, *Pinus Strobus* L. (See Proc. Nat. Sci. Assoc. Staten Is. vol. 9, p. 47, Ap. 15, 1905, and ibid. p. 50. May 20, 1905.)

2. Specimens described in a paper by Dr. Arthur Hollick on Some Botanical and Geological Features of the Silver Lake Basin, read at the meeting of the Staten Island Association of Arts and Sciences, October 17, 1914. (See Proc. Staten Is. Assoc. Arts and Sci. vol. 5, pp. 60-65, pls. 2-5. Oct. 1914.)

(a) *Polypodium vulgare* L. Common polypody fern. Rare on Staten Island.

(b) *Lorinseria areolata* (L.) Underw. Net-veined chain fern. Recorded from but few localities on Staten Island.

(c) *Brasenia purpurea* (Michx.) Casp. Water shield or water target. Silver Lake was the only known station for this species on Staten Island. It is now probably exterminated from our local flora.

(d) *Dentaria laciniata* Muhl. Cut-leaved toothwort or pepper grass. Recorded from but few localities on Staten Island.

(e) *Prunus pennsylvanica* L. f. Wild red or pigeon cherry. A single tree, now destroyed, was the only one known on Staten Island.

(f) *Diospyros virginiana* L. Persimmon. A few of these trees formerly grew on the northwestern border of Silver Lake. They are more or less common in the vicinity of Tottenville and Kreischerville, and a few may be found in the vicinity of Bull's Head and Watchogue, but not elsewhere on Staten Island.

(g) Peat from the northeastern end of Silver Lake basin.

(h) Semi-lignitic wood from peat bed.

(i) Hickory nuts from peat beds.

(j) Wood from the silt at the inner margin of the peat bed.

(k) Silt from near the center of the lake basin, exposed by draining off the water, covered with a growth of *Eleocharis acicularis* (L.) R. & S.

(l) Sandy silt, representing the lowest deposit in the basin.

(m) Glacial till from beneath the peat bed and silt deposits, representing the original lake bottom.

3. Pictures illustrating the paper mentioned under Exhibit 2, reproduced from photographs taken by H. H. Cleaves, September 29, 1914.

(a) View, looking northeast across the partly drained lake basin.

(b) Beginning of a crevasse in the marginal silt.

(c) A slip, following a crevasse in the marginal silt, exposing the original lake bottom.

(d) Shrinkage cracks in the surface of the silt toward the middle of the drained lake basin.

(e) View, looking across the northeast end of the receding water, showing advancing terrestrial vegetation.

(f) Part of the drained lake basin, northeast end, showing zone of *Decodon verticillatus* (L.) Ell. in the background and *Bidens laevis* (L.) B. S. P. in the foreground.

(g) *Decodon* zone on former shore margin of the peat bed at northeast end of the lake basin.

(h) Ditch cut through the peat bed, about seven feet in depth.

4. (a) Silver Lake as it was in 1859. Photograph by H. Hoyer, enlarged. View is from the eastern side, looking toward the northwest.

(b) View from approximately the same point as that from which the above mentioned picture was taken, showing the marginal grading and the partly drained basin of the lake, in preparation for its conversion into a reservoir. Photograph by H. H. Cleaves, September 29, 1914.

5. (a) Silver Lake as it was in 1896. Photograph by Otto Loeffler, enlarged. View is from the northeast end, looking toward the south.

(b) View from approximately the same point as that from which the above mentioned picture was taken, showing the trees cut down, the water mostly drained off, and the sides of the basin raised and graded in order to convert it into a reservoir. Photograph by H. H. Cleaves, September 29, 1914.

6. Silver Lake Reservoir, completed and filled with water. Photographs by J. A. Rundlett, October 8, 1917.

This reservoir is now the southern terminus of the Catskill water supply system. Capacity = 438,000,000 gallons. Area of water surface = 54 acres.

(a) View from the northeast end, looking toward the northwest.

(b) View from the northeast end, looking toward the west.

The reservoir is constructed in two sections. The northeastern section, shown in the foreground, was made by erecting a dam across Logan's Spring valley. The southwestern section, shown in the background, is the old Silver Lake basin in which the original water level was 200 feet above tide. By the erection of a dam across the natural outlet at the southwestern end the level of the water has been raised to 228 feet above tide.

7. Logan's Spring. Photograph by William T. Davis, November 30, 1911, enlarged.

The site of this formerly well-known spring is now at the bottom of the northeastern section of the reservoir.

8. The Hessian Springs. Photograph by Edward C. Delavan, jr., 1902. These springs were located in the valley of the Jersey street brook, between Jersey street, Westervelt avenue, Fifth street and Crescent avenue, New Brighton They were formerly an important source of water supply for the neighborhood.

9. Views illustrating the growth of population in the section of Staten Island nearest to New York, from the time when local natural springs and shallow wells were adequate sources of individual and neighborhood water supply to the present time, when it is necessary to bring water through an elaborate aqueduct system from a distance of more than one hundred miles.

(a) Steel engraving, entitled "New York from Staten Island," from "The Picturesque Beauties of the Hudson River and Its Vicinity, etc."' published by J. Disturnell, 156 Broadway, New York, in or about 1835-36. The view is from the top of Pavilion Hill, with New York in the distance and the shore front of Staten Island in the foreground. Only four houses are shown, exclusive of the old Quarantine buildings at Tompkinsville.

(b) Two views taken from the same place and showing the same section occupied by hundreds of dwellings, apartment houses, stores, warehouses, public buildings, etc. Photographs by William T. Davis, September 29, 1917, enlarged.

10. Pictures of the pumping stations, and reservoirs of the several water supply systems constructed prior to the introduction of the Catskill water. The supply was obtained entirely from driven wells.

This exhibit is contributed by the Department of Water Supply, Gas and Electricity, Borough of Richmond, through John W. McKay, Borough Engineer in charge of water supply.

(a) Enlarged photographs, framed, of the (1) Tottenville, (2) Bull's Head, (3) New Springville, and (4) Clove pumping stations. (5) Architect's colored drawing, framed, of the Grant City station. (6) Photograph of the West New Brighton station, by J. A. Rundlett, October 1917.

(b) Exterior and interior views of the Grant City station, erected in 1911. This is the main pumping station of the Southside Boulevard water development system, which is being held in reserve in event of an emergency. Pumping capacity = 6,500,000 gallons per day of 24 hours. Photographs by J. A. Rundlett, October 1917.

(c) Exterior and interior views of one of the four auxilliary stations on Southside Boulevard. Total pumping capacity of the four stations = 9,000,000 gallons per day of 24 hours. Photographs by J. A. Rundlett, October 1917.

(d) High service standpipe, Grymes' Hill. Elevation of top = 452.8 feet above sea level. Capacity = 234,000 gallons. Size = 100 feet high by 20 feet diameter. Photograph by J. A. Rundlett, October 1917.

(e) Clove reservoir, Richmond Turnpike and Little Clove Road. Elevation of flow line = 250 feet above sea level. Capacity = about 2,080,000 gallons. Photograph by J. A. Rundlett, October 1917.

(f) Fort Hill or New Brighton reservoir, between Bismarck, Downey and Lynch avenues, New Brighton. Elevation of flow line = 211.9 feet above sea level. Capacity 800,000 gallons. Put in service August, 1881. Abandoned 1917. Photograph by J. A. Rundlett, October 1917.

11. (a) Members of Staten Island Battery, Veteran Corps of Artillery, at headquarters, Ardsley Sector, Catskill Aqueduct, September 1917. Photograph.

The Staten Island battery was Battery A, First Provisional Regiment, New York State Militia.

(b) Hon. Howard R. Bayne, Staten Island Battery, Veteran Corps of Artillery, returning from inspection of culvert under Catskill Aqueduct, while on guard duty at fixed post No. 8, Ardsley Sector. September 14, 1917. Photograph.

12. A newspaper account of the Catskill water supply project fourteen years ago. New York Sun, October 11, 1903.

13. List of works and articles relating or containing references to sources of water supply for Staten Island. Twenty-eight titles are listed, arranged in chronological sequence, all of which are in the library of the Association, where they may be consulted on application at the office of the Director.

Contribution of

STEVENS INSTITUTE OF TECHNOLOGY

to the

CATSKILL AQUEDUCT CELEBRATION

In Coöperation with the Work of the

Sub-Committee on

Art, Scientific and Historical Exhibitions

(Reprinted from The Stevens Indicator, October, 1917)

THE MAYOR OF NEW YORK'S CATSKILL AQUEDUCT CELEBRATION COMMITTEE

GEORGE MCANENY, *Chairman*

ISAAC N. SELIGMAN, *Treasurer* EDWARD HAGAMAN HALL, *Secretary*

Executive Committee

ARTHUR WILLIAMS, *Chairman*
WILLIAM C. BREED
WILLIAM HAMLIN CHILDS
EDWARD HAGAMAN HALL
GEORGE FREDERICK KUNZ
J. W. LIEB
SAMUEL L. MARTIN
GEORGE MCANENY
WILLIAM MCCARROLL
ISAAC N. SELIGMAN
CHARLES H. STRONG
HENRY R. TOWNE

Sub-Committee on Art, Scientific and Historical Exhibitions

Chairman

DR. GEORGE FREDERICK KUNZ
409 Fifth Avenue

UNIVERSITIES AND COLLEGES

Columbia University
Dr. Nicholas Murray Butler, *President*
Prof. William H. Carpenter, *Librarian*
Milton J. Davies

New York University
Dr. Elmer Ellsworth Brown, *Chancellor*

Stevens Institute of Technology
Dr. Alexander C. Humphreys, *President*

College of the City of New York
Dr. Sidney E. Mezes, *President*

LEARNED SOCIETIES AND INSTITUTIONS

American Geographical Society
John Greenough, *President*

New York Historical Society
John Abeel Weeks, *President*
Robert H. Kelby, *Librarian*

New York Genealogical and Biographical Society
Capt. Richard Henry Greene, *Representative*

Long Island Historical Society
Judge Willard Bartlett, *President*

Brooklyn Institute of Arts and Sciences
Dr. A. Augustus Healy, *President*

Staten Island Association of Arts and Sciences
Hon. Howard R. Bayne, *President*

American Numismatic Society
Edward T. Newell, *President*

Cooper Union for the Advancement of Science and Art
Miss Sarah Cooper Hewitt, *Trustee*
Miss Eleanor G. Hewitt, *Trustee*

American Scenic and Historic Preservation Society
Col. Henry W. Sackett, *1st Vice-President*

ENGINEERING SOCIETIES

United Engineering Institute
Charles F. Rand, *President*
Calvin W. Rice, *Secretary*

American Society of Mechanical Engineers
Dr. Ira N. Hollis, *President*

American Institute of Electrical Engineers
E. W. Rice, Jr., *President*

American Institute of Mining Engineers
Philip N. Moore, *President*

American Institute of Civil Engineers
E. W. H. Pegram, *President*

LIBRARIES

New York Public Library
Dr. Edwin H. Anderson, *Director*

New York Society Library
Frederic dePeyster Foster, *Chairman*

MUSEUMS

Metropolitan Museum of Art
Dr. Robert W. de Forest, *President*

Brooklyn Museum
William H. Fox, *Director*

American Museum of Natural History
Dr. Henry Fairfield Osborn, *President*

Museum of the American Indian
George G. Heye, *Founder*

Van Cortlandt Museum House
(The Colonial Dames of the State of New York)
Mrs. Hamilton R. Fairfax, *President*
Mrs. Elihu Chauncey, *Chairman*

Jumel Mansion, Washington Headquarters Association (The Daughters of the American Revolution)
Mrs. George Wilson Smith, *President*
William H. Shelton, *Curator*

Fraunces' Tavern
(The Sons of the Revolution)
Henry Russell Drowne, *Secretary*

CLUBS

National Arts Club
John G. Agar, *President*

City History Club of New York
Mrs. A. Barton Hepburn, *President*

PARKS AND GARDENS

Department of Parks, Manhattan and Richmond
Hon. Cabot Ward, *Commissioner*

Department of Parks, Brooklyn
Hon. Raymond W. Ingersoll, *Commissioner*

New York Botanical Garden
Dr. Nathaniel L. Britton, *Director*

New York Zoological Garden
Madison Grant, *Vice-President*

New York Aquarium
Dr. Charles H. Townsend, *Director*

Brooklyn Botanic Garden
Dr. C. Stuart Gager, *Director*

CHURCH

The Collegiate Church of St. Nicholas
Rev. Dr. Malcolm James MacLeod, *Pastor*

THE INFLUENCE OF THE WORK OF THE STEVENS FAMILY AND OF GRADUATES OF STEVENS INSTITUTE OF TECHNOLOGY ON ENGINEERING WORK LEADING UP TO THE CONSTRUCTION OF THE CATSKILL AQUEDUCT.*

THE engineering colleges of the United States have exerted a strong influence on the rapid development of engineering progress that has lead up to great undertakings that are distinctively American. The Catskill Aqueduct, the Panama Canal, the New York State Barge Canal, are recent examples. Referring only to one engineering college, Stevens, and to only one of these great works, the Catskill Aqueduct, there are distinct outcroppings of technical influence in the work of Mr. John A. Bensel, Stevens '84, who was at one time Chairman of the Catskill Aqueduct Board, and of Mr. Nicholas S. Hill, Jr., Stevens '92, who was chief engineer of the water department of New York City at the time that the Commission on Additional Water Supply was called in to report on the best means of supplying the city with additional water. The report of this committee led to the construction of the present Catskill Aqueduct.

Just as outcroppings indicate there are veins underneath, so do these two examples suggest that there have been great educational forces quietly at work in the past producing

*Written at the request of Dr. George F. Kunz, Chairman of the sub-committee on Art, Scientific and Historical Exhibitions of "The Mayor of New York's Catskill Aqueduct Celebration Committee," by Franklin DeR. Furman, M.E., Professor of Mechanism and Machine Design at Stevens Institute of Technology, Castle Point, Hoboken, N. J.

engineering developments which have influenced the methods of living of the people, congregating them in communities great and small, and thus introducing further engineering problems, such as the present Catskill Aqueduct which is a grand climax.

In the beginning of these vast developments, there was no greater influence at work in the United States than that exerted by the three noted engineering members of the Stevens family during the years from 1788 to 1868. John Stevens the father, and Robert L. and Edwin A. his two sons, worked together and singly, one taking up the tasks of the other in the order named when one had passed away. John Stevens was the grandson of an officer of the Queen's Court who came to this country early in the eighteenth century. His father was vice-president of the Council of the first legislature of New Jersey, and president of the New Jersey State Convention which adopted the United States Constitution. John Stevens had a strong bent toward scientific invention and mechanical development and in 1788 began experiments on steamboat navigation leading to the successful operation of a small screw propelled vessel on the Hudson River in 1804, and of a larger and commercial type of vessel which was burned shortly before Fulton brought over his engines from England and placed them on the *Clermont.* With the commercial honors thus lost, John Stevens who had built his own engine and boilers in his own shops, set about rebuilding the vessel which he named the *Phoenix,* and early in 1809 sent her around to Philadelphia to operate on the Delaware River because Fulton and his associates had secured a monopoly of the Hudson River from the New York State Legislature. Stevens was thus the first to navigate the seas with a steam-propelled vessel which successfully withstood a fierce storm that drove an accompanying schooner far out to sea and which was lost for many days.

When the plans for a great waterway construction of a canal to connect Lake Erie with the Hudson River was before the New York State Legislature, John Stevens presented a memorial to that body exhaustively treating of the plan to make "an inclined plane from the lake to the river, to be fed in its whole length by the waters of the lake," and comparing with this plan the advantages of a steam railroad to take its place. At this time, 1812, there were no steam railroads in the country. Stevens himself was the first to operate a steam locomotive in a small way in Hoboken, in 1826, although it was in 1817 that he applied for and obtained a railroad charter, the first in America, from the state of New Jersey to operate a steam railroad from "the river Delaware, near Trenton to the river Raritan, near New Brunswick." John Stevens' inability to construct his railroad more promptly was due principally to the successful operation of the new steamboats and to the successful adoption of canal waterways in Europe which influenced capital and legislation in this country.

There is no doubt, however, but that the activity of John Stevens, both in the engineering field and in legislative halls, spurred the efforts of those interested in canal development, and thus was laid an early and effective foundation for waterworks construction. The value of a canal across New York State was greatly increased in 1814 when Robert L. Stevens placed in operation a fast steamship line between New York and Albany, the monopoly law of the state of New York having been meanwhile overruled by the Constitution of the United States. This was the first "day line" between New York and Albany and was a valuable feeder to the canal. The first ship was the "New Philadelphia," being large and commodious and traveling at a rate of thirteen and one-half miles per hour, against about seven miles per hour for all previous vessels.

While the remainder, and by far the greater part of the

engineering work of the Stevens family led away from all direct influence on waterway construction, one can not help but feel that their enterprise in navigating the Delaware, Hudson and Connecticut rivers, including ferryboat service between New York City and adjacent shores, in establishing railroad connection between New York and Philadelphia, in developing many detail inventions which made these larger enterprises successful, and in establishing manufacturing centers for carrying on their work, contributed to the more rapid growth of urban communities calling, in succession, for larger and larger sources of water supply and for greater and greater scientific knowledge in construction and conducting that supply. The many ingenious inventions and improved adoptions of the Stevens family, notably that of the screw propeller by John Stevens; the expansive use of steam, the burning of anthracite coal, the wrought-iron walking beam, the use of the "hog-frame" on steamboats, the use of balanced valves, the use of tubular boilers, and perhaps best known, the invention of the present form of T-rail, by Robert L. Stevens; the use of several methods of forced draft for boilers, the introduction of armor plate, the invention of the ploughshare, the introduction of the two-horse dirt-wagon with loose sides and bottoms of narrow planks for cleaning up the débris after the great fire in New York City in 1842, by Edwin A. Stevens, all contributed to the development of tools, machines and methods that made the construction of such a great work as the Catskill Aqueduct possible.

Although the two generations of the great engineers of the Stevens family have long since passed away, engineering science since their time and of the present day owes much to them, for it was Edwin A. Stevens, the youngest and the surviving member of the trio, who, dying in 1868, left generous provision, for those days, for "an institution of learning," which "institution" was established in 1870 under the leadership of the late president Henry Morton as a college of Mechanical Engineering, the first in America.

The engineering contributions of the Faculty and the graduates of Stevens, along with those of other mechanical engineering colleges since established, have made possible to a large extent the mechanical, electrical, structural, hydraulic, and other equipment necessary as an aid to the older profession of civil engineering in the construction of the aqueduct. It is only through the work of many that such great undertakings are successfully achieved, one man's work being built on another's so that in the last analysis each one who toils produces that of which he cannot see the end. The work of such toilers as have had a technical mechanical training may be exemplified in a brief way by enumerating collateral experiences of some of the Faculty and alumni of one of the mechanical engineering colleges. In this enumeration only such cases as have had to do directly with waterworks supply are included, omitting all reference to those who have worked on various engines, machines and structures that are necessary to aqueduct construction but which have a much wider and more general usefulness; omitting also those whose work have been along the lines of technical analysis and investigation, all of which is essential in large engineering undertakings. Early in the days of scientific study of water supply Dr. Albert R. Leeds, professor of Chemistry at Stevens Institute of Technology was largely engaged in investigations, analyses, and recommendations in the matter of water supply for Jersey City, N. J., Newark, N. J., Brooklyn, N. Y., Philadelphia, Pa., Hoboken, N. J., Albany, N. Y., Wilmington, Del., Reading, Pa., Brockton, Mass., New London, Conn., and Minneapolis, Minn. One of his most extended investigations was for the city of Brooklyn, N. Y., to determine the cause of the offensive condition of the water supply. After several hundreds of miscroscopical and bacteriological as well as chemical analyses covering a period of several years the trouble was found to be due to an enormous multiplication of one species of diatomaceous algae. Upon the death of Dr. Leeds, Professor Stillman, his successor, conducted extensive investigations along the same line.

In the matter of detail mechanical construction of city water supply Dr. James E. Denton, professor of Engineering Practice, became interested in special rock drilling machinery about 1882 and later the drills made under his direction were used on a three-mile section of the Croton Aqueduct tunnel. It was to this section that Wegmann, in his work on "The Water Supply of the City of New York," pp. 151–218, refers when he speaks of the "record for the most rapid rate of excavation reached during the construction of the aqueduct."

On the side of general engineering direction the official positions of Mr. John A. Bensel, class of 1884, and Mr. Nicholas S. Hill, Jr., Class of 1892, have already been referred to. In addition, in 1908, Mayor George B. McClellan appointed Mr. H. deB. Parsons, Class of 1884, as engineer to a Committee of the Board of Estimate and Apportionment to determine the question of damages to the Ulster and Delaware Railroad Company due to the removal of about twelve miles of tracks made necessary to permit of the building of the Ashokan reservoir. This work embodied a careful study of the property owned by the railroad within the territory flooded by the reservoir, and an estimate of the cost of the new construction and equipment, such as signals, stations, etc. This work alone required three years.

Numerous other instances in which Stevens' technical graduates have been associated in water supply work in both minor and major capacities may be readily found in a casual inspection of the records of the alumni, as for example, the installation of a gravity water filter plant of 4,000,000 gallons daily; surveys, maps, etc. for water supply work; pumping machinery; irrigating plant equipment; power canal construction; filtering plant; rock-drills; special pneumatic tools for water works construction; invention and construction of integrating and registering instrument which made practical the utilization of the principles of Torrecelli's theorem and the Venturi tube for the commercial purpose of measuring the quantity flowing through large water ducts. Of this invention the Journal of The Franklin Institute CXLVII No. 2 states: "Its invention, design and perfection are the fruit of great ingenuity and of much knowledge and painstaking labor and they (the inventors) have been of vast benefit to the community by making the Venturi meter a practical working tool. Its inventors, Messrs. Frederick N. Connet and Walter W. Jackson [both of Stevens, Class of 1889] are therefore entitled to distinguished honor at the hands of the Franklin Institute, and we take pleasure in recommending the award to them of the John Scott Legacy Premium Medal for their registering apparatus."

Other collateral work in the line of water supply construction conducted by Stevens graduates include dredging water supply for Toms River, N. J., Allegheny City, Pa., Jersey City, N. J., Minneapolis, Minn., including pipe line under Mississippi River, Passaic, N. J., Pittsburgh, Pa., Baltimore, Md., New York City, Milwaukee, Wis., Peoria, Ill., Chicago, Ill., including waterworks tunnel under Lake Michigan; pollution work, professional paper on water supply of Memphis, Tenn.; engineer in charge of shop and field of largest and longest system of conveying city water then in existence (1892) at Newark, N. J., the line consisting of twenty-two miles of 48-inch pipe and five miles of 36-inch pipe all rivetted together in a continuous shell without expansion joints, this part of the work alone costing $1,750,000 and the whole $6,000,000; storage reservoir construction of two and one-half billion gallons capacity; numerous reservoir dams and walls, filtration work, inspector of masonry and construction on Croton Aqueduct and Jerome Park reservoir; jetty and breakwater building, engineer of engine house and line stations of the Brooklyn, N. Y., water supply; surveyor of waterworks system for Americus, Ga.; sanitary and chemical examination of Passaic River water as a supply for Paterson, N. J.; invention of registering and continuous recording devices for pressures, temperatures, electric currents and all phases of aqueduct construction where such records are used and kept.

www.ingramcontent.com/pod-product-compliance
Lightning Source LLC
LaVergne TN
LVHW010547110826
845149LV00003B/590

* 9 7 8 1 4 1 8 1 8 7 7 4 3 *